David Edgar
Plays: 1

The Jail Diary of Albie Sachs, Mary Barnes, Saigon Rose, O Fair Jerusalem, Destiny

This volume contains the best of David Edgar's work from the seventies on subjects ranging from South Africa (*Jail Diary*) to schizophrenia (*Mary Barnes*), from venereal disease (*Saigon Rose*) to the Black Death (*O Fair Jerusalem*), and on to the rise of fascism in contemporary Britain (*Destiny*).

The Jail Diary of Albie Sachs: 'A remarkable, persuasive picture.' *Observer*

Mary Barnes: 'A brilliant piece of pure theatre . . . promulgating the theory that schizophrenia can be effectively treated through behaviourist methods alone.' *Los Angeles Times*

Saigon Rose: 'Intriguing and entertaining . . . Edgar handles his themes – loss of innocence and a sense of betrayal – in a bitty, playful style laced with black comedy.' *Independent*

O Fair Jerusalem: 'In all its aspects a big play.' *Sunday Times*

Destiny: 'A play which astonished me with its intelligence, density, sympathy, and finely controlled anger.' Dennis Potter, *Sunday Times*
'I cannot remember a play that coupled so much urgent topical information with such dramatic force.' Irving Wardle, *The Times*

David Edgar was born in 1948 in Birmingham. His stage work includes *Excuses Excuses* (1972); *Dick Deterred* (1974); *Saigon Rose* (1976); *Wreckers* (1977); *Mary Barnes* (1978); *Teendreams* (with Susan Todd, 1979); *That Summer* (1987) and *Entertaining Strangers*, a community play first commissioned by Ann Jellicoe and the Colway Theatre Trust and adapted for performance at the National Theatre, London in 1987–8. He has written five plays for the Royal Shakespeare Company: *Destiny* (1976); *The Jail Diary of Albie Sachs* (1978); *Nicholas Nickleby* (1980); *Maydays* (1983); and *Pentecost* (1994). Plays for the National Theatre include *Entertaining Strangers* (revised version 1987) and *The Shape of the Table*. He received the John Whiting award for *Destiny*, the Society of West End Theatres Best Play award for *Nicholas Nickleby* (which also won him a Tony award in New York), the *Plays and Players* Best Play award for *Maydays* and the *Evening Standard* Play of the Year award for *Pentecost*. His television work includes adaptations of *Destiny*, *Jail Diary* and *Nicholas Nickleby*, *Buying a Landslide* (1992) and a three-part play *Vote for Them* (BBC, 1989). His radio work includes *Ecclesiastes* (1977), *A Movie Starring Me* (1991) and *Talking to Mars* (1996). His first film, *Lady Jane*, was released in 1986. He is Professor of Playwriting Studies at the University of Birmingham.

by the same author

DAVID EDGAR PLAYS: 2*
Ecclesiastes, Nicholas Nickleby Parts I & II,
Entertaining Strangers (the National Theatre Version)

DAVID EDGAR PLAYS: 3*
Teendreams, Our Own People,
That Summer, Maydays

THE SHAPE OF THE TABLE
THE STRANGE CASE OF DR JEKYLL AND MR HYDE
PENTECOST

EDGAR: SHORTS
Ball Boys, The National Theatre, Bloodsports,
The Midas Connection, Baby Love

THE SECOND TIME AS FARCE
A book of essays

also available
by Susan Painter

EDGAR THE PLAYWRIGHT*

* published by Methuen Drama

DAVID EDGAR

Plays: 1

The Jail Diary of Albie Sachs
Based on Albie Sachs's 'Jail Diary'

Mary Barnes
Based on
'Mary Barnes: Two Accounts of a Journey
through Madness'
by Mary Barnes and Joseph Berke

Saigon Rose

O Fair Jerusalem

Destiny

with an introduction by the author

Methuen Drama

METHUEN CONTEMPORARY DRAMATISTS

This edition first published in Great Britain in 1987 by Methuen London Ltd

Reissued in this series in 1997 by Methuen Drama

Methuen Publishing Ltd
215 Vauxhall Bridge Road
London SW1V 1EJ

www.methuen.co.uk

Methuen Publishing Ltd reg. number 3543167

The Jail Diary of Albie Sachs first published in 1982 by Rex Collings Ltd and
reprinted here in a revised version by arrangement with Rex Collings. Copyright
© 1982, 1987 by David Edgar
Mary Barnes first published in 1979 by Eyre Methuen Ltd. Copyright
© 1979, 1984 by David Edgar
Saigon Rose first published in 1987 by Methuen London Ltd, revised 1994. Copyright
© 1987, 1994 by David Edgar
O Fair Jerusalem first published in 1987. Copyright © 1987 by David Edgar
Destiny first published in the Methuen New Theatrescripts series in 1976 by
Eyre Methuen Ltd. Fully revised and reprinted in 1978 in Methuen Modern Plays.
Copyright © 1976, 1978, 1986 by David Edgar

Introduction copyright © 1987 by David Edgar
This collection © 1987, 1994 by David Edgar

The author has asserted his moral rights

A CIP catalogue record for this book is available at the British Library

ISBN 0 413 15220 0

Transferred to digital printing 2002.

Contents

David Edgar

A Chronology of Plays and Screenplays

Two Kinds of Angel (Bradford University, July 1970; Basement
  Theatre, London, February 1971) Published by Burnham House,
  London, 1975

The National Interest (General Will Theatre Group, July 1971)

Tedderella (Pool Theatre, Edinburgh, December 1971; Bush Theatre,
  London, January 1973)

Excuses Excuses (Belgrade Theatre Studio, Coventry, May 1972;
  Open Space, London, July 1973)

Death Story (Birmingham Repertory Theatre Studio, November
  1972; New End Theatre, London, November 1975)

Baby Love (Soho Poly Theatre, London, May 1973; BBC–TV Play
  for Today, November 1974)

The Eagle Has Landed (Granada Television, April 1973)

Operation Iskra (Paradise Foundry Theatre Group, September 1973)

Dick Deterred (Bush Theatre, February 1974) Published by Monthly
  Review Press, New York, 1974

I Know What I Meant (Granada Television, July 1974)

O Fair Jerusalem (Birmingham Repertory Theatre Studio, May
  1975)

Blood Sports/Ball Boys (Birmingham Arts Lab, July 1975; Bush
  Theatre, June 1976) *Ball Boys* published by Pluto Press, London,
  1978

The National Theatre (Open Space, London, October 1975)

Saigon Rose (Traverse Theatre, Edinburgh, July 1976; BBC Radio
  Three, April 1979)

Destiny (Royal Shakespeare Company at the Other Place and
  subsequently the Aldwych Theatre, September 1976, May 1977;
  BBC–TV Play for Today, January 1978; BBC Radio Four,
  January 1979) Published by Methuen, London, 1976/78

Wreckers (7:84 Theatre Company, February 1977) Published by
  Methuen, London, 1977

Ecclesiastes (BBC Radio Four, April 1977)

Our Own People (Pirate Jenny Theatre Company, November 1977)

The Jail Diary of Albie Sachs (Adaptation) (Royal Shakespeare
  Company at the Warehouse, June 1978; Manhattan Theatre
  Club, New York, October 1979; productions in Los Angeles, San
  Francisco and Seattle; BBC Television, 1981) Published by Rex
  Collings, London, 1978

Mary Barnes (Based on book by Mary Barnes and Joe Berke)
  (Birmingham Repertory Studio, August 1978; Royal Court,
  January 1979; productions in New Haven, New York, Los
  Angeles and San Francisco) Published by Methuen, London, 1979

Teendreams (with Susan Todd) (Monstrous Regiment, January 1979) Published by Methuen, London, 1979

Nicholas Nickleby (Adaptation from Dickens) (Royal Shakespeare Company, Aldwych Theatre, July 1980; Plymouth Theatre, Broadway, New York, October 1981; Channel Four, November 1982) Published by Dramatists Play Service, New York, 1982 and Methuen Drama, London, 1990

Maydays (Royal Shakespeare Company, Barbican Theatre, October 1983) Published by Methuen, London, 1983, 1984

Entertaining Strangers (Colway Theatre Trust, Dorchester, 1985; National Theatre, October 1987) Published by Methuen, London, 1986

Lady Jane (Paramount picture, 1986)

Entertaining Strangers (new version) (National Theatre, Cottesloe Theatre, London, 1987) Published by Methuen, London, 1988, 1990

That Summer (Hampstead Theatre, London, July 1987; BBC World Service, August 1993) Published by Methuen, London, 1987

Vote for Them (with Neil Grant) (BBC Television, June 1989) Published by the BBC, 1989

Heartlanders (with Stephen Bill and Anne Devlin) (Birmingham Repertory Theatre, October 1989) Published by Nick Hern Books, 1989

The Shape of the Table (National Theatre, Cottesloe Theatre, London, November 1990; BBC Radio Four, June 1993) Published by Nick Hern Books, 1990

The Strange Case of Dr Jekyll and Mr Hyde (Royal Shakespeare Company, Barbican Theatre, London, November 1991) Published by Nick Hern Books, 1992

A Movie Starring Me (BBC Radio Four, November 1991)

Buying a Landslide (BBC Television, September 1992)

Citizen Locke (Channel 4 Television, April 1994)

Pentecost (Royal Shakespeare Company, The Other Place, Stratford upon Avon, October 1994) Published by Nick Hern Books, 1995

Talking to Mars (BBC Radio Three, October 1996)

Introduction

Most of the plays in this volume can be called social-realist pieces. That is, unlike symbolist or absurdist or agitprop plays, they present what aspires to be a recognisable picture of human behaviour as it is commonly observed — but, unlike naturalistic drama, they set such a picture within an overall social-historical framework. The characters and situations are thus not selected solely because that's how things are — but because they represent a significant element in an analysis of a concrete social situation. The most popular definition of this endeavour is by Lukács, who said that social-realism presents 'typical' characters in a 'total' context.

The most obvious example of such a play in this book is *Destiny*. The play presents an analysis of British society in the seventies, and in particular of those sections of society who were then (and might again in the future) tend towards support for an emerging neo-fascist organisation, and of the response that other forces in society were mounting or might mount against such a movement. The characters in the play were chosen quite carefully to add up if not to a total then to at least a representative picture of the forces of fascism and their various opponents, and in a scene like the meeting scene early in Act Two several of the characters were invented purely to contribute to the socio-political mosaic. But *Destiny* is not an agitprop play: the accessibility of what it has to say relies not just on its argument, but also in large part on the recognisability of the situations it portrays. So, in that particular scene, the audience might well have no point of contact (or *think* they have no point of contact) with the arguments being expressed, but they could recognise and acknowledge their recognition of the observed reality of badly organised public meetings, from the dicky microphone and the broken guitar string to the echoing silences, bowel-shrivelling crossed-purposes and agonising non sequiturs, which to anyone who has ever attended a public meeting of anything is all to familiar.

On the surface, *Mary Barnes* and *The Jail Diary of Albie Sachs* fit less easily into the social-realist mould — not least because their protagonists are so dramatically *un*typical. But although the real (and I hope the dramatised) Albie and Mary are quite exceptional people, they remain paradigmatic figures for their times. Even more importantly, the contexts in which their individuality is expressed — early sixties Afrikanerdom, a late sixties alternative household — certainly strove to be representative if not typical. Both plays are in fact analogous to orchestral concertos, seeking to achieve a balance of tension between the central characters and the social matrix into which they are catapulted and against which (in both cases, I think) they struggle. So although both plays are about the literal loneliness of solitary confinement and the metaphorical isolation of lunacy, they are essentially social plays, as much about the commune and the jailhouse as they are about the schizophrenic and the prisoner.

In this respect, it is clear that both *Saigon Rose* and *O Fair Jerusalem* fit into the same, broadly social-rather-than-domestic pattern of playmaking. But these two previously unpublished plays are significantly different from *Destiny*, *Mary Barnes* and *Jail Diary*, and represent I think a significant departure from the social-realist model. Both plays are built in fact around a clash of metaphor — in the case of *Jerusalem*, based on a chronological coincidence; in *Saigon* a kind of pun. And although both plays have a clear subject and indeed message, they are in my view less interesting for what they say than for how they say it. For although they were the first plays in this book to be produced (*Destiny*'s early drafts were written earlier), they are the most modern, or perhaps more accurately the most post-modern, of this crop of plays. For while the other three use a variety of contemporary, disjunctive techniques (most particularly, the episodic format), they are all basically engaged in the project of *explaining* social phenomena, of making superficially irrational and in some cases seemingly arbitrary behaviour emotionally and intellectually intelligible to an audience. Whatever other theatrical virtues *Destiny*, *Mary Barnes* and *Jail Diary* may possess, the plays have not worked unless Dennis Turner's racism, Mary Barnes's madness and Albie Sachs's fortitude are both individually and socially comprehensible by the end of the evening. And while I hope that the behaviour of their characters is credible and indeed recognisable, there's no doubt in my mind that the architecture of *Jerusalem* and *Saigon* is built on metaphorical rather than strictly realist foundations.

I've recently come to the rather obvious conclusion that these two types of play need not be incompatible, and indeed that they are (or should be) the component antitheses of a dramatic synthesis which might, at one and the same time, show how things feel and also how they are. In my more self-congratulatory moments, I think that some at least of most of these plays achieve such a synthesis already. What I am certain about is that the social-realist form has significant limitations when it comes to representing the contemporary world to itself. But whatever takes over from it in my work or anybody else's is not a matter for this volume.

I should however acknowledge in conclusion that by a happy accident the plays in this volume were directed in their première productions by the five people who have had the greatest influence on my work. Ron Daniels bludgeoned the Royal Shakespeare Company into doing *Destiny* (and later *Maydays*). Howard Davies battered me into adapting Albie Sachs's diary (and then let me interfere in his rehearsals of *Henry VIII* and Trevor Griffiths' *The Party*). Christopher Honer (*O Fair Jerusalem*) gave me my first professional production, and went on to introduce me (as a writer) to the Birminghan Repertory Theatre, a relationship which culminated in Peter Farago's premiere production of *Mary Barnes*. And Chris Parr (who directed *Saigon Rose* at the Traverse) presented my first plays at the University of Bradford, and has remained a favoured director, mentor, confidant and friend.

David Edgar, 1987

The Jail Diary of Albie Sachs

Based on Albie Sachs's 'Jail Diary'

THE JAIL DIARY OF ALBIE SACHS was first presented by the Royal Shakespeare Company at the Warehouse Theatre, London, on 15 June 1978, with the following cast:

ALBIE SACHS	Peter McEnery
SERGEANT	Peter Clough
CONSTABLE	John Burgess
WAGENAAR	Philip Dunbar
FREEMAN	Charles Dance
DANNY	Jeffrey Kissoon
ROSSOUW	Ian McNeice
SNYMAN	Edwin Richfield
2nd SERGEANT	Charles Dance
COLOURED CONSTABLE	Jeffrey Kissoon
VLOK	John Burgess
McINTYRE	Peter Clough
3rd SERGEANT	John Burgess
KRAAL	Philip Dunbar
SAMOLS	Peter Clough
2nd CONSTABLE	Peter Clough
CAMERA-MAN	Peter Clough
SWANEPOEL	Edwin Richfield

Directed by Howard Davies
Designed by Chris Dyer
Lighting by Brian Wigney
Sound by John Leonard

The play takes place in Cape Town, South Africa, in the early 1960s.

The set consists of a cell, with a heavy metal door, concrete walls and, in the corner, a practical toilet; an office, to the side; and a downstage area that serves as the prison yard.

Act One

Scene One

The cell is empty.
Downstage of the set stands ALBIE SACHS.
He is 29, short black hair, thin, even scraggy.
He wears a business suit, white shirt and tie.
He is addressing a meeting.

ALBIE. You know, that it's traditional, at gatherings, in certain circles, to propose a vote of thanks. And that is what I'd like to do today, propose a vote of thanks, not to the people who set up this meeting, nor to the speakers, you've applauded them already, nor to you.

In fact, especially, not to you.

Because I want to thank a man who isn't here, unable to attend, but with us, I am sure, in spirit. And I'd like you to acknowledge, in the usual way, our thanks to J.B. Vorster.

Without whom, all of this would certainly have been — a great deal easier. Without whom, many more would now be here.

So what is it, in particular, for which we should express our gratitude, to Balthazar Vorster, here today?

You know, you may have read George Orwell's 1984. If so, you will remember, there's four Ministries, described in that; the Ministry of Peace, which deals with War, the Ministry of Plenty, deals in scarcities, the Ministry of Truth which pumps out lies, and finally, the Ministry of Love, the secret police. And why that's of significance to us, here in South Africa, is that the man who's locking people up indefinitely, without trial or hearing, the man who passed the Bill to do that, he is called the Minister of Justice.

Twenty-one years before George Orwell's 1984.

And, as it happens, this new Law is being used, not just against the blacks and coloureds, but against the whites, here in South Africa.

To which you may *with* justice, say, so what, about time too. But it's important, to us all, it really is, because it shows us just how scared they are, of what is happening, the movement for black justice and emancipation, throughout Africa.

And that's not bad. It's good, that they're so scared, they're scared enough to use it on the whites, on us, because it makes *us* choose what side we're on, it tells us, and we didn't know, it tells us what it's like.

So thank you, Dr Vorster. You have told us what it's like.

Pause.
The speech is over.
He turns upstage, looks at the cell.

So this is what it's like.

Scene Two

Lights on the cell.
A sudden clatter.
The cell door being unlocked.
It opens.
Enter a SERGEANT and a CONSTABLE, who carries a roll of rush matting, six blankets and a grip.
ALBIE wanders into the cell set as:

SERGEANT. OK. Sit dit daar neer. Gee my die sak. Roer jou! (Put it down. Give me the bag. Quick!)

The CONSTABLE gives the bag to the SERGEANT, and lays out the matting.
The SERGEANT rummages through the grip, takes out ALBIE's things: a change of clothes, a bright checked beachtowel, sandshoes, pyjamas, dressing-gown, shaving and washing tackle.
The SERGEANT finds a comb and razor.

SERGEANT. Los die komberse daar. (Leave the blankets there.)

ALBIE. So this is what it's like.

SERGEANT. Wat? (What?)

ALBIE. Nothing.

SERGEANT stands.

SERGEANT. Das. (Tie.)

ALBIE. I'm sorry?

SERGEANT. Gee my joue das. (Give me your tie.)

ALBIE (*takes off his tie*). Oh, yes. Of course.

SERGEANT (*taking the tie*). En die gordel ook. (And the belt.)

ALBIE takes off his belt, gives it to the SERGEANT.

ALBIE. I'm not planning to hang myself.

SERGEANT. I'm not planning letting you. (*To the* CONSTABLE:) OK. Goed. (OK. Good.)

The SERGEANT, *with the tie, belt, comb and razor, turns to go.*

ALBIE. Um, Sergeant —

SERGEANT. Em?

ALBIE. I wonder, could I ask —

SERGEANT. Ja? What?

ALBIE. I would like a copy of the regulations governing my detention here.

SERGEANT. Oh, yuh?

ALBIE. Yes, and books. I would like to ask permission for reading matter to be provided for me.

Slight pause. SERGEANT *laughs.*

SERGEANT. Boeke en regulasies.

He turns to go.

ALBIE. Well? My request?

SERGEANT. You see the magistrate, OK? Me, I'm only a policeman.

ALBIE. Well, whatever —

SERGEANT. OK, you want a book? You can have it. You can have a good book.

To the CONSTABLE:

Bly daar. (Stay there.)

SERGEANT *goes out.*
ALBIE *looks at the* CONSTABLE.
Pause.
ALBIE *takes off his jacket and hangs it on a stud on the cell wall.*
Pause.
The SERGEANT *re-enters with a Bible.*

SERGEANT. Here, you have a good book. The Good Book. That you're allowed. OK?

ALBIE (*takes the Bible*). I see. Thank you.

SERGEANT *going again,*
ALBIE *glances at his watch.*
CONSTABLE *notices, gestures to* SERGEANT, *taps his wrist.*

CONSTABLE. Horlosie. (Watch.)

SERGEANT (*to* ALBIE). Watch.

ALBIE. I'm sorry?

SERGEANT. Jou horlosie, gee dit hier. (Your wrist-watch, give it here.)

ALBIE. Why?

SERGEANT. The regulations.

Pause.
ALBIE *gives his watch to the* SERGEANT.
As he goes:

Vokken Kommie moer.

The CONSTABLE *follows the* SERGEANT *out. The door is locked.*
Pause.
ALBIE *opens the Bible.*
He reads:

ALBIE. If I be wicked, woe unto me: and if I be righteous, yet will I not lift up my head. I am full of confusion, therefore see thou my affliction:

For it increaseth.

He shuts the Bible, puts it down.
He looks round the cell.

No bed. No bunk. No *chair.*

He looks round.
He goes and sits on the bed.

There's something wrong with this room.

He looks up.

It isn't a room. It's a concrete cube. With me inside. And no outside.

He stands, jumps up, trying to see out of the window. Several times.

No hurry. Lots of time.

He looks up. Sees something behind the partition.
He goes and opens the partition, revealing the lavatory.
A metal loop juts through the wall.
He pulls it.
The lavatory flushes.
He lets go, the wire snakes back into the wall.

That's a relief.

He pulls it again.
It flushes.

That's very good.

He pulls it again.
It flushes.

That's most efficient.

And once more.

That is a most efficient lavatory.

He is about to pull it again.

Maybe — don't tempt providence.

He goes to the pile of his possessions on the floor. He puts the
spare clothes on the bed.
He hangs the beachtowel on two studs on the wall.
He sees he's been left his tube of shaving cream. He picks it
up, feels the sharp end of the tube.
He goes to the wall of the cell. He sits.

I was entering my chambers this morning. I had parked my car
and I was at the entrance of the building. I felt a hand on my
shoulder. There were men in suits all round me.

I am detained under the 90-day Law. After 90 days I can be
re-arrested for a further 90-days. And then again. Ad infinitum.

He scratches 1/10/63 on the wall.

It is Tuesday, October the first, 1963.

He scratches his initials.

I am Albert Louis Sachs.

He scratches a single scratch.

Day One.

In the distance, the hour chime of a clock.
ALBIE instinctively looks for his watch.
He listens.
The clock chimes six.

Thank God for that.

He stands, puts the tube into his grip.
As he does so, he sings the hour-chime to himself:

Dong dong ding-dong, dong dong ding-dong.

He hums the same tune.
Then he has an idea.
He 'dongs' the first eight notes of Beethoven's Fifth.

Ding ding ding dong.
Ding ding ding dong.

He waits to see if anyone will sing back, from elsewhere in the prison.
Nothing.
He tries the Marseillaise:

Ding ding dong dong ding ding dong ding-dong
Ding ding dong ding dong ding-dong.

Pause.
Nothing.

Well.

He tries the words:

Something, something ma patrie, something, um —

Pause. Then, quietly:

The people's flag is deepest red
It shrouded oft our martyred dead . . .

Realising that singing so softly, he can't be heard, he la's the last four lines of the Red Flag, very loudly.
Pause.
Nothing.
Then, suddenly, a rattle at the door.
ALBIE looks round in some alarm.
The CONSTABLE *admits* LT. WAGENAAR *and* PHIL FREEMAN.
WAGENAAR *is a tall, burley Special Branch Officer.*
FREEMAN *is better dressed. When he speaks, we will hear his British accent.*
For the moment, he is detached, looks round the cell.

ALBIE. Hallo.

WAGENAAR. You've got a voice.

ALBIE. Thank you.

WAGENAAR. I meant loud, not good.

ALBIE. Well, still.

WAGENAAR. My name's Lieutenant Wagenaar.

ALBIE. Yes. We met this morning.

WAGENAAR. So we did.

ALBIE. You were going through my clients' private
correspondence.

WAGENAAR. Was I now.

Pause.

Just came to check, on how you were.

ALBIE. That's nice of you.

WAGENAAR. Yes, isn't it.

Pause.

ALBIE. Well, since you ask. I am, in fact, being kept in rather uncivilised conditions. I'm locked up in a bare cell without books or writing materials. I'm being held in solitary confinement without trial.

WAGENAAR. Well, that's easily solved.

ALBIE. How.

WAGENAAR. Are you prepared to answer questions?

ALBIE. No.

WAGENAAR. Ach, then it's not so easy.

He looks away. To FREEMAN:

Laat staan dit nou, hy . . . (We'll leave it now, he . . .)

ALBIE. You know, it doesn't say much for you police.

WAGENAAR. What doesn't?

ALBIE. That you can't do your job without using methods like this.

Pause.
WAGENAAR *turns back.*

WAGENAAR. All right. Our job is to protect the people of this country. What methods should we use?

ALBIE. The usual police methods.

WAGENAAR. Like what?

ALBIE. Well, methods used in civilised countries throughout the world.

Slight pause.

WAGENAAR. Well?

ALBIE. Well, patient, investigation, contacts, interviews, informers, all the usual —

FREEMAN *coughs.*
ALBIE *looks to him.*

FREEMAN. Oh, but they do. The police already do have informers, Mr Sachs. They give them information.

Pause.

ALBIE. I am not prepared to answer any questions.

WAGENAAR. Ag, hy is koppig. Kom ons loop. (He's being stubborn. Let's go now.)

WAGENAAR *pretends to go.*
Then turns back to ALBIE.
With a sympathetic smile.

Albie.

ALBIE. Yes.

WAGENAAR. Albie, don't just think of yourself, hey?

ALBIE. Who should I think of? My country?

WAGENAAR. No. Think of your family.

ALBIE. My family —?

WAGENAAR. Think of your wife and children. And the suffering you'll cause them, hey?

ALBIE. I'm sorry, what d'you say?

WAGENAAR (*harder*). Think of your wife and children.

Slight pause.

ALBIE. Yes. OK. I will.

WAGENAAR *and* FREEMAN *go out.*
The door is closed.
It is locked.

ALBIE. Or would. If I had any.

A slight laugh.
Suddenly, he shouts:

NO wife. NO children.
Don't you know that, policemen?
Don't you even know —

He is delighted.
He sings, loudly this time:

The People's Flag is deepest red
It shrouded oft our martyred dead
And when their limbs were stiff and cold
Their blood red-dyed its every fold.
So raise the scarlet standard high . . .

That's silly. The Africans' flag is black, gold and green.

He sings the first few lines of the African song Samlandela Lutuli.
He stops.
Nothing.
Shrugging, he lays out his blankets, lies down, singing to himself:

Let's twist again, like we did last summer,
Let's twist again, like we did last year:
Remember when, we did the Twist last summer —

He stops.
He's heard something.
We hear it too.
It's someone whistling the 'Going Home' theme from Dvorak's New World symphony.
Pause.
Then again.

It's 'Going Home'.

ALBIE *stands, whistles a few notes.*
Pause.
They are answered, the same phrases.
He goes on, through the tune, a few more phrases.
The whistler takes them up, goes on.
They whistle in antiphony.

Oh whistler.
You have turned me into we.

Blackout.

Scene Three

ALBIE *lies on the mat.*
He wears a vest, shorts and sandshoes.
His towel, shaving cream and a clean vest lie on the floor by him.
In the outside area, a bucket of water, ALBIE's razor, comb, and a metal mirror and a piece of soap.
The ten o'clock chime.

ALBIE. It is the fifth day.
It is ten o'clock. Time for exercise.

He sits up.

I always rather hope they'll be late.
Then I'll be further through the day when exercise is over.

Pause.

He jumps up.
He goes and pulls the lavatory chain.
He is going back to the mat, changes his mind, pulls the chain
again.
He turns back.
He sees the Bible, picks it up, flips idly through it.
Then the door opens.
The CONSTABLE.

ALBIE. Hello, Konstabel.

CONSTABLE. Hallo, Mineer Sachs.
Oefening-tyd. (Exercise time.)

ALBIE. Right.

ALBIE *goes out with the* CONSTABLE. *As they come on*
again, going towards the open area, they meet the SERGEANT
who is escorting a COLOURED PRISONER.

ALBIE. Good morning, Sergeant.

SERGEANT *looks at* ALBIE.
As he turns to go, ALBIE *a look at the* PRISONER.
Nothing we can see passes between them.
SERGEANT *takes the* PRISONER *out.*
ALBIE *and the* CONSTABLE *to the yard.*
ALBIE *to the bucket.*

ALBIE. Warm water today?

CONSTABLE. No, sorry.

ALBIE. Doesn't matter.

ALBIE *props up the mirror and lathers his face.*

Before I exercise, I shave. This is the only time of the day I
have a mirror, so I must peruse my face. I notice things I've
never seen before. My nose is bent, it veers, just like my views,
quite markedly to the left.

ALBIE *shaves.*

Then I see the right side of my lower lip is slightly more
bulging than the left side. I feel sorry for the poor old left side,
and laugh at myself for being such an indefatigable supporter
of the underdog.

ALBIE *rinses and towels his face.*

I know the coloured prisoner. His name is Danny Young. I
have defended him three times. I don't know if I'm sad or glad
to see him. Sad that he's here, and glad we're here together.
P'raps he is my whistler.

He puts down his towel.

Now for my exercise. To keep myself in trim. I tried to do press-ups in the cell. I found it very hard. So, I must exercise myself, here, in the sun.

Suddenly, ALBIE *jumps up and down, drops into a crouch. Then off, running very fast, round and round the yard. The* CONSTABLE *looks on. Blackout.*

Scene Four

ALBIE *in his cell. He wears his dressing gown and sandshoes.* WAGENAAR, FREEMAN *and* CAPTAIN ROSSOUW *are in the cell.*
ROSSOUW *is about 50, broad physique, black hair with a centre parting, a thin dark moustache. He smokes a cigarette.*

WAGENAAR. This is Captain Rossouw.

ALBIE. Yes, I know. I've seen him in court.

WAGENAAR. You're not in court now.

ALBIE. I know that. Perhaps soon you'll charge me and I'll be back there again.

ROSSOUW (*puts out his hand*). Pleased to meet you.

Pause.
ALBIE *shakes* ROSSOUW's *hand.*

Well, we shouldn't be too long.

There are just a few questions I want to ask you and then we'll be off.

ALBIE. Well, go ahead.

ROSSOUW. So, you're prepared to answer questions?

Glance at WAGENAAR.

ALBIE. What are the questions.

WAGENAAR *a 'told you so' look back to* ROSSOUW.

ROSSOUW. Now, first you must tell us whether you will answer them.

ALBIE. How can I say, if I don't know what the questions are?

ROSSOUW. Ah, yes, but if we tell you what they are, you'll have time to think about your answers.

Pause.

ALBIE. I think Lt. Wagenaar can tell you what my attitude is.

ROSSOUW. When did you join the Modern Youth Society?

ALBIE. I'm not prepared to answer any questions.

ROSSOUW. Or we could start with the Congress of Democrats.

ALBIE. My answer is the same.

ROSSOUW. Or perhaps the Coloured People's Congress. That's all right, it doesn't exist any more.

ALBIE. The answer is the same.

ROSSOUW. How old are you again?

Slight pause.

You're 28, aren't you?

Slight pause.

Remind me.

ALBIE. No comment.

ROSSOUW. No comment?

ALBIE. That's what I said.

ROSSOUW. No comment on how old you are?

WAGENAAR *laughs.*

Your age, a vital military secret?

ALBIE. I'm not prepared to answer any —

ROSSOUW. I mean, for God's sake, we already know how old you are.

ALBIE. Then there's no need to ask me.

Pause.

Look, take me to court and I'll answer anything you —

ROSSOUW. Look, man, you know full well. It's nothing to do with the courts. Under the 90-day law we have to detain you till you answer questions.

ALBIE. That's not correct. The law says you *may* detain me, it doesn't say you *must.*

WAGENAAR. Ach, that's lawyer's shit. We're not concerned with politics.

Slight pause.

ALBIE. It isn't politics. It's what the law is.

Pause.

ROSSOUW. Is there anything at all you'd like to say?

ALBIE (*with feeling*). Oh, plenty. There's lots I'd like to say.

ALBIE waits for reaction.
None, so he goes on to amplify the point:

I mean, there's lots of things, I'd like to tell you, but it wouldn't do me much good if I did.

ROSSOUW doesn't understand.
He looks at WAGENAAR.

WAGENAAR. Hy grap. Hy wees sarkasties. (He's joking. He's being sarcastic.)

ROSSOUW. Sarkasties?

ALBIE (*in some desperation*). I mean, there's, um, a lot of rude things, I'd like to say. About my conditions, all that.

ROSSOUW. Ach, I see. Rude things.

Pause.

ROSSOUW. You know you're just wasting your time.

ALBIE. I'm delighted to waste my time. The more of it I waste, the better.

Pause.
Suddenly, WAGENAAR, a cheap effect.

WAGENAAR. We've got Sarah, you know. We've got her, and she's singing like a bird. Mostly she sings about you.

Pause.

ALBIE. Tweet tweet.

ROSSOUW (*angry*). I think we'll be seeing a lot of each other. I think we'll get to know each other very well. You said you've got time to spare. You could be thinking about your statement. You could be thinking about the sabotage school you attended at Mamre. You know, the charges that you face. It could be 30 years. We charge you, and you could face 30 years.

Oh, you've got time to kill.

He nods to the OTHERS.
They move towards the door.

ALBIE. Oh, Captain . . .

ROSSOUW turns back.
He is affable.

ROSSOUW. Yes?

ALBIE. Please, next time, before you come, could you give me a few moments' warning, so I can put my pants on and receive you properly.

ROSSOUW. I couldn't give a shit about your bloody pants.

He goes out.
WAGENAAR follows.
ALBIE turns away, slightly smug.
FREEMAN has a word with the CONSTABLE, who goes out.
ALBIE aware of FREEMAN, turns back.

FREEMAN. Well, there we are.

ALBIE. Yes. There you are.

FREEMAN looks round the cell.
He notices the scratching.

FREEMAN. Ah. Scratching already. Quite the convict.

He has a look.

Nine down. Eighty-one to go. At least.

ALBIE. I'm sorry, I don't think I ever got your —

FREEMAN. Freeman. Phil Freeman. Do you mind if I smoke?

ALBIE (*glances at ROSSOUW's smoking butt on the floor*).
No-one else asks.

FREEMAN. I do. This is your home.

ALBIE. Then be my guest.

FREEMAN takes out his pipe, and reaches in another pocket for his matches.
He takes out his matches and a photograph.
He hands it to ALBIE.
He strikes a match.

FREEMAN. Who's this chap here?

He lights his pipe.

ALBIE. I'm afraid I'm not prepared —

FREEMAN. Yes, so you said. Repeatedly.

ALBIE. I was asked repeatedly.

ALBIE gives him the photograph back.

FREEMAN. Why wouldn't you tell them how old you are?

ALBIE. You know why.

FREEMAN. Tell me.

Pause.

ALBIE. Because if I answer any questions . . .

FREEMAN. Yes?

ALBIE. How old are you, Mr Sachs? Answer. When did you go to University, Mr Sachs? Answer. How long has your friend so-and-so been in the ANC? No, I'm sorry, that I will not answer.

FREEMAN. Right. Well done.

Pause.

Any complaints? About the way they treat you?

ALBIE. Well, they're not beating me up or anything like that.

FREEMAN. Good.

ALBIE. But I do think, now you ask, I think it is extremely cruel and uncivilised to subject a person to prolonged isolation. Also the facilities are rather primitive.

FREEMAN (*quietly*). Primitive. Uncivilised. You want to build a state like Ghana or the Congo and you say that South Africa is primitive and uncivilised.

Slight pause.

Or, for that matter, Hungary.

Slight pause.

ALBIE. Well, all —

FREEMAN *interrupts, with a glance at his watch.*

FREEMAN. I'd better go now.

ALBIE (*over-suddenly*). Look, my mother always sends far too much fruit, would you like an orange?

FREEMAN (*abruptly*). No, of course not.

Slight pause.

No, thank you.

Slight pause.

You know, you ought to try the old army dodge. You know, get a tin and leave the peel in it and make some booze.

He goes to the door.
Turns back.

They won't let people see you. You do realise. People from outside. You'll have to make your mind up on your own.

They know the way your mind works, Albie. It's their job. They do it for a living. They know what happens on your own.

FREEMAN *goes out.*
The door is locked.
ALBIE *is alone.*

ALBIE. All right then.

He bangs round the walls of the cell.

Oh, if you want it. On my own.

He is at the lavatory.
He reaches for the chain.
He stops, goes and sits down.
He flicks open the Bible.
About to read.
Stops.
Snaps it shut.
He sits and waits.
The half-hour chimes.
ALBIE *gets up, takes off his gown.*
He lies down, to do press-ups.
After a few, the sound of the WHISTLER.
The WHISTLER *whistles 'Going Home'.*
ALBIE *stops press-ups.*
Listens.
Then, without responding, he carries on his exercise.
Lights fade to blackout.

Scene Five

In the darkness, the eight o'clock chime.
Lights.
ALBIE *sits on his bed.*

ALBIE. It is the fifteenth day. It is eight a.m. Each day it is a shock waking here. Night is normal, I could be at home. Sleep has no geography. Sleep is instant time.

I woke up first two hours ago. All my life, I've had trouble rising. Now I'm grateful for my sloth. Since six o'clock, I dozed.

At first, my mind is thick and lazy. Then emotion stirs.

It's lousy.

Clatter.
Door opens
Enter CONSTABLE *with a plate of porridge.*

CONSTABLE. Breakfast, Mr Sachs.

ALBIE. Thank you. I'm the last today?

CONSTABLE. That's right.

ALBIE *eats.*
CONSTABLE *watches.*
Enter the SERGEANT. *To the* CONSTABLE:

SERGEANT. Weet ju hoe laat die is?
(Do you know how late it is?)

ALBIE. Good morning, Sergeant.

SERGEANT (*surly*). Morning. (*To* CONSTABLE:) Ek wil die
borde terug hê in tien minute, hy! (I want these plates back in
ten minutes, yuh?)

CONSTABLE. Ja.

SERGEANT (*to* ALBIE). Breakfast all right?

ALBIE (*unconvincingly, waving a spoonful*). Well, yes, it's —

SERGEANT. Good for you. Stop you being constipated. (*To*
CONSTABLE, *as he strides out:*)

Spoedig! (Quick!)

ALBIE *looks at the* CONSTABLE.
CONSTABLE, *to* ALBIE's *surprise, a grin.*
ALBIE *spoons up the last mouthful, holds out his plate.*

ALBIE. You can take this now.

CONSTABLE *goes and takes the plate.*

CONSTABLE. Um, Mr Sachs.

ALBIE. Mm?

CONSTABLE. You're a lawyer, yuh?

ALBIE. That's right.

CONSTABLE. I know a joke about lawyers.

Pause.

ALBIE. Tell it then.

CONSTABLE. Well, there's this woman, you see, whose son
swallowed a sixpence. And she was very worried, and she was

going to take the son to the doctor, when her husband said, don't bother with the doctor. Take him to a lawyer he'll get it out of him quicker.

Pause.
ALBIE *laughs a lot.*

It's a good joke?

ALBIE. It's a very good joke.

CONSTABLE, *pleased, takes out* ALBIE's *plate.*
As he goes:

CONSTABLE. Take him to a lawyer, he'll get it out in no time.

ALBIE *smiles, not at the joke, but at the pleasure of human contact.*
Broken by the slamming and locking of the door.
Pause.

ALBIE. In fact, constipation is not a problem. I defaecate at least three times a day. I enjoy it greatly, as it is the only activity I have not programmed. It is spontaneous and unpredictable.

I wait. My next activity, timed half-way between breakfast time and exercise, is to fold my blankets and then pile them up to be a chair. The day is made of fractions, punctuated by activity. Right now I am nearly half-way to the first activity of the first quarter of the fifteenth day. I am half-way to being a third of the way through my first 90 days, which is half-way to the second, which is two-thirds of the way to the third.

I am like the Constable. Like him, I have a joke. It's when I clean my water-jug with toilet-paper. The jug is plastic. I am not allowed anything made of metal or glass, but anything plastic is allowed. The joke is, that if keys were made of plastic, I would doubtless be allowed plastic keys. Every day my joke amuses me. Today it will amuse me.

My joke will make me laugh in just an hour's time.

Lights to blackout.
Then up again.
ALBIE *sits on his piled-up blankets, in the same position.*

ALBIE. It is now half past three.

The morning was a hive of activity. I piled my blankets, cleaned my jug, had my exercise, scratched my calendar, read my Bible and ate my lunch. After lunch, I slept. The worst part of the day, the first half of the afternoon, it stretches like a desert, but today I slept and slept, and now its back is broken.

Usually, at this time, I play draughts, on my check towel, with orange peel and toilet paper. This was fine to start with, but as time went by it palled. My right hand always knew my left hand's strategy. I made a third team — pea-pods — and the fact of playing matches on a small-league basis saved the project for a day or two. But now I'm quite relieved that orange peel can retire the winner.

Pause. He enjoys the revelation.

Cos I've got a new activity.

He jumps up, finds a small paper bag, full of bits of paper, orange peel, etc. He finds a small fishbone.

Fishbone. Knew'd come in handy.

He goes to the toilet, gets a piece of toilet paper.

Toilet paper.

He sits again, lays out the fishbone and the toilet paper in front of him.
Then he feels under the blankets, and produces, with a flourish, a comb.

During this morning's exercise, I stole my comb.
It's clogged with dirt.
It's *filthy.*
It'll take at least a quarter of an hour to clean.

He picks up the fishbone and starts to gouge out the dirt from between the teeth of the comb.
He chatters on.

After the comb, I will do my physical jerks. I hate this activity, but it must be gone through. Today, it will not be too bad, because I have another new activity I can look forward to. My mother sent a tube of cheese. I plan to try and write with it.

Cheese-writing is my substitute for nurturing my caterpillar.
I fed him peas from lunch, and over two days he grew to quite enormous size, and yesterday he disappeared. I hope he made it to the world outside.

My comb, cheese-writing, jerks, and then my second Bible reading — what a crowded afternoon it's turning out to be!

Lights to blackout.
Then up again.
ALBIE in the same position.
Then he gets up, puts on his trousers and a red sweater.

ALBIE. It is nearly a quarter to eight.
    After supper.

Time for my concert.
The high spot of my day.
My rendezvous with the whistler. Nearly time.
For a long time, whenever I heard it, I would whistle back.
Now, however, I am silent, waiting for this time. It does not
interrupt my day's routine. We sing and whistle at a set time,
and we know, all day, that it is going to happen, that we'll
never let each other down. Nearly time.

My concert consists of a number of melodies: the Going Home
theme, Nkosi Skilele Afrika, political songs like If I Had a
Hammer. Recently, I have begun to perform an Alphabet
Medley. A for Always to which I have set my own words,
B for Because, which I have to 'la' a lot of because I can't
remember it, C for Charmaine, D for Daisy. Sometimes I
cheat, for X I sing Deep in the heart of Texas, but I do manage
something for each letter.

The three-quarter chime.

And now it's time.

He sings:

I'll be living here, always
Year after year, always
In this little cell
That I know so well
I'll be living swell
Always, always
I'll be staying in, always
Keeping up my chin, always
Not for but an hour
Not for but a week
Not for 90 Days
But Always.

And on I go. Through all my songs. And he or she, my whistler,
whistles back. It it an act of love.

And it has been quite wonderful today. The best so far.

And I wonder, sometimes, on the good days, if I am coping
far too well. And if I'm suffering enough.

Blackout.

Scene Six

ALBIE *asleep.*
A chime.
He wakes, grovels about. Sits up.
Suddenly, he lifts his vest. It's splattered with blood.
He looks round, teeth clenched, for the culprit.
He snaps at a flea.
He misses.

ALBIE. Damnation.

> *He points to his vest, explaining to us.*

Not the brutality of the apartheid state. The violence of probably unsegregated fleas. Who have become intolerable.

So. Today.

> *The* CONSTABLE *comes in.*

CONSTABLE. Good morning, Mr Sachs. How are you today?

ALBIE. Well, I'd prefer to be outside than in.

> CONSTABLE *grins.*

But in fact there is something, Constable.

CONSTABLE. Mm?

ALBIE. I wonder if it would be possible to have clean blankets sent in by my mother. These are full of fleas. It's most uncomfortable.

CONSTABLE. There's powder. What's wrong with the powder?

ALBIE. Well, what's wrong with the powder is that it doesn't have any effect on the fleas, in fact they seem to thrive on it, but it's nearly killing me. As soon as I lie down I start sneezing. I can't breathe and I can't sleep.

CONSTABLE. Well, I'm not allowed to do anything. You'll have to see the Sergeant.

ALBIE. All right, then. I'll ask the Sergeant.

CONSTABLE *(as he goes).* Don't worry, Mr Sachs. The Sergeant, he'll see about the blankets.

> *Exit* CONSTABLE.
> *Door closes.*

ALBIE. And the Sergeant comes that evening. And he wishes me a good evening, and I wish him one back. And he asks me how I am. And I tell him that I would prefer to be outside than in, he grunts, and asks me if I have any problems. And I tell him about the blankets.

And, yes, they are treated with powder but all that does is encourage them and suffocate me.

And, yes, I see that it is not a matter with which he is permitted to deal, and of course I will and when can I see the Station Commander?

And he says Sunday and I say right.

And on Sunday there is the Station Commander, on his way to church, neat in his grey suit.

Good Morning Mr Sachs, he says.
Good Morning, Mr Kruger, I reply.

And he enquires after my condition, and I reply to the effect that I would much prefer to be outside than in — he smiles — and then I move without ado to the question of my blankets.

Is there no powder, he enquires.

Oh, yes, I say, there's powder, heaps of it, there's mountains of the stuff, but all they do is eat it. As a hors d'oeuvre to me.

And Mr Kruger then explains, in detail, that he is not instructed to permit me to receive anything from outside, except for food and clothing.

Ah, I riposte. At once. Ah, ah, I reply, quick as a flash, but aren't blankets really the same as clothes? I mean, like, really?

No, he says.
No, blankets aren't the same as clothes. And my instructions speak of clothes, at length, but they say nothing on the matter of your blankets. You had better see the Special Branch. It's their domain.

And off he goes, in his grey suit, to church.

And Tuesday, it's the Captain.

Good day, Mr Sachs, and I return the salutation, and he questions my general state of health, and I vouchsafe that I would most definitely prefer to be outside than in, and now, dear Captain Rossouw, what about my blankets.

Blankets?

Yes, that's right, my blankets, this is one of them, it's full of fleas, look there's some blood, that's mine, and full of powder, have a sniff, acute asphyxiation, can my mother send me clean ones from outside.

Well. Says the Captain. If you answered questions — Captain Rossouw this has nothing whatsoever — Well, I'm sorry, but it's not my function to concern myself with your facilities.

Well, then, whose function is it?

There's a pause.

Well, I'm afraid that your request can only be authorised by Pretoria.

Pause.

Pretoria?

That's right. Pretoria.

Pretoria? My request for blankets has to go to Pretoria?

That is correct, he says, Pretoria, and turns to go.

Then how in God's name do I get my request for clean blankets to Pretoria?

Pause.

You'd better see the Magistrate.

The Magistrate.

That's right. If anyone can do it, he can. He has, and at this point, in a strange gesture, the Captain waggles his earlobe at me, more or less the direct ear of Pretoria.

And off he goes. And then, on Thursday, there's the magistrate.

Good Afternoon, Good Afternoon, how are you, well, on balance, I would much prefer, but as it happens, I do have this small complaint, to which I'd like to draw your eye, or bend your direct ear, in fact, to wit, my blankets have been colonised by fleas, they're biting me to death, can't sleep, my clothes are bloody, please can I have clean ones sent in from outside.

Hm. Blankets, eh?

That's right.

Well, blankets . . .

Yes?

Not really my department.

No? But what about your ear?

My ear?

The Captain swore you had the direct ear of Pretoria!

ALBIE *waggles his earlobe.*

Oh, I understand! You are responsible for complaints. And asking for blankets isn't a complaint. It's a request. And, yes,

I see, you are not responsible for requests. There's nothing you can do.

Exactly, says the magistrate.

And by the time that I spot the flaw in this, the fact that my request is in essence the consequence of a complaint, about the fleas and powder, he is gone.

Pause.

And at this point, I must confess that my resolve is somewhat on the wane.

Pause.

But then, on Tuesday, there is Major Riebeeck. Now Major Riebeeck is *all right*.

Good morning, Mr Sachs, and morning Major. Are you all — no, Major, not all right, I'm not all right at all, I have a request, no not a request, a complaint, and I have made it to the Constable, who is not allowed, and the Sergeant, who is not permitted, and Mr Kruger, who is not instructed, and Captain Rossouw, who is not concerned, and the Magistrate, who is not responsible, and in the faint and indeed rapidly diminishing hope that somebody somewhere may conceivably be authorised to deal with it I am making it to you.

Pause.

Uh?

Pause.

I can't remember.

Pause.

I've forgotten the complaint.

Pause.

Well, then.
I'm sorry to have . . .

Yes, perhaps I will.
Well, thank you for your patience, Major Riebeeck.

And that evening, the Sergeant once again.

Lights down.
Lights up.
The SERGEANT *stands there.*

Sergeant, do you recall, I was asking for something last week, do you remember what it was?

Slight pause.

SERGEANT. Well, I do remember something . . .

ALBIE. Yes?

SERGEANT. But, no, I can't remember what it was.

Slight pause.

I can't remember everything.

ALBIE. No, of course not.

SERGEANT *turns to go.*

Sergeant?

SERGEANT. Hm?

ALBIE. I heard this joke. Perhaps you'd like to hear it.

Pause.

SERGEANT. All right, go ahead.

ALBIE. Well, there was this woman, whose son swallowed a
sixpence. And she was very worried, and she was going to take
her son to the doctor, when her husband said, don't take him
to a doctor. Take him to a lawyer. He'll get the money out of
him faster.

Pause.
The SERGEANT *laughs.*

SERGEANT. Ja, that's good. That's very good. I'll tell my wife
that joke.

Slight pause.

Hope you remember, eh? The thing it was.

ALBIE (*smiles*). Hope so.

The SERGEANT *goes out.*
Door closes.
ALBIE pleased about his relationship with the SERGEANT.
He sits on his blankets.
He sneezes.
He looks at the blankets.
He falls back on the bed, partly in a gesture of mock despair.
Partly real.
Suddenly, the clatter.
ALBIE up.
Puts on his jacket.
Just in time.
The CONSTABLE *admits* ROSSOUW *and* WAGENAAR.

ALBIE. Good evening, Captain.

ROSSOUW. Evening.

Slight pause.

How are you?

ALBIE *smiles.*
He glances at the blankets.

ALBIE. Well, I would prefer . . .

He looks at ROSSOUW.
Still smiling at his private joke.

Well, If you don't mind, not to answer any questions at this stage.

WAGENAAR *looks at* ROSSOUW.
ROSSOUW *nods.*

WAGENAAR. OK. You're moving.

WAGENAAR *starts collecting* ALBIE's *things.*

ALBIE. Where?

ROSSOUW. You'll see.

He goes.

WAGENAAR. Now, can we go?

The SERGEANT *enters with handcuffs.*
ALBIE *looks at them, puts his hands out.*
The handcuffs are snapped on.

SERGEANT. 'Get it out of him in no time.'
Eh, Mr Sachs?

ALBIE. Yes.

WAGENAAR. Let's go.

ALBIE *picks up the grip. It's difficult to hold. He goes out.*
Blackout.

Scene Seven

In the darkness, loud, the noise of the new prison.
Shuffling and mumbling, prisoners being shunted down corridors.
Shouts of GUARDS.

GUARDS. Maak gou, julle vokken donders!
Dink julle ons kan die hele blêrrie dag rondstaan! (Get a move on, move your fucking arses! You think we've got all day?)

Halt! almal halt! (Stop! All of you stop!)
Wat's jou naam? (What's your name?)
Hy ken nie sy vokken naam nie. (He doesn't know his fucking
name.)

*Then lights on the cell. A 2nd SERGEANT stands there.
And ALBIE stands in his new cell. His handcuffs are off. The
same basic set, but a bunk rather than a mat. ALBIE's stuff is
piled on the bunk. Not sorted out.*

ALBIE. Thank you, Sergeant.

2nd SERGEANT goes out. Slams and locks door.

ALBIE. My new cell. It's shaped like a loaf of bread. The walls,
covered by filthy scrawlings. Outside, the din is deafening.
Everyone shouts, at everybody. Me. I am wretched and jangled
and alone.

*He goes and looks at a window, high in the fourth wall. A
shout in the corridor — a harsh, metallic voice:*

VOICE. Waar's hy? Waar's die blêrrie Kommie? (Where's the
bloody Commie?)

ANOTHER VOICE. Hier, meneer — (In here, sir.)

VOICE. Maak die blêrrie deur oop! (Open the bloody door!)

*The door is opened.
A COLOURED CONSTABLE admits Warrant Officer
SNYMAN.
SNYMAN is elderly, balding and capless.
He has a thick accent.*

ALBIE. Oh, good after—

SNYMAN. Well, have you got all your stuff?

ALBIE (*not understanding*). Uh?

SNYMAN. All the stuff you brought from Maitland, is it here?

ALBIE (*gesturing at the jumble on the bunk*). Well, I hope so, I—

SNYMAN. You people always come along and say your stuff is
missing and you blame us. So, I'm asking you, right now,
have you got all your stuff?

ALBIE. Well, it seems to be all here, but, I could make sure . . .

*ALBIE, disorientated, goes and looks at his stuff.
SNYMAN impatient.*

Look, I should say, I don't think you'll find me troublesome.

SNYMAN. You'd better not be.

ALBIE. You can ask the people at Maitland.

SNYMAN. Maitland? I'm not interested in Maitland. This isn't Maitland. It's Wynberg.

ALBIE looks up.

ALBIE. To whom am I speaking?

SNYMAN. Me? I'm Warrant Officer Snyman. I am the Station Commander. You will be under my control and I don't want any nonsense.

ALBIE can't concentrate, he's just turning over his stuff, to look busy.

ALBIE. No.

SNYMAN. Well, for the last time, have you got all your stuff?

ALBIE. There doesn't seem to be anything missing.

SNYMAN. Good. Well, all I say is, don't come along later with a lot of lies.

To the COLOURED CONSTABLE.

Kom, robbish.

ALBIE (*assertive*). Mr Snyman, before you go, can I ask when my exercise will be?

SNYMAN. Exercises? Whenever we can find the time. We're very busy here. We can't worry about you all day long.

ALBIE. Yes, well, in Maitland —

SNYMAN. I told you, I'm not interested in Maitland. Anything else?

ALBIE. Only — does my mother know I'm here?

SNYMAN. How should I know? It's not to do with me.

Slight pause. ALBIE and SNYMAN look at each other.

Look, I know you. I know all about you Communists. I studied you. I am an expert, see? I know all there is to know about you Communists.

Pause.
ALBIE, *deeply upset, scrabbles about, finds his razor, thrusts it at SNYMAN.*

Wat's dit?

ALBIE. It's my razor. Don't you want it?

SNYMAN. What do you mean? Why should I want your things, cluttering up my office?

Slight pause.

If you want to cut your throat, you'll cut your throat. Who cares if someone's watching, hey?

To the COLOURED CONSTABLE:

Come on, rubbish.

SNYMAN *and the* COLOURED CONSTABLE *go out.*
Door slams.
Pause.
ALBIE *throws himself on his bunk, on top of his stuff.*
He puts his forearms across his eyes.
A moment.
Then ALBIE *suddenly stands up.*
He grabs his razor.
He waves it at the high window.

ALBIE. No, you fool. No, you clumsy oaf. I won't cut my throat. Up there, that window bar, it's solid, it'll hold my weight, don't worry, that's the way I'll do it, if I need to.

Blackout.

Scene Eight

ALBIE *lies on his bunk. The junk has been struck.*

ALBIE. At Maitland. I read the book of Job. It is one of the most compelling stories I have ever read.

It is about a man of privilege, hedged against suffering, who, as the result of a kind of cosmic competition, a bet-settling experiment between God and Satan, is made to suffer terribly.

And Job discovers, on his dung-heap, with his false friends, that if God made everything he made not just the good but also evil; pain, disease, oppression, suffering. And thus had God destroyed, for Job, the Hope of Man.

Job's suffering is not noble. It does not make him pure and fine. It makes him wretched. He abhors his pain.

But he can't hate it quite enough. And having looked up to the skies and found them dark and empty, he looks up again and the sky is full of God, in all fearful majesty, in all his vengeful glory, and Job submits. And instead of hating pain and suffering, abhors himself.

Job hates himself for hating God, through his hatred of his pain.

And God had won his bet with Lucifer.

Lights fade down and straight up again.
Suddenly, ALBIE sits up.
He has heard something.
Then we hear it too. It is a WHISTLER.
The WHISTLER is whistling 'If I Had a Hammer'.
ALBIE whistles too.
The WHISTLER stops.
ALBIE whistles Beethoven's Fifth.
The WHISTLER repeats 'If I Had a Hammer'.
. ALBIE responds with the same tune.
But then we hear the WHISTLER getting closer.
ALBIE stops whistling.
The whistling stops outside the door.
It's opened by the 2nd SERGEANT.

2nd SERGEANT. They want you in the office, Kom.

Pause.

ALBIE. ALBIE. What for?

SERGEANT. How should I know? Interrogation.

ALBIE stands, puts on his jacket.
Blackout.

Scene Nine

Warrant Officer VLOK and LT. WAGENNAR are in the office.
VLOK is oldish. He has very bad teeth.
WAGENAAR has a pad of paper. VLOK has a typewritten list of questions.
ALBIE.
The 2nd SERGEANT goes out.

VLOK. Hallo, Mr Sachs. I'm Warrant Officer Vlok. You know Lt. Wagenaar?

ALBIE. Yes, indeed I do.

VLOK. Please sit down.

ALBIE sits.

VLOK. Now, Mr Sachs. I have certain questions to put to you. Before I do so, however, under Judges Rules, I must give you a caution. I'm sure you know it well enough.

ALBIE. There's different kinds of caution. Depending on whether I am merely suspected of a crime, or whether I'm going to be charged.

VLOK. Oh, yes, of course. Well, you are being detained under the

90-Day law at the moment. What happens afterwards depends on the Attorney-General. He will decide whether to prosecute you or not. In the meantime I must warn you under the judges' rules that we are going to put certain questions to you, and any answers you give will be recorded by Lt. Wagenaar, and may be used in evidence if you are brought to trial.

Pause.

ALBIE. The point being, of course, that I am not obliged to answer questions.

Pause.

VLOK. No, you are not obliged, under the judges' rules.

ALBIE. But under the 90-Day law, if I don't you can keep me locked up for ever.

VLOK. Yes, Mr Sachs, that's right, I'm not very impressed that you know the law so well, it is your job.

Now, the questions. One. When you were arrested, a copy of the May 1962 issue of 'Fighting Talk' was found in your office. Did you know it was banned?

ALBIE. I am not prepared to answer at this stage.

VLOK. Two. For how long had you possessed it.

ALBIE. I am not prepared to answer at this stage.

VLOK. Three. Did you have permission from the Minister to have it in your possession?

ALBIE. I am not prepared to answer at this stage.

VLOK. Four. In December, 1962, did you attend a camp near the village of Mamre?

ALBIE. I am not prepared to answer at this stage.

VLOK. Five. When did you arrive there?

ALBIE. I am not prepared to answer at this stage.

VLOK. Six. Why did you tell people that they must be careful of police spies and of agents and provocateurs?

ALBIE. I am not prepared to answer at this stage.

Pause.

VLOK. Are you going to answer any of the questions?

ALBIE. I'll answer them all in court. Does this mean I'm going to be charged?

Pause.

VLOK (*hands* ALBIE *the list*). Read them.

ALBIE. What?

VLOK. There's no point in my reading them all out to you.

> ALBIE *takes the typescript.*
> *He reads the questions.*
> VLOK *lights a cigarette.*
> *A few moments. Then:*

VLOK. Look, you're a clever man. You must have a defence to the Possession of Banned Literature.

> ALBIE *looks up.*
> *Then back to reading.*
> *Pause.*

And the sabotage camp, I mean, you might not have known. Or you might not have been there all the time.

> ALBIE *looks up.*
> *Then back to reading.*
> *Finally, he hands the typescript back.*

ALBIE. My defence is the truth.

VLOK. Are you prepared to answer any of the questions?

ALBIE. No.

> VLOK *looks at* WAGENAAR, *shrugs.*
> VLOK *stands.*

ALBIE. However —

VLOK. Yes?

> *Pause.*

ALBIE. There is one thing, I could say.

VLOK. There is?

ALBIE. And I'd like it written down.

VLOK. Of course.

> *A glance at* WAGENAAR.

ALBIE. Right. Here it is.

> *Slight pause.*

I can say quite honestly and on my honour as an advocate and officer of the court —

WAGENAAR. Beg pardon.

> ALBIE *looks at* WAGENAAR.

You said officer of what?

ALBIE. The Court.

WAGENAAR. Oh, yes.

He carries on writing.

ALBIE. That I am not guilty of any offence in relation to any of the questions put to me.

Pause.

VLOK. I see.

Slight pause.

That's it?

ALBIE. That's it.

VLOK (*stands*). It isn't much. And it isn't up to us. But I'll see what I can do.

Blackout.

Scene Ten

The cell. Evening.
ALBIE sits on his bunk. He has just finished his dinner. His plate and his chipped enamel mug beside him.
SNYMAN stands there.

SYNMAN. Hm. Is it all right?

ALBIE. I'm fine, thank you, Mr Snyman.

SNYMAN. The food.

Slight pause.

ALBIE. Oh, fine.

SNYMAN. You sure?

ALBIE. Well, there is —

SNYMAN. Go on, man, spit it out.

ALBIE. It's just — it's very good, there's plenty of it, but it's just a bit more starchy than I'm used to.

SNYMAN. Starch? What's wrong with starch? The old Bantu at the back, he loves it.

ALBIE. Yes, well, p'raps it's rather better than the food he can afford at home.

Quickly.

It's just a matter, of nutrition.

Pause.

SYNMAN. Ah. Nutrition. Yes, well, perhaps you're right. In fact, you are right.

ALBIE. I am?

SNYMAN. I know, you see. As it happens, I am something of an expert on nutrition.

ALBIE. Are you?

SNYMAN. Yes. I've read a lot about it.

Pause.

Is that your mug?

ALBIE. Yes, it is.

SNYMAN. Hm. A white man shouldn't have a mug like that.

ALBIE. Well, I —

SNYMAN. You know, when I first came here, I was shocked, white prisoners were made to drink from metal mugs. And so I bought five proper cups, for them, out of my own pocket.

ALBIE. Oh, that's very —

SNYMAN. And you know what happened?

Slight pause.

Yes. That's right. They bust them all. Within a week. That was their gratitude.

Slight pause.

Then they come here and complain that we don't treat them properly. People like you. You know, Communists and lawyers. You're a lawyer, right?

ALBIE. Yes, I —

SNYMAN. You lawyers think you know it all. You think that no-one else knows anything. Like, for example, me. But as it happens, I've done a lot of reading, of my own. You'd be surprised. You could say, I am something of an expert on the law.

ALBIE. I'm sure you are.

Pause.

Actually, about the law, or lawyers, I did hear this joke . . .

SNYMAN. I haven't time for jokes. I'm very busy.

ALBIE. Yes, of course.

SNYMAN. I've twenty things to do.

Pause.
ALBIE, *thinking* SNYMAN *wants to go, hands him his plate.*
SNYMAN *goes to the door, shouts:*

Hey! Jy! Robbish!

COLOURED CONSTABLE *appears.*

Vak dit. (Take this.)

The COLOURED CONSTABLE *takes the plate out.*

ALBIE. Thank you.

SNYMAN *still stands there.*

Um, Mr Snyman?

SNYMAN. Hm?

ALBIE. I do have one request.

SNYMAN. What's that?

ALBIE. At Maitland —

SNYMAN. For the last time —

ALBIE. They did let me have a Bible.

Pause.

SNYMAN. Bible? You read the Bible?

ALBIE. Yes I do.

SNYMAN. And you understand it, do you?

ALBIE. Well, I'm learning a great deal. Of course, there are things that I find it hard, at first, to understand.

SNYMAN. Well, that's to be expected. The Bible needs a lot of study.

Slight pause.

As it happens, I myself have studied it for over 20 years.

Slight pause.

You could say, I am something of an expert on the Bible.

ALBIE *looks at* SNYMAN.
Blackout.

Scene Eleven

ALBIE *sits on his bunk.*
SNYMAN *perambulates.*

SNYMAN. Yes, I have studied the Bible, now, for nearly 30 years. In fact, I was once a rebel, just like you, and it was the Bible saved me. Since then, I've made a study of it. It's all there, you know.

Slight pause.

So. What have you been reading?

ALBIE. Well, at the moment I'm reading Kings. Kings One. The story of King Solomon.

SNYMAN. Ah, yes. That's a very interesting story.

ALBIE. Yes, I find it —

SNYMAN. For what it tells us. You see, King Solomon, he sinned with the heathen, and that was the beginning of the fall of the House of Israel. Even before Solomon, the same thing was happening, the Bible contains many such stories, on the same theme. To take an example, there is the story of the Samaritans.

ALBIE. You mean the good Samaritan?

SNYMAN. No, before that. You see, the Samaritans were a mixed breed, just like the Coloureds here in South Africa, and they also caused trouble all the time. You see, when the Jews arrived in Canaan, after wandering through the desert, they were very tired and hungry and thirsty. Now the people that they fell among had strange sexual customs. The girls were not allowed to marry anyone from their village, they had to marry strangers. And so they told the Israelites they would give them food, provided the Israelites sent young men for their daughters. Well, they needed the food, and the young men had been in the desert a long time, and unlike the Israelite women, who were all hard and bony, from their years wandering about the place, the girls in the village had soft flesh. So they took up the offer, and went to the girls of the village, and had knowledge of them. And that's how the Samaritans came to pass, they were the issue of the knowledge. And they lived side by side with the Israelites in Israel. Making trouble.

Pause.

The *Good* Samaritan, you see, he was an exception; he didn't make trouble. In fact, he made good. But the point of the story is how exceptional he was.

ALBIE. Oh, I see.

Pause.

I wish I had a book that told me things like that.

SNYMAN. Do you? Really?

ALBIE. Yes, I do. Really.

Pause.
SNYMAN, *with great magnanimity, goes and shouts off:*

SNYMAN. Hey! You! Rubbish! Stop lazing about and come here!

The COLOURED CONSTABLE *appears.*

You go to my office, now, OK? And on the table near the desk, you find a big book, it's called Encyclopedia, it has a picture on the front of a lot of men with beards and skirts on. You go and get it. OK?

The COLOURED CONSTABLE *salutes and goes off.*

ALBIE. That's very kind of you.

SNYMAN (*still looking after the* COLOURED CONSTABLE). Hm. You know, some of these coloured police are very good. Some are nearly as good as white police. You shout and swear at them as much as you like, and they don't mind. But most of them are rubbish. That one's rubbish. You can tell at once, if you've been in the police force as long as I have. Which are good and which are rubbish.

He turns back.

So, have you any other questions? About the things you've read?

Pause.

ALBIE. Well, there was . . .

SNYMAN. Yes?

ALBIE. There was the Book of Job.

Slight pause.

SNYMAN. Ah. Yes. Now that's a very interesting story.

ALBIE. Please, do tell me.

SNYMAN. Yes, of course. You see, Job was a very good man, who feared God and possessed a large family and a great deal of property and many men and maidservants. And God used to show Job off to Satan, as a man who was completely good in every way. And Satan waxed sore at this, and plagued Job with boils, and set fire to his farm and slew his family. And Job was very miserable, and covered himself with ashes, and rent his mantle, and cursed God. And he had three friends — one was a Temanite, one a Shumite and one a Nathamite — and they tried to stop Job, who was cursing God, and saying that he was dust, and should never have been born, and going on about how kings and rulers were all corrupt and wicked, very much as Communists like yourself do here in South Africa. And these three friends couldn't stop Job cursing everything, but a fourth man, called Elihu the son of Barachel the Buzite of the kindred of Ram, he told Job to snap out of it and get back to fearing God. And Job did fear God again, and God was so pleased that he restored unto him all the riches he'd had before. In fact, he gave him rather more, for example, he was given an thousand she-asses rather than the five hundred he'd had to start with. Just for fearing God so much.

Slight pause.

That's Job.

Pause.

ALBIE. That's — quite amazing.

SNYMAN *looks questioning.*

I mean, an thousand is an awful lot of she-asses.

SNYMAN. Oh well.
Oh well, it might be. But you mustn't always take the Bible to be exactly right.

ALBIE. No?

SNYMAN. Oh, no, you see, when they wrote in Moses' time, they didn't know things we know today. For instance, according to the Bible, the world was created exactly 5,724 years ago. Now you mustn't take that to be exact. In fact, scientists have gone into the question very thoroughly and they have finally worked out that the creation was at least 300 years earlier than the Bible says.

The COLOURED CONSTABLE *is back with the book.*

Ah, here's the rubbish.

He takes the book, an Afrikaans Biblical encyclopedia, from the COLOURED CONSTABLE.

You can bugger off now.

The COLOURED CONSTABLE *goes.*

So here you are. You can borrow my encyclopedia.

He presents the book to ALBIE.

ALBIE. Well, thank you very much, Mr Snyman.

SNYMAN. It's nothing.

ALBIE. Well, still.

ALBIE decides to seize the time.

Mr Snyman, I wonder if I could ask you something else?

SNYMAN. Yes, go ahead.

ALBIE. I wonder if, you know, that chap, sweeps out my cell. I wonder if I might be permitted to sweep it out myself?

Pause.

SNYMAN. No.

Slight pause.

No, it's not your place, to sweep out cells.

Pause.

Well, I must go. I'm very busy. They've made me Secretary of the Committee for the Police Widows' and Orphans' Ball. It's one big nuisance. I don't know why, they make me secretary of everything.

Pause. To ALBIE:

You know, it isn't possible, for me, to convert a person.

ALBIE *looks at* SNYMAN.

That's God's work, to convert. A person, can't convert a person.

Slight pause.

You know, I heard, they want to find a way they can release you.

Exit SNYMAN.
ALBIE *looking after him.*
Blackout.

Scene Twelve

ALBIE *stands in his suit.*
The 2nd SERGEANT *stands outside the open door.*

ALBIE. It is the 81st Day.

If what the Station Commander says is true, then I have much to think about. I am innocent of any possible charge they may bring against me.

There is an offer I could make. It wouldn't affect anyone else.

It might be possible.

Crosscut lights to office.
VLOK *there.*
ALBIE *comes in with the* 2nd SERGEANT.

ALBIE. Hallo, Mr Vlok.

VLOK. Sit down.

ALBIE *sits.*

Mr Sachs, I'm sorry. Headquarters are quite adamant. No statement, no release.

Pause.

Look, if there's nothing else you are prepared to say, then we're in deadlock.

Pause.

Look, to me personally, I couldn't give a shit. But it would be good to get the matter —

ALBIE. Well —

VLOK. Yes?

ALBIE. Well, there's one idea, that I was thinking over.

VLOK. Yes?
What is it.

ALBIE. I would be prepared, to clarify to the Attorney-General, anything he wants to know about those questions. I could do it through a colleague, you can choose who you like, or through one of the Attorney General's assistants.

Slight pause.

I must be absolutely clear, however, that I will discuss only those questions, and only matters concerned with me alone. That's all.

Pause.

VLOK. Hm. Good. It's something.

Slight pause.

I'll do my best. I'll try for an answer on Monday or Tuesday.

ALBIE. Well, that would be splendid. Wednesday is Christmas
  Day.

VLOK (*stands*). Indeed.

  Pause.

  You know, your type, you don't belong in here.

  He goes out.
  Blackout.

Scene Thirteen

ALBIE *sits in his cell.*
*His plate is in front of him, with the remains of his Christmas
dinner.*

ALBIE. It is Christmas Day in the jailhouse.

  The Station Commander brought me a special Christmas
  dinner. Cooked by his wife. From his own table.

  It didn't work. They won't release me. 'Sorry'. But no.

  Pause.

  I am the only prisoner left. The others are on bail. A girl,
  supposed to be a prostitute, she couldn't raise ten rand. So I
  thought, good, an opportunity to give a Christmas gift, quite
  selflessly, she'd never know her benefactor. But she raised the
  money somehow, and I got my ten rand back.

  The best of both worlds, really.

  Pause.

  I cannot understand the cruelty. I do believe, still, just, that
  men are basically good and fine and splendid.

  But I can understand the pain. It's not an attitude, a state of
  mind, it is a matter of one's circumstances. It is real. I think of
  medieval monks, who volunteered to suffer silent isolation.
  There's no glory there. There is no glory, in a suffering which
  drives out love.

  Self-sacrifice with love may well be fine. But self-denial
  coupled with an individual pain, that is absurd.

  The pain I feel is not ennobling.
  It is useless.
  It's destroying me.

  Pause.

  About a month ago, I was exercising. And the policeman

guarding me, he had a newspaper. And there was a huge headline on the newspaper, and I tried, as I flashed past, to read it. The first letter on the headline was clearly a K. Then an E, and then an S or perhaps an N. K-E-N, I thought, Kenya, but why headlines that size for Kenya? An election, here, perhaps, I wondered, but the Afrikaans for election is verkeising — or is it Kiesing, choosing? Perhaps it was a K-I-E. And it wasn't till three days later that they told me Kennedy's been killed. And all I thought of was, if there is war, detainees will be shot. The President was dead, and all I thought of was, maybe I'll be shot.

And when I thought they'd charge me, all I thought of was me standing up in court, addressing it, all eyes on me, the crowded hush.

And when I thought they might release me, all I thought of was the people coming up to me and saying, good old Albie, well done, man, you showed them, you held out.

And when they told me that I wouldn't go to court, I wouldn't get released, I fantasized about a life outside South Africa.
Living and working, writing, somewhere else.
Marrying, and having children.
Leaving everything and everyone behind.
To turn my back. To wash my hands.
A happy ending.

Pause.

Where did they get their stamina. The freedom fighters, tortured in Algeria. The resisters to the Nazis, under the Gestapo. All those bloody heroes.

Where did those bloody heroes find their will.

Pause.

And here's me, in my concrete cube, sat nursing my own useless pain.

Blackout.

Scene Fourteen

ALBIE *in his cell.*
The plate has gone.

ALBIE. It is, as it happens, the 90th day.

The clatter.
ALBIE *hardly looks up for a moment.*

Then he goes, slowly, and puts his jacket on.
A twitch of the shoulders, to try and snap out of his apathy.
The door opens.
Enter ROSSOUW *and* COLONEL McINTYRE, *a small man in a neat brown suit.*

ALBIE. Hallo, Captain.

ROSSOUW. This is Colonel McIntyre. He is in overall charge of security in Cape Town.

ALBIE. Hallo, Colonel.

McINTYRE. Hallo.

Pause.

This is for you.

He hands him a document.

ALBIE. Thank you. What is it?

McINTYRE. It's the order for your release.

Pause.

ALBIE. I'm sorry?

ROSSOUW. Read it.

ALBIE (*reads*). . . . hereby ordered that Albert Louis Sachs who is presently being detained in Wynberg Police Station, Cape Town, be released forthwith . . .

Pause.

Well.

Pause.

Colonel, haven't we met before? Weren't you in charge of the police who dispersed the crowds at the Remember Sharpeville meeting? In '61?

McINTYRE. That is correct. You'd better pack your things.

Pause.

ALBIE. I'm really free?

ROSSOUW. You're really free.

ALBIE. Right then.

He packs, quite quickly, but not too quickly.
Lights fading up on the office.
VLOK *is there.*

ALBIE. You know, it's ridiculous, but I reckon I run about three.

miles a day here, and I've had this thing, throughout, to run to Muisenberg Beach when I'm released, which I reckon is about six miles, d'you reckon that's right?

ROSSOUW. Yes, I think that's about right. It's quite a marathon.

ALBIE has finished packing.

ALBIE. I'm ready.

McINTYRE. Right.

They go out of the cell.
VLOK stands and goes out of the office.
ROSSOUW, McINTYRE and ALBIE reappear, go into the office.

ROSSOUW. Now all you have to do is sign the receipt for all your property, and you can go.

ALBIE signs the receipt.

ALBIE. I can go home?

ROSSOUW. You can go anywhere you like.

ALBIE. You're not going to arrest me again?

ROSSOUW. You are completely free.

Pause.
ALBIE believes it.

ALBIE. Oh, am I. Oh, am I.

Oh, I don't know whether to say thank you or fu . . .

ROSSOUW a slight, sympathetic smile.
Even McINTYRE a smile.

Can I, phone my mother?

ROSSOUW looks at McINTYRE, who nods.

ROSSOUW. Certainly. The phone is there.

McINTYRE goes out.

In fact, hold on, I'll have to get a line for you.

He sits, dials.

Won't be a moment.

ALBIE has to lean against a wall, he's almost shaking.
Enter VLOK followed by McINTYRE.

VLOK (*smiling*). Hallo, Albie.

ALBIE turns to VLOK.

ALBIE. Oh, Mr Vlok, I —

VLOK. A great day, eh?

ALBIE. I mean, we brought it off, after all that, I'm actually —

VLOK. I am placing you under arrest.

> *Pause.*
> ROSSOUW *puts down the telephone.*

ALBIE. What.

VLOK. Under Section 17 of Act 37 of 1963.

> ALBIE *sits.*

ROSSOUW. You'd like a glass of water.

> *He stands, pours a glass of water from a carafe on the desk.*
> *He gives the water to* ALBIE.
> *Pause.*
> ALBIE *drinks the whole glass.*
> McINTYRE *moves easily behind the desk.*

McINTYRE. We are keeping you because we are satisfied that you have information about certain offences, and we cannot release you until you answer all our questions satisfactorily. That's all.

> *The telephone rings.* McINTYRE *sits.*
> McINTYRE *answers the telephone.*

> Yes.
> This is Colonel McIntyre.
> Yes, good morning.
> No, he's still here.
> No, I'm afraid I can't give you any more information.
> He will be kept here in Cape Town.
> That's up to him.
> I can tell you nothing more.
> Goodbye.

> McINTYRE *puts down the telephone.*

> Your mother.

> ALBIE *stands, picks up his grip.*

ALBIE. My cell, please. Now.

McINTYRE (*stands*). Of course. Warrant Officer Vlok will get a Constable.

> *Blackout.*

Scene Fifteen

ALBIE *in his cell.*

ALBIE. At first it was a book. But books are flat, controlled. The stuff of life is rolled up flat and sliced in two-dimensional pages. I wanted something more immediate, more active, more alive. So it had to be a play.

And working on the play is fighting back. The worse the things they do, the more I suffer, then the better, richer, deeper is the play.

He stands, growing in enthusiasm.

There will be singing, Africans will sing, to start the play. The play's in Africa. I see these cubes, they look opaque, in fact they are transparent, made of gauze, and they light up, you see people in them. Danny, me, the other 90-days.

But first, the stage is dark. The singing. Then I come on — actually me, or someone who's made up to look like me -- and I — or whoever's playing me — explains the play, that it is true, that this is what occurred. And then he's in the cell. He prods the walls, and says out loud, so this is what it's like.

The thoughts, perhaps, are pre-recorded, or the actor has a tiny microphone to whisper in.

Through him, we see his life, inside the cell. One scene, perhaps, will show me exercising, and the pain of it, and how it must be gone through. In another, there will be the caterpillar, and the draughts, the cleaning of my comb, the writing with the cheese, and, most of all, the singing. From my cube, from me, and the other cubes, the fact that isolation is the worst thing of them all, the crowd is not an enemy, that singing is an act of love.

And then perhaps I'll tell the audience — myself, or who is playing me — will tell the audience of how I thought that I would write a play, a play-within-a-play, or rather, a playwright within a play; and the play may even somewhere have the playwright writing it, and thinking of the opaque cubes, and working out the dialogue, and saying 'this is what it's like', the playwright writes his play within the play.

But as I think of it, I am aware, increasingly, the real problem is to show just what it's like, in isolation, the disintegration, and the horror of it all, to people who are not alone, because they are together, watching, as an audience, my play.

And then, I think.
Perhaps the best thing is, not in the play, but in the audience,

for them to see, for me to come out, to the audience, and say, my day is sitting staring at a wall, now I am going to make you sit and stare, you mustn't talk, or read your programmes, look at other people. For two minutes, you must sit and stare.

And then, perhaps, they'd know.
Just what it's like.

Pause.
For about 15 seconds.
Then ALBIE *goes to his bunk.*
He lies down.
Another three-quarters of a minute.
ALBIE *puts his forearms across his face.*
He does not move, for another half minute.
Then he puts his arms by his side.
Another half a minute.
Then he swings his legs out, stands.
He speaks, not to the AUDIENCE, *briskly, as he walks out, through the fourth wall of the cell.*

ALBIE. When this is over, I will leave South Africa. I owe that thing to me.

ALBIE *walks out of the set, off the stage.*

Act Two

Scene One

ALBIE sits.
The door is open. It's light behind the door.
The COLOURED CONSTABLE *stands there with a broom, in the light.*
ALBIE stands. Then he talks to the COLOURED CONSTABLE.

ALBIE. I'm a banned person. I am not allowed to publish, or to meet a group of more than two. I am forbidden, also, to travel away from what must be one of the most brilliantly beautiful places on the earth.

Cape Town. Surrounded by dazzling beaches. Forests on one side, and wild bush on the other. Behind, the huge stone mountain. For the perfect holiday. By day, you swim, or surf, or take a cable-car up Table Mountain, and at night, stand on a beach-side balcony, look out across the shimmering sea, and catch the twinkling of the lights of Robben Island.

I have no problem with the policy of armed struggle for the overthrow of White South Africa. Since Sharpeville, since the banning of the ANC, there's been no other way. If when people organise they are banned, if when they demonstrate they are shot, if disparities of wealth and power are actually growing, then there is no question why and only questions how.

But, still, I think back to the early days, the fifties, days of innocence, so good to be alive, we saw ourselves as storming heaven. Saw it as an act of love. But now it's different. Now, the sacrifices that we'd only sung of, suddenly came real.

It's all too simple, elevate our lack of courage to a principle, and call that principle non-violence. It's all too easy, build your fear of being hurt or killed into a principle that people should not hurt or kill the people who are hurting and are killing them. It's all too, neat, to say that change must be controlled and ordered, that our world here can revolve that far without a revolution, that crops will grow without the plough, that we can have the rain without its thunder, we can seize the sun without the fierceness of its burning.

But where do I locate that. Me, Albie Sachs, the boy who always broke up fights at school. The natural mediator. Where can I find my hatred and my rage?

Oh, yes, I loathe apartheid, its complacent grubbiness, the fact that in here, even as a prisoner, I'm better off than you are as a jailer, I don't have to sweep my cell, I don't even have permission, I'm patted all over with petty privilege.

And I abhor its cunning. What it's done to me, by splitting me from my comrades, isolating me. Removing me from that collective strength, that stops me being just a white man with an upset conscience, places me in history, and gives my conscience scale.

But I can't hate the *people*. I am jealous of the Africans. I'm sick with envy for their rage. I hear the canings in the courtyard, of the boys, their screaming and the cackles of the policemen beating them, and I feel pity, and disgust, I cannot understand how people act like this, but still I wish I had their hatred and their rage.

I'm furious with what my jailors do, but not with what they are.

I hate the whip but not the men who wield it.

Pause.

So?

Blackout.
Then lights.
ALBIE sits.
The door is open. It's light behind the door.
SNYMAN stands there.
ALBIE looks up, stands.

ALBIE. Good morning, Mr Snyman.

SNYMAN is not in a good mood.

SNYMAN. Where's the boy who sweeps your cell?

ALBIE. He hasn't been yet.

SNYMAN (*looks at his watch*). Tt.

ALBIE. Perhaps he's been delayed.

SNYMAN. I try to run a station.

Pause.
SNYMAN looks at ALBIE.
ALBIE looks back, not sure what SNYMAN is thinking.
SNYMAN takes a document from his pocket.

This was served on me last night.
The person asked me to show it to you.
Here it is.

ALBIE. What is it?

SNYMAN. It's the result of your application.

ALBIE. I haven't made an application.

SNYMAN. You're supposed to read it.

He gives ALBIE *the document.*

It's your books and writing paper.

ALBIE. What?

ALBIE *turns the pages rapidly.*

Oh, what —

He looks up at SNYMAN.

SNYMAN. You've got to read it.

ALBIE. Yes, of course, I'll . . .

(*Reads*): 'In the Supreme Court of South Africa, Cape of Good Hope Division . . . Having read the files of record, ladida, the court declares the applicant entitled to be supplied with, or to be permitted to receive and use, a reasonable supply of reading matter and writing material.'

Pause.

Oh, boy.

SNYMAN (*with another paper*). Now you've read it, sign here.

ALBIE. Yes, of course.

He looks at SNYMAN.

SNYMAN. It doesn't help, you know.

Your people, making a fuss, and keeping on at me. The telephone's not stopped. I said I would consider it, when I had studied what the judgement said.

Pause.

ALBIE. But you are — you will, I mean, it is the order of the court . . .

SNYMAN. If they'd listened to me this whole thing wouldn't have been needed. Policemen are so obstinate. I'd have given you a book or two, and there'd have been no case.

ALBIE. Well, yes, you did, your encyclopedia, I'm very grateful —

SNYMAN. Now they come serving orders on me.

Pause.
The COLOURED CONSTABLE *has appeared.*

COLOURED CONSTABLE. Erm —

SYNMAN. Hey, wat maak jy? (What you playing at?)

CONSTABLE. Ek —

SNYMAN. Ja, ek kan dit sien. Jy is twintig minute laat. (Yes, I can see. You're 20 minutes late.)

The COLOURED CONSTABLE *shrugs.*

Here, give me that broom.

COLOURED CONSTABLE, *surprised, gives* SNYMAN *the broom.*

Now bugger off. Off!

COLOURED CONSTABLE *shrugs and goes.*
SNYMAN *holds the broom out to* ALBIE.

Here's the broom. You can sweep out your cell.

Slight pause.

I'll leave the door open, so you can sweep the dust into the yard.

Slight pause.

It's sunny in the yard.

Slight pause.

I'll be back in about ten minutes.
You understand?

Slight pause.

There's ways of doing things.

Pause.
ALBIE *takes the broom.*

ALBIE. Thank you, Mr Snyman.

SNYMAN. Hm. We'll talk about what books you want tomorrow.

SNYMAN *goes out.*
ALBIE *holds the broom.*

ALBIE. Thank you, Louis. Thank you, Basil. I know you're judges in South Africa, but still I thank you.

Blackout.

Scene Two

ALBIE *in his cell.*
A pile of books beside him.

ALBIE. It is Friday evening. It is the 116th Day.

And I have my books.

Long books. Can read 600 pages in a day. And novels. Don't want books of politics, philosophy and criticism. Books about people. Want escapist books. Books about normal life.

The door opens.
SNYMAN *comes in.*
His shirt is open, and he wears shorts.
He has no shoes on. CONSTABLE *is behind him.*

SNYMAN. Hey, gee my die sleutels. (Give me the keys.)

He takes the keys.

You can go back to the charge-room.

SNYMAN *half-closes the door.*
ALBIE *looks at* SNYMAN's *feet.*
SNYMAN *notices.*

SNYMAN. Athlete's foot. The doctor says I should walk barefoot as much as I can. It's good for you.

ALBIE. I see.

SNYMAN. Makes feet of steel. When I was small, we were so poor, we didn't know what shoes were. Hard as steel.

Slight pause.

ALBIE. Would you like to sit down?

SNYMAN. Hm. Thanks.

He sits.

We've just been celebrating. Bit of a party, celebrating the success of the Widows and Orphans Ball. The ball took place last night. I didn't go myself. I'm not a drinking man. Of course, I have a drink or two at home, but not the bar. This afternoon, just one or two, to celebrate the success we had, the ball.

ALBIE. I'm very pleased.

SNYMAN. Yes, we were very poor. My grandfather, in fact, he was a Justice of the Peace. That was when the Cape was a separate province. He had seven farms, but the British took them, because he was a rebel. Life was hard. That's why I joined the police force.

ALBIE. When was that?

SNYMAN. Oh, yes, you see. The police force, at the time, it wasn't like it is today. It was run, then, by the English and the Irish and the Scots. And the English hated the Irish, and the Irish hated the Scots and the Scots hated the English.

Slight pause.

But they could agree on one thing.

ALBIE. What was that?

SNYMAN. D'you want to know what it was? I'll tell you. They all agreed to hate the Afrikaaner.

Slight pause.

You know, before the war, I wrote my Sergeant's exams, and because I was Afrikaans, they failed me. And again, in 1947, I wrote them all again. And still they failed me. It was like that. If you asked an English Sergeant anything, he'd say fuck off. Just like that, he'd say it, fuck off, Afrikaner. Now that's one phrase that you'll not hear in my station. No-one says fuck off. You will not hear a person in my station, use that phrase. Fuck off.

Slight pause.

But that is how it was, for Afrikaaners, in those days. But now, of course, it's changed. Now being Afrikaans is all right.

Pause.

ALBIE. I see.

SNYMAN. It's all much better now.

Pause.

In fact, as it happens, after 1948, the Nationalists took over, I wrote my exams another time. And they still failed me. Some reason or another.

Slight pause.

It's because of that experience that I gave up politics and became a student of the Bible.

ALBIE. You were in politics before?

SNYMAN. The OBs went ahead, of course. You know, the people who cut wires and blew things up, to make us fight the Russians with the Germans. I wouldn't blow things up. I mean, I wouldn't fight, I'm not prepared, I said, to fight, unless it's fighting in South Africa, for South Africa. But, still, they said I was pro-German, nearly put me here in jail, in fact. But I'd refused to blow things up.

Pause.

And so, when the Nationalists came in, they failed me. Politics! It hasn't done me any good. Look what it's done to you.

ALBIE. Indeed.

Pause.

SNYMAN. I mean, why should I hate you, just because you're Jewish and a Communist?

Slight pause.

Doesn't the Bible tell us we should love our enemies?

Pause.

ALBIE. Does it say that?

SNYMAN. Oh, yes. Yes. It says it in the Bible. That's why we get on, you and I. Cos God says, we should love our enemies.

He stands to go.
Suddenly, he falters, almost falls, the keys jangling.
ALBIE reaches out to steady him.
SNYMAN recovers.

Birmingham.

ALBIE. I'm sorry?

SNYMAN. Birmingham, America.

ALBIE. You mean, in Alabama?

SNYMAN. Yes, that's right. They tried desegregation there. And look what happened. Riots. People killed. Those little black girls, all blown up.

Slight pause.

We don't want that.

Slight pause.

It doesn't work. You read your Bible. Doesn't work, you see.

Pause.
He goes out.
Door slams.
ALBIE goes and sits.

ALBIE. I could have knocked him down, and stole the keys, and gone.

But I thought he might be ill.

I was worried that *he* might be ill.

Suddenly, rattle of keys.
Door opened.
ALBIE looks up in surprise.
Enter VLOK and FREEMAN.

ALBIE. Hallo.

VLOK. Hallo. Is everything all right?

ALBIE. It's fine.

VLOK. Where's Mr Snyman?

Slight pause.

ALBIE. How should I know. He's not here.

VLOK. Mm. I'd heard he was here.

Pause.

Some time ago, perhaps. Alone with you. For quite a time.

ALBIE. Well, he was here.

VLOK. Alone with you? How long?

Pause.

Ten minutes? Twenty minutes?

ALBIE. I think you'd better ask him that yourself.

VLOK. Yes.

Pause.

Is everything all right?

ALBIE. It's fine.

VLOK looks at FREEMAN.
VLOK goes out.
ALBIE looks at FREEMAN.
FREEMAN lights his pipe, leans against the wall of the cell.

ALBIE. Well?

FREEMAN. You wanted to protect him. ·

ALBIE. Did I?

FREEMAN. Very sweet of you.

Pause.

The man's a Nazi, Albie. Loathes you Jews. Should hear him.
Vokken Jood.

ALBIE. He wasn't an OB. Like Vorster was.

FREEMAN. Now there you go again. Defending him.

Slight pause.

Too scared, I would imagine. Or too dumb. Or both.

Slight pause.

Why do you protect him?

Pause.

Mm?

FREEMAN *takes a duplicated leaflet from his pocket.*

'Solitary Confinement'.
Interesting and not inaccurate.
We don't know quite who wrote it.

'Some of the consequences are strange and unexpected.
You might fear you are going mad.'
'There may be changes in the way you see and hear. There may be fluctuations, drifting and swirling of objects in the visual field.'
'You will be shouted at, insulted, told you will be kept in prison for ever or even hanged.'

Well, that's a little, purple. But this one is spot on:
'After a time you will feel a terrible urge to talk, to anyone. About anything. This urge is almost irresistible.'

Pause.

And so you talk to Snyman.
And so you're not going to talk to Snyman any more.

Pause.

Of course, it isn't Snyman as such. It's anyone you can protect. It makes you feel, a human being.

Pause.

And part of the idea, of course, is quite precisely not to let you feel a human being.

Pause. He waves the document.

One thing, it doesn't mention, oddly, is sleep deprivation.

Slight pause.

I mean, if you want to drive a man quite potty, have him gibbering, you keep him up all night. I saw it once, in Mozambique. It's quite — degrading, as a spectacle.

Slight pause.

ALBIE. That is a threat.

FREEMAN. I found it markedly unpleasant.

ALBIE. You don't like seeing people suffer.

Slight pause.

FREEMAN. Well, I've always been, fastidious. It's a very British trait. I was in Kenya with the British Army. There was only one problem there. The British didn't really want to win. We have this draining pedantry, obsession with the other fellow's case. That's what I mean, fastidious. Like you.

ALBIE. There's no doubt at all in my mind. It's very simple. I want to see justice and equality in South Africa. I don't see apartheid's case because it hasn't got one.

FREEMAN. Do you see Ghana's?

ALBIE. All I know is this country. And I've no doubt at all that things will have to change here. And when they do, if I am ever able to influence anyone or anything, then there will never be anything like this solitary detention, anywhere, at any time.

Pause.

FREEMAN. Are you quite sure, Albie? Anywhere? At any time?

ALBIE. Oh, yes. Quite, quite sure.

Slight pause.
FREEMAN a light laugh.

FREEMAN. Yes. Yes, you probably are.
Equality and justice. Late night chats with Nazis.

Pause.

Tell me about Sophiatown.

ALBIE. I'm not prepared to answer any —

FREEMAN. Oh, for heaven's sake. It's an illustration.

Pause.

All right, then. Sophiatown, Johannesberg. In 1955, they moved the blacks out, make an all-white suburb. Blacks protested, and refused to go. Defiance of Unjust Laws Campaign. Defied away. But then, eventually, they did get moved, and Sophiatown became an all-white suburb. And then they decided to rename it. And the name they chose was Triumph.

Pause.

And some, you know, the liberals, progressives, thought it rather tactless. Pointed out, it's lack of, well, fastidity.

Pause.

So you defy. You carry on, defying. We'll continue triumphing.

Pause.

You hate the whip but not the man who wields it, Albie. You do that because, in here, you've no-one. And to hate and fear your guards would make you feel so small and tiny and alone that you'd give in. We aim to make you feel that, Albie. That is what we're doing to you.

Pause.

Just to let you know.

FREEMAN *goes out.*
The door shuts behind him.
ALBIE *left alone.*
Blackout.

Scene Three

ALBIE *sits with a pad of paper and a pencil in his cell.*

ALBIE. When I first received the paper it was dazzling white and the pencil felt clumsy between my fingers. I rested my hand on the pad and waited for my fingers to start moving. First I thought of my name, but that seemed a bit silly. And then I thought of drawing, but I'm hopeless at drawing, and finally I made a blob. A tiny black blob, on the corner of the page, and thought, here it is, paper and pencil, the power of communication, the summit of civilization, and all that I can manage is a blob.

And I suppose, that I was frightened, too, that they would read it, what I wrote, and see inside my mind.

And so I blobbed on for a week or two.

But then I started games. Word games. I have developed quite a repertoire. First there are word ladders. Dog to cat in three, dog cog cot cat. Sick to well, four, sick silk, sill, sell, well. But jail to free is a little longer. Jail fail fall fell feel feet fret free. Jail to free in seven.

Very faintly, the sound of GUARDS *shouting orders.*

GUARDS. Staan in die lyn, julle moere.
(Stand in line, you cunts.)
Kom, hotnot, trap, trap gou.
(Come on, niggers, go, go fast!)
Wag nou, bobbejaan, moenie stoot nie.
(Wait, you baboon, don't push.)

ALBIE. From word-games, it is not a big step to cross-words, and
I have been working on a special 90-day variety. I'm pleased
that all the clues fit so well into my theme. For example, there
is 'See you later, plainsclothesman', 12 letters, which is
'Investigators'. 'To begin with for keeping prisoners, but
altogether for keeping wine' is six, 'cellar'. 'Hath April, June,
November and certain types of prisoner', six and four, is
'Ninety Days'.

The GUARDS *are closer.*

GUARDS. Stil, julle blerrie donders.
(Quiet, you bloody loudmouths.)
Het julle nie vokken ore nie.
Hou jou vokken mond bobbejaan.
(Don't you have fucking ears, shut up you fucking baboon.)

ALBIE. 'Prisoners in Flight'. Four and five. 'Jail Birds'. In fact, I
gave the crossword to the Station Commander, in the hope
that it might be published in the Police Magazine. Sadly, they
thought it was a kind of code. Which indeed it is. But not the
kind of code they thought.

*ALBIE is increasingly aware of the sounds and what they
mean, and is trying to block them out.*

GUARDS. Nou sal julle bobbejane sweet.
(Now you baboons will sweat.)
Mou gaan julle kak, jong.
(Now you will shit, man.)

ALBIE. Many of my pages are devoted to what I call the Quick
Brown Fox game. The idea is to write a sentence which
contains all the letters of the alphabet but which is shorter
than the famous 'Quick Brown Fox jumped over the Lazy
Dog', which is 33 letters. My best effort, I feel, is 'Quick
Brazen fights vex jumpy world', with only 30 letters. Even
shorter is 'Wild brazen fights vex jumpy quack' which has only
29 letters, but little sense, and 'Why just quiz and vex grim
black fop' must be rejected on the grounds of poor political
content. My personal favourite is 'Beg crazy cops fix with
vim quick end jail', which although it has all of 34 letters is
highly topical and accordingly worthy of a consolation prize.

Sound of a bench being scraped along the ground.

If I am released, perhaps a newspaper will be interested in this game too.

GUARD. OK, let's start.

A swish.

ALBIE. And finally, there are memory games, which are quite important to me as my memory's so terrible, I have forgotten half the license number of my car, and this I hope will help revive my powers of remembering.

GUARD *(calls)*. Magebula!

CHILD'S VOICE. Ja, baas.

GUARD. Kom hierso.

ALBIE. I have spent a day, for instance, going through the states of America, alphabetically, geographically, and related to major towns. By now the first 45 or so come easily, but two or three remain elusive every time. I write my list and then I go through all the permutations till I find the ones I've missed. Today I've three to find.

Sound of a caning.
Six strokes.
A little male laughter.

So, alphabetically, there's Alaska, Arizona, Arkansas, the Cs are Colorado, California and Connecticut, ah, missed out Delaware, there's Florida and Georgia, and Hawaii, Idaho and Illinois, um, Indiana, Iowa, then Kansas and Kentucky . . .

GUARD. Ngela!

ALBIE. For a while, confused myself by thinking that New Brunswick's an American state, in fact it's Canadian. Two left.

GUARD. Wilfred Ngela!

CHILD'S VOICE. Ja, Baas.

ALBIE. And now the towns. The easy ones. Boston, Massachusetts, Detroit in Michigan, Oklahoma City more or less by definition, as of course New York New York. Dallas or Houston Texas, Atlanta Georgia, Las Vegas is Nevada, LA, San Francisco California, Tucson Arizona . . .

A cane stroke. Laughter.

Why the hell do I remember Tucson?
Memphis —

Remembers one,
as another stroke.

Tenn-e-ssee.

Two strokes.
Laughter.

For a long time, tried to restrict myself to state capitals, but that proved ridiculously frustrating. I mean, who knows the capital of New York State?

Three strokes.
Laughter.

In fact, I did remember, it was Albany. One left. So geography, starting from the north west, going round the coast, there's Maine, Vermont, Massachusetts . . .

GUARD. 'Sekgane! J. Sekgane!'

ALBIE. Connecticut, New York, New Jersey, Maryland, Virginia, both the Carolinas, Georgia, Florida . . .

CHILD'S VOICE. Ja Baas.

GUARD. Kom, hotnot!

ALBIE. Mississippi, Louisiana, Texas, New Mexico . . .

A cane stroke. Laughter.

Oh, no. Missed it.

Another.

Next to Georgia. First in the bloody alphabet. And as in Birmingham.

Another.

Al. Abama.

Much laughter. A stroke. For the first time, a scream.
ALBIE goes and sits on his bed.
Stroke. Scream
ALBIE puts his check towel over his head.
Stroke. Scream. Stroke. Scream.

ALBIE. Lock look loom doom door.

Laughter.
Blackout.

Scene Four

ALBIE *asleep.*
The door opens.
Enter WAGENAAR.
ALBIE *snaps awake.*

WAGENAAR. Ok, Albie.

ALBIE (*quickly up*). Hallo, Lieutenant —

WAGENAAR. Get packed. You're moving.

ALBIE. Where to?

WAGENAAR. Does it matter? Kom nou, loop. (Come on, move.)
Hurry!

ALBIE (*beginning, vaguely, to find his things*). These days, I'm
not used to doing things in a hurry.

WAGENAAR. Well, you better start learning.

ALBIE, *angry, as he packs his stuff.*

ALBIE. You keep me here for 130 days doing nothing, and then
you expect me to hurry.

WAGENAAR. That's right.

ALBIE *looks at* WAGENAAR.

Come on, we haven't got all day.

ALBIE *drops a pile of books in his bag.*

ALBIE. All right. I'm ready.

SNYMAN *appears in the doorway.*
He has a pair of handcuffs.
He looks at ALBIE.
He looks at WAGENAAR.

SNYMAN. I have come to oversee the transfer of the detainee.

Pause.

I am the Station Commander. It is my job to supervise the
prisoners.

WAGENAAR. Of course it is.

Slight pause.

SNYMAN. Whatever's said.

SNYMAN *looks at* ALBIE.
ALBIE *goes and gets the encyclopedia.*
He gives it to SNYMAN.

ALBIE. Goodbye, Mr Snyman. I won't say it's been a pleasure
being here, but . . . We've had some interesting conversations,
and for that I'm very grateful.

SNYMAN. Hm! Hope we don't see you back in here.

ALBIE. Well, so do I.

Pause.
SNYMAN *speaks to* WAGENAAR, *gesturing with handcuffs.*

SNYMAN. They asked me to bring these.

ALBIE. All right.

ALBIE *sticks his hands out to* SNYMAN.
SNYMAN *hands the handcuffs to* WAGENAAR.

SNYMAN. So now you've got them.

He turns and goes out.
ALBIE *puts out his hands to* WAGENAAR.
WAGENAAR *clicks on the handcuffs.*
Blackout.

Scene Five

In the darkness, the sound of a Radio Patrol room.
A jabble of voices, mixed up, following each other like a fugue.
'Hallo. Dis 414 radio patrollie. Your name? Where are you calling
from? Yes, I know it's a phone booth, but where, man? Don't be
stupid, of course it's in the street, but what's the name of the street?
In the main road? What main road? Where are you man? What
part of town? Look I can't send off the van unless you tell me
where you are.'
'Ons roep C2, ons roep C2. Kom in C2. C2, there's a fight at
number 24 Blumfeld St. The complainant's name is van der Bijl.
Did you get that? I don't know. OK, C2, over and out.'
'Hey, how old did you say you are? You can't be 12, you sound
at least 15. What are your measurements? Hey, man I don't
believe you. Well, I go off duty at 10 o'clock, OK? What's your
name? Hey, Bathsheba, that's a pretty name.'
Lights on the cell.
There is a bunk, in a different position.
ALBIE *stands there.*

ALBIE. At Caledon Square I suffer another drop in my standard
of living. The cell is tiny, and so little natural light that the
electric light has to burn all day. The only good thing about
the cell is the window, which is at eye level, and although
it's heavily gridded I can see through it. Unfortunately, the

view is blocked by a red brick wall a yard away. Through the window comes the incessant jabber of the radio patrol room. It goes on all day.

A 3rd SERGEANT *opens the cell door.*
He admits McINTYRE.

McINTYRE. Mr Sachs.

ALBIE. Good morning, Colonel.

Slight pause.

Would you like to sit down?

McINTYRE. No thank you.

Pause.

I am told by my men that you still refuse to answer any questions. Is that the case?

ALBIE. Yes, that is the position.

McINTYRE. You won't answer any questions at all?

ALBIE. No.

Pause.

McINTYRE. I am afraid, then, that the outlook for you is very bleak.

Pause.
He goes out.
The 3rd SERGEANT *closes the door.*
It is locked.
Blackout.

Scene Six

ALBIE *in his cell.*

ALBIE. It is the 138th Day.
It's started.
It's been going on for weeks.

It started mildly. I would feel, when going to the yard, a strange light-headedness, a dizziness, my head becoming a balloon. I feel as if I'm in some kind of, growing void.

And it got worse. A periodic shock, a kind of spasm, when my mind's at rest, off guard, my limbs will suddenly contract and kick out and my body's shaken, as if an electric current's passing through me.

Sometimes, also, when I'm showering, I have this fantasy. I stand there, in the wet, all soapy, slippery, and get this urge to tumble down and crack my skull, and watch it split apart, my brains burst out like pomegranite pips, the red stuff splurging out across the wet cement.

I think, perhaps, the idea in my mind is, if I fall and let my head break open, then I can't be blamed if the policemen see inside my mind.

But worst of all's the splitting. I am lying in my bed, and feel my soul is separating from my body. My limbs and trunk and head lie there inert, a vegetable mass, while my soul floats gently to the ceiling, where it coalesces and becomes embodied.

Usually, the soul becomes an owl. It sits there, calmly, watching me. It's I. I'm staring at myself. My owl is watching me. My owl. My me.

Blackout.

Scene Seven

ALBIE *in his cell.*
DR KRAAL *stands there.*

KRAAL. You asked to see me.

ALBIE. I'm sorry to bother you, Doctor, but I —

KRAAL. You've got a bed, I see.

ALBIE. Yes, it's reasonably comfortable.

   KRAAL *goes and looks at the bunk.*

KRAAL. So. What's your complaint?

ALBIE. Would you like to sit down?

KRAAL. No thank you.

   Slight pause.

   I know what you're going to say.

ALBIE. Do you?

KRAAL. Yes. You'll say we doctors are useless, we don't do anything to help. But, of course, there's very little we can do.

   He turns from looking at the bed.
   He looks at ALBIE.

   It's up to you.

ALBIE. Don't think I caught your name.

KRAAL. I'm Doctor Kraal.

ALBIE. Well, Dr Kraal, I've asked to see you because I'm worried about certain symptoms I've been having. They're not things I'd normally bother with.

KRAAL *looks at the bunk again.*

. . . there's nothing serious, I'm sure, but in here I feel I can't take chances with my health.

KRAAL *does not respond.*

Do you want to hear my symptoms?

KRAAL. Yes. All right.

ALBIE. Well, doctor, I've a number. The first is, I have this dizziness. When I'm walking to the yard, my head becomes very light. It's not easy to describe, but I feel as if I'm in a kind of expanding void.

KRAAL (*not turning to* ALBIE). Expanding what?

ALBIE. Void.

Slight pause.

And the second thing, I get these shocks, it's a kind of spasm, when my mind's at rest, when I'm off guard, my limbs suddenly contract and kick out. It's a bit like an electric shock.

KRAAL (*light laugh*). Hm.

ALBIE. And third . . . Doctor, do you want to note this down at all?

KRAAL (*prodding the mattress*). No, no.

ALBIE. Well, third I have this feeling, it's a bit hard to describe, when I'm lying on my bed, as if my soul is, sort of, separating —

KRAAL. Your soul? Are you religious?

ALBIE. Well, it's a physiological sensation, I only . . . I'm trying to describe it.

KRAAL *turns to* ALBIE.

KRAAL. You know, you're very lucky here.

ALBIE. I am?

KRAAL. Prisons are much better places than they used to be.

You get three meals a day. And a bed, with blankets. I can't see what you're fussing about.

ALBIE. Well, I'm just telling you, that I —

KRAAL. I can't see why you're complaining.

Pause.

ALBIE. I'm not complaining. I'm reporting an illness.

KRAAL. If you don't like it here, then there's a very simple way out.

ALBIE. Doctor, I'm not sure it's your function —

KRAAL. I think it's my job to decide my function.

Slight pause.

Have you finished?

Slight pause.
ALBIE*'s given up.*

ALBIE. Yes.

KRAAL. Right. I'm satisfied that your conditions are perfectly adequate.

He goes and bangs on the door.

ALBIE. Doctor?

KRAAL (*turns back*). Mm?

ALBIE. Would it, what would you say if my arm was broken? Or blood was pouring out of my mouth?

The 2nd SERGEANT *opens the door.*

KRAAL. Your arm isn't broken. There is no blood pouring from your mouth.

He goes out. The door shuts.

ALBIE. Or if I said I was Napoleon? The Queen of Sheba? Elihu the son of Barachel the Buzite?

ALBIE *out front.*

I pace backwards and forwards in my narrow cell. This man's job is to heal the sick. I've been five months in solitary confinement. And instead of examining me he gives me a lecture. How dare the Government employ a man like that to care for prisoners.

Pause.
He realises what he's just said.

How dare the Government of the Republic of South Africa.

Pause.
He sits on the bed, picks up a book.

I decide I'd better try and take my mind off it. I realise that now I must rely on my own resources to keep my mind together. I try and read. My eyes are skimming through the lines, they're not absorbing any of the sense. They're brimming up with tears of anger.

He throws the book across the room.

How dare he. How dare he accuse me of malingering. What kind of person does he think I am?

The locks being opened.
The door opens.
Enter SAMOLS. *He carries a black case.*

ALBIE. Who are you?

SAMOLS. My name is Samols. I'm a doctor. I believe you are worried about your health.

ALBIE *looks at him.*

ALBIE. I've just seen Dr Kraal.

SAMOLS. I know. He's just reported to me. I thought it best if I came here myself.

SAMOLS *picks up the book.*

Is this your book?

ALBIE *stands, goes to* SAMOLS, *takes the book.*

ALBIE. Would you like to sit at all?

SAMOLS. Thank you.

He sits.

So what's the problem?

ALBIE. Well, I've got these symptoms. They're not things I'd normally bother with . . .

SAMOLS. Then why are you bothering?

ALBIE. Because I'm abnormally locked up in solitary confinement.

SAMOLS *takes out a notebook.*

SAMOLS. Yes.

Slight pause.

Is it true you refuse to answer questions?

ALBIE. Yes.

Slight pause.

SAMOLS. Tell me your symptoms.

ALBIE. Really? You want to hear them?

SAMOLS (*smiles*). Yes, of course.

Slight pause.

It's not my job to lecture you.

ALBIE. Then thank you. For being a doctor. Thank you, prison
doctor.

SAMOLS *doesn't understand.*
He looks at ALBIE.
Blackout.

Scene Eight

ALBIE *stands with a bottle of pills.*

ALBIE. He gave me pills. I haven't taken them. I don't know
what they'll do to me.

He sits on the floor, holding the bottle of pills.
He looks up at his owl.
Lights fade to darkness.
Then fade up again.
ALBIE *still sits on the floor.*
Surrounding him are ROSSOUW, WAGENAAR *and*
FREEMAN.
But ALBIE *still looks up at his owl.*

ROSSOUW. Why's he not talking, d'you suppose?

WAGENAAR. Well, I don't know.

ROSSOUW. Perhaps he's worried, he'll betray his Comrades in
The Struggle.

WAGENAAR. P'raps he is.

ROSSOUW. Although they'd hardly thank him for it.

WAGENAAR. Seeing as how they've talked, the lot of them,
they've talked and now they're free.

Slight pause.

FREEMAN. It's rather touching, isn't it, the way he seems
prepared to suffer everything. For people who won't suffer

anything for him.

Pause.

ROSSOUW. Why's he not talking, d'you suppose?

WAGENAAR. It's hard to say.

ROSSOUW. It could be his ideals. His long participation in the struggle.

WAGENAAR. Well, that could be so.

ROSSOUW. Grand gestures. Making Africans sit down on all-white benches. Sitting down himself on benches marked Nie Blankes.

Slight pause.

FREEMAN. I wonder what he thinks he will achieve. I wonder what he thinks he has achieved.

Pause.

ROSSOUW. You know, I think I've got it. Albie wants to be a hero.

WAGENAAR. You know, I think you're right. He wants to be St Joan.

ROSSOUW. He wants to be a Freedom Fighter in Algeria.

WAGENAAR. He wants to be a French resister, captured by the Nazis.

Slight pause.

FREEMAN. He wants to do a far far better thing than he has ever done before.

Pause.
Quickly:

WAGENAAR. Why be a hero, Albie? It isn't like the books. Not clench your fist against the firing squad. Not the short walk, and shout defiance on the gallows. Just the empty cell, and all those endless days.

ROSSOUW. Of course, he'll tell us that's the same.

FREEMAN. Why be a hero, Albie? Haven't you read the sacred texts? It's not the individual, it's the masses. Not the man that matters, it's the movement.

WAGENAAR. Of course, the man's got little choice. Now he's the only one that's left.

ROSSOUW. Why be a hero, Albie? Justice? Liberation? Come on, you read the papers. You know what's happening in Ghana and the Congo. You know what bombs do to people, Albie. Must have doubts. You must have reservations? Haven't you?

Pause.

FREEMAN. Why be a hero, Albie. When you know we're certain. And you're really not quite sure.

Suddenly, ALBIE starts to speak.
The OTHERS listen.

ALBIE. I've always said, tomorrow is another day. Sufficient unto this day be its evil. But I have had an awful lot of yesterdays. And every day, it's harder, find the stamina, sufficient stamina, to get me through until the next tomorrow, drag through that, and add another yesterday.

And I'm convinced it's not the information any more. It's just you want to prove that nobody survives, a kind of trial of strength for you, and you won't let go until I've broken.

And I'm sure, that all the trials in train when I was taken must be over.

And I know that all I'm doing's suffering. A year, two years. I'm bound to break eventually, and why not now.

And I don't think it matters any more. It won't hurt anyone, it won't hurt me.

And so, on Friday, when you come, I'll speak to you.

Pause.
He opens the bottle of pills.
He takes out a pill.
He looks at it.
He puts it back in the bottle, screws down the cap.
He stands and puts the bottle on the bed.
Fade to Blackout.

Scene Nine

In the yard, a 2nd CONSTABLE with ALBIE's washing bucket.
ALBIE prepared for exercise, in the cell. The 3rd SERGEANT also in the cell.

ALBIE. And it is the Friday. Time for exercise.

SERGEANT. Kom.

ALBIE and the SERGEANT into the yard.
ALBIE to his bucket. Starts to wash his hair.

His two GUARDS *light cigarettes.*
ALBIE *has an idea.*

ALBIE. Hey, Sergeant.

SERGEANT. Hm?

ALBIE. Do you like jokes?

SERGEANT. Depends on the joke.

ALBIE. Well, it's about this woman, whose son swallowed a sixpence. Have you heard it?

SERGEANT. No.

ALBIE. Well, she told her husband about this, and said, we must take him to the doctor. And the husband said — no, don't bother with that, take him to a lawyer: he'll get the money out of him in no time!

Slight pause.
CONSTABLE *looks at the* SERGEANT.
The SERGEANT *laughs.*
The CONSTABLE *laughs.*

SERGEANT. Ja, that's very good. I will remember that.

Laughs.

Ja, very good.

SERGEANT *goes out.*
ALBIE *rinsing his hair.*

ALBIE. The Sergeant seemed to like the joke.

CONSTABLE. Oh, yes. He likes a joke.

ALBIE. What's he like? To work under?

CONSTABLE. Oh, you know . . .

ALBIE. Go on?

CONSTABLE. Most time, he's OK. Sometimes, we say it must be better to be one of his prisoners than one of his constables.

ALBIE *laughs.*

He used to be a prisoner, so I suppose he's, you know, sympathetic.

ALBIE. He used to be a prisoner himself?

CONSTABLE. Oh, yes. Two years.

ALBIE. And they let him have his job back?

CONSTABLE. Oh, Yes. You know, the police are not too bad
'bout that.

ALBIE. What was he in for?

CONSTABLE. Oh, it was something 'bout a bandiet . . . Think he
filled this kaffir up with water, and then jumped on him till
he died.

ALBIE, his head dripping, stares at the CONSTABLE.

ALBIE. What?

Re-enter the 3rd SERGEANT.
He looks at ALBIE.
He laughs.

SERGEANT. Get it out of him in no time.

ALBIE. I'm sorry?

SERGEANT. Joke.

ALBIE. Oh yes.

SERGEANT. They want to see you now.

ALBIE. Who?

SERGEANT. The interrogators.

ALBIE. But I'll need — (ALBIE *picks up his towel. Then, to the*
SERGEANT:) How long did it take?

The SERGEANT doesn't understand.

I mean, it must have taken quite a time.

SERGEANT. You what?

ALBIE. It doesn't matter.

Enter ROSSOUW, WAGENAAR and FREEMAN.

ROSSOUW. Albie.

ALBIE. Ah, Captain. Look —

FREEMAN. Now, Albie. It's been 150 days. We know you want
to talk. But something holds you back. What is it?

ALBIE. Well —

WAGENAAR. Look, Albie. It's the others, is it? Really, you
know, there's no-one need discover. We can promise secrecy.
If you don't want to be a witness, then you needn't be. We'll
see you all right.

ALBIE. Yes —

ROSSOUW (*angrily*). Why are you so stubborn? Why? Your precious self-respect? Your honour? What a medieval word. Your dignity? You think that you look dignified? You think it matters? To us or anybody?

Pause.

ALBIE. No. I don't.

Pause.

I am not prepared to answer questions at this stage.

Pause.

Sorry. But no.

. *Pause.*

It matters to me.

ROSSOUW (*with a vague, dismissive gesture*). Ag, vat hom terug na die sel. (Take him back to his cell.)

ALBIE *stands. The* SERGEANT *leads him out.*
Lights fade up on the cell.
ALBIE *taken to the cell, as* WAGENAAR *and* FREEMAN *look at* ROSSOUW.
ROSSOUW *lights a cigarette.*
ALBIE *in his cell.*

ALBIE. Sergeant.

SERGEANT. Ja?

ALBIE. Just thank you. Thank you very much.

ALBIE *takes off his jacket, begins to fold it.*
Suddenly, ROSSOUW *stands, goes out of the interrogation room. The* OTHERS *will go as the lights fade.*
ROSSOUW *bumps into the* 2nd SERGEANT *leaving the cell.*

ROSSOUW (*to the* SERGEANT). Maek oop die deur. Maek die vokken deur oop! (Open the door. Open the fucking door.)

The 2nd SERGEANT *goes back and opens the door, admits* ROSSOUW, *and stands outside.*

ALBIE. I thought we'd finished, Captain.

ROSSOUW (*blurted*). You know — you do realise —

ALBIE. What?

ROSSOUW. We won't be soft on you.

ALBIE. I'm aware of that.

ROSSOUW. You can't complain, we didn't tell you what we meant.

ALBIE. Oh, no, I can't complain.

ROSSOUW. And any time. Just ask for me, the day or night, I'll come.

ALBIE. You will?

ROSSOUW. I will.

ALBIE. Oh, thanks. Thanks very much.

Pause.

But I don't think, it will be necessary.

ROSSOUW. Someone else?

ALBIE. Not necessary. Thank you, all the same.

Slight pause.

It's nothing personal. It is your orders, after all. You are just doing what you're told.

Pause. ROSSOUW stands, smoking, looking at ALBIE. Then he tosses the butt on the floor, goes out. Shuts the door. The locks.
ALBIE stubs out ROSSOUW's cigarette carefully. He 'tt tts'. He puts it down the toilet.
He pulls the chain.
He leans against the wall.

ALBIE. You needn't be a witness.
Oh, we'll see you right.

What kind of person do they think I am.

Fade to Blackout.

Scene Ten

The cell.
ALBIE sits.
WAGENAAR stands smoking.
ALBIE looks questioningly at WAGENAAR.
WAGENAAR turns away, looks at the wall.
He sees ALBIE's scratchings.
He crouches.

WAGENAAR. What's that. 167 days?

ALBIE. 168, in fact. I haven't done today.

WAGENAAR. Nearly six months.

WAGENAAR stands.

ALBIE. It is.

Pause.

Did you want something?

Pause.

WAGENAAR. This is for you.

He takes a document from his pocket.
He tosses it on the floor in front of ALBIE.

ALBIE. What is it?

WAGENAAR. I'm only the messenger boy.

WAGENAAR goes out.
The door remains open.
ALBIE picks up the document.
He doesn't read it.
Because he's noticed the open door.
He stands and walks slowly forward, out of the cell, through
the fourth wall.
Lights fade to a spot on ALBIE.
And ALBIE, *on the spot, starts to run.*

Scene Eleven

ALBIE *running.*

ALBIE. I am free,
I am FREE.
I am off to the SEA.

It is a quarter to five, the sun is low, and I am running to the
sea. As I pass the magistrate's court I fling my arms in the
air -- I'm free! I'm free!

People stare at me. They think I'm one of those cranky
runners trying to keep fit. Well, let them stare. If only they
knew. They think I look funny. Well, that's fine. A man
should look funny when he's free.

It's six miles to the beach. I've never run six miles before. But,
then again, I've never been released after nearly six months in
jail before. They've lost and I HAVE WON. So I'm running to
the sea.

I pass a stadium, it's empty, I'm the only athlete here.
I cross a patch of grass, and feel it soft beneath my feet.

I pass a police station, and I shout, oh, no, you cannot touch
me now!

And I am near. The mountain rises. I can see the water sparkle, hear the crashing of the waves. I think of what the sea will feel like, water washing over me.

I'm free! I'm FREE.

And then at last the beach. And there he is, the man I'd hoped for, with his camera, and taking pictures of the mountain and the beach. And one more thing to do, before I throw myself into the sea.

A spot finds the CAMERAMAN.

ALBIE. Hey. Hallo!

CAMERAMAN. Hullo?

ALBIE (*running round the* CAMERAMAN). Look, could you do me a favour?

CAMERAMAN. What favour?

ALBIE. Look, please don't think I'm mad, but —

A VOICE (*from the darkness*). Hey, Albie!

ALBIE. . . . but I've just been released from prison, I've been held as a 90-Day detainee . . .

VOICE. Hey, Albie, you bugger!

ALBIE *waves into the darkness, keeps running round the* CAMERAMAN.

ALBIE. . . . those are my friends, they've come to celebrate, but I'd like you to take my picture.

VOICE. Hey, hallo, Albie!

CAMERAMAN. Eh?

ALBIE. Look, my name is Albie Sachs, I know it must sound crazy . . .

2nd VOICE. Hey, Louis, where's Albie?

ALBIE. . . . but if you do this for me, I'll pay for the whole spool.

VOICE. He's there on the beach, look at him!

2nd VOICE. Hey, Albie, how's it feel?

ALBIE. You see, this is a wonderful day for me, and I want a record of it, I mean, do you see?

3rd VOICE. Hey, Albie! How are you!

CAMERAMAN. Well. OK. If you like.

ALBIE. That's wonderful.

3rd VOICE. Albie!

CAMERAMAN. You'll have to run that way, because of the sun.

ALBIE. OK.

2nd VOICE. What is he *doing?*

> ALBIE *runs a little way from the* CAMERAMAN, *they are both still in spots.*
> ALBIE *jumps up and down in one place.*

ALBIE. Is that OK?

CAMERAMAN. That's OK.

> *The* CAMERAMAN *lines up the shot.*

VOICE. Hey, Albie!

2nd VOICE. Albie!

3rd VOICE. Hey, hallo, Albie!

CAMERAMAN. Now.

> *And* ALBIE SACHS *leaps up, punching the air with his fist, a cry of triumph:*

ALBIE. OUT — SIDE.

> *Snap Blackout.*
> *In the darkness, at once:*

ROSSOUW. Well, hallo, Albie.

Scene Twelve

Cold, grey lights.
The CAMERAMAN *has gone.*
We see the people playing ALBIE's *friends.*
They are ROSSOUW, WAGENAAR *and* FREEMAN.
They stand there.

On the edge of the set stands another MAN.

ALBIE. Oh no.

ROSSOUW. Well, Albie. How are you?

ALBIE. But I thought —

ROSSOUW. Yes, Albie, what did you think?

ALBIE. It was made clear to me, when I was released, that no further proceedings would be taken against me.

ROSSOUW. That was two years ago.
A lot has changed.

The 3rd SERGEANT *enters to the office with pads of paper, cans of beer, a large pile of cigarette packets, and a hamper of food.*

WAGENAAR. Things hotting up.

ROSSOUW. Your people, killing people. Nasty business, in Johannesberg Station.

FREEMAN. We think, some chums of yours involved. We'd like to know.

ROSSOUW. Oh, yes, a lot has changed.

ALBIE. Yes, I know things have changed. Now you're beating people up, depriving them of sleep. You're using electric shocks. You're driving people beserk, so beserk that some of them have jumped out of eighth floor windows. Oh, I'm aware that things have changed.

Pause.

Are you going to deprive me of sleep?

ROSSOUW. Please sit down.

They are in the office, which the 3rd SERGEANT *has set up.*
WAGENAAR and FREEMAN sit. The SERGEANT stands.
ROUSSOUW still stands. ALBIE sits opposite the desk.
The MAN on the side walks into the set.
He is a big, ugly man with short-cropped red hair and bloodshot eyes.
He is CAPT. SWANEPOEL.

ROSSOUW. This is Captain Swanepoel
He and his team have come down specially from Pretoria.

ALBIE. Good afternoon, Captain.

SWANEPOEL. Good afternoon, Mr Sachs.

ALBIE. Have I been brought here for interrogation.

SWANEPOEL. Have I been brought here for interrogation?

ALBIE. What happens if I want to leave here?

SWANEPOEL. What happens if I want to leave here?

ALBIE. Are you planning to deprive me of sleep?

Slight pause.

SWANEPOEL. You'll see.

SWANEPOEL sits behind the desk.

ALBIE. I'd like to make my position clear.

SWANEPOEL. Please, make your position clear.

ALBIE. I was brought here as a witness, and the law doesn't
entitle you to subject me to prolonged interrogation.

Pause.

And if you do, then I'll see to it that the whole profession
gets to hear — judges, lawyers, prosecutors, everyone.

Pause.

Last time I was detained, one of my colleagues saw the
Minister of Justice, who promised to keep a personal eye on
me.

The INTERROGATORS laugh.
SWANEPOEL lets it run a little.
Then:

SWANEPOEL. No. No more laughing.

The OTHERS stop laughing.

It used to be a laughing matter. Bit of fun. Two years ago, it
was good football. Play up, play the game, shake hands, and
let the best man win.

It's not so funny now. And now, we are the best one, every
time.

We've got the whiphand, Albie.

ROSSOUW goes out.
SWANEPOEL lights a cigarette.
ALBIE looks at FREEMAN.
FREEMAN looks at ALBIE.
He takes out his pipe.
The lights fade to blackout.

Scene Thirteen

In the darkness.
ALBIE on tape.

ALBIE. I, Albert Louis Sachs, state as follows: I am at present a
180-day detainee held at Caledon Square police station, and I
am making this statement under duress. The circumstances are
that I have been deprived of sleep for 21 hours in order to
induce co-operation, counter to natural justice and the law. I
collapsed on several occasions and was re-awakened by sudden

noise and, on three occasions, being doused with water. I was on two occasions physically held up in a chair by six officers, one of whom forced open my eyes with his hands. I have been threatened with violence by teams of interrogators, operating in relays. The following statement has thus been extracted from me illegally. On the 14th of December 1962 I attended a camp near the village of Mamre. I had been invited to lecture on the history of the white colonisation of South Africa.

Lights.
It is ALBIE's *office.*
Sunlight streams through the window.
The room is almost empty, a stick or two of furniture, a pile of books, a few packed packing cases.
ALBIE *is in his suit and tie.*
DANNY YOUNG *stands there.*

ALBIE. Hallo, Danny.

DANNY. Hallo, Albie. I hope I'm not disturbing you.

ALBIE *smiles, gestures at the room.*

ALBIE. No, not at all. How are you?

DANNY. Fine. And you?

ALBIE. You win some. Some you lose.

Pause.

I mean, I lost quite well. I fought quite hard. I didn't give them everything. I lied. But lost.

Slight pause.
ALBIE *waves his hand.*
There's a scar in his palm.

I tried — I'd seen it in a film — I tried to keep myself awake, by gouging with a pin, into my hand. The scar's still there. My very own stigmata.

Pause.

Not that it seemed to —

DANNY. Everybody breaks.

ALBIE. I'm sorry?

DANNY. Everybody breaks, sleep deprivation. Anyone'll tell you. And it's worse, the people who hold out the longest, break the hardest. More that you resist, the more you'll give. You know that. Everybody knows.

ALBIE. Oh, yes. Not only everybody. Me.

Slight pause.

DANNY. You know, I still remember Maitland. And your running. Really cheered me up.

ALBIE. It did?

DANNY. Oh, yes. Your running and your whistling.

ALBIE. Going Home.

DANNY. Yes, Going Home.

ALBIE *looks out of the window.*

ALBIE. I knew that it was worse for you. I was locked up, while blacks and coloureds were being sleep-deprived. And I was sleep-deprived, while blacks were beaten up. And whites are being beaten up, and non-whites getting tortured with electric shocks.

You see, I never got that back. That thing at Maitland. That elan. When I went in, I was kind of innocent. And inside, I lost that.

And when I came out, I found that people still, still had that innocence, and it was good and tough, but it was wrong. And it was wrong to say, it's wrong, you just don't understand, you can't base all your plans on people holding out, they won't, you need to take precautions, need to plan on human failure. I couldn't say that, so I didn't; and I lay about, and swam, and climbed the mountain.

We were nice people. We weren't gangsters, thugs. It's different now. Now people realise.

And what it leaves you with's a kind of fatalism. Crippled spirit. What the hell. And intellectually, of course, it's still all there, but all the feelings, all the passions, all that wild-eyed innocence, been shorn away. What's left is the belief, a little core, as hard as steel, quite pure. But rather cold.

DANNY. That doesn't matter.

ALBIE. Doesn't it?

DANNY. You had it once. It kept me going, Maitland, that did matter. That was real.

Pause.

ALBIE. And now I'm going. Off to England. And of course, it always has been, down to you. But now, all down to you.

Pause.

DANNY. I brought you greetings. There are many people, hope that when South Africa is free, we'll see you once again in Cape Town. Many people, won't forget, the things you did for them.

Pause.

Even if, they know it's down to them. And always has been. Really.

Slight pause.

Won't forget.

ALBIE. I'll probably, I don't know, write another book. I'll get a job; a university. I'll speak at meetings, write for left-wing periodicals.

DANNY. They won't forget.

ALBIE. I'm planning to get married. Have some children. Buy a house. A big house, hope for, lots of room. A big and cosy house in England.

DANNY. No, they won't forget.

Oh, no. They'll say still, Albie Sachs. The one locked up alone for all those days, who ran off to the sea.

ALBIE. And Albie Sachs, the one who —

DANNY (*interrupts, an order*). They'll say still, Albie Sachs. That one, the one locked up alone for all those days, who ran off to the sea.

Pause.

ALBIE. You're right. That is the one. They must remember.

Lights fade.

Mary Barnes

Based on 'Mary Barnes: Two Accounts of a Journey through Madness' by Mary Barnes and Joseph Berke

To my Mother and Father

Author's Note

Mary Barnes: Two Accounts of a Journey Through Madness is a
true story, set in the recent past, about a group of people who
believed fiercely in a particular view of the nature of madness, and
who attempted to live that belief in a peculiarly intense and
passionate way. This has led to problems in adapting the book for
the stage. The first was that I needed to fictionalize the characters
in the book in order to give myself the freedom to represent their
community dramatically. Mary Barnes and Joseph Berke quoted,
liberally and in retrospect, third parties. I have gone further, and
invented many statements and actions by people involved in Mary's
journey. For this reason, Mary Barnes herself is the only named
character in the play. Other people often say and do things that
were really said and done; what the characters *are*, however, is my
own invention.

Second, the exigencies of time and clarity forced me to telescope
and even alter many of the events in the book, to combine
functions and people, and to find ways of making publicly clear
what was occurring in the privacy of people's minds and souls.

I should like to thank Mary Barnes and Joseph Berke for their
tireless patience with my questions, and for their generosity in
accepting my interpretation of their story. I must also acknowledge
my gratitude to Peter Farago, who not only realized the play as its
director, but who also contributed, above and beyond the call of
duty, to its writing. And, finally, my thanks to Patti Love, who
suggested the project in the first place, and whose performance
in the name part was as near perfection as I had always, quite
unreasonably, expected it to be.

David Edgar

MARY BARNES was first presented at the Birmingham Repertory Theatre Studio on 31 August 1978 and subsequently at the Royal Court Theatre, London, with the following cast:

DOUGLAS	Tim Hardy
KEITH	Teddy Kempner
BRENDA	Ann Mitchell
MARY	Patti Love
HUGO	Donald Sumpter
ZIMMERMAN	Alan Aldred
EDDIE	Simon Callow
BETH	Katherine Kitovitz
LAURENCE	Timothy Spall
ANGIE	Judy Monahan
ANGIE'S MOTHER	Judith Harte
ANGIE'S BROTHER	Roger Allam
SIMON	David Gant

Directed by Peter Farago
Designed by Andrea Montag
Lighting by Mick Hughes

The set is divided into two areas, connected by stairs. Downstairs is a general living and eating space, with exits to the kitchen, the stairs and the street. Upstairs is a bedroom, with an iron bedstead and washstand. At the beginning of the play, the set is almost empty; by the end of the first act, it has developed the fittings of occupation. The play takes place in a large old house in East London and starts in 1965.

Act One

Scene One

In the DARKNESS, *the first few bars of the Beatles' "Dizzy Miss Lizzy", performed energetically but inaccurately. It peters out in a mass of wrong notes, lack of rhythm and feedback.*
    LIGHTS. *The main set. A microphone stands centre. In the room, also, a side-drum, cymbal, and a screwdriver on the floor.*
    DOUGLAS, *who is 30, dressed in a three-piece suit, stands. He carries a good quality suitcase and briefcase. He puts them down, looks round. He taps the head of the microphone. It's dead. He can't work out what it's doing there. He notices a mirror, in the fourth wall. He looks at himself, his neatness, his suit.*
    From offstage, the same burst of Beatles, petering out.
DOUGLAS *looks off, towards the noise. Then looks at the mirror. Decision. He lays down his suitcase, opens it, takes out a floppy old sweater, on which is pinned a CND badge, a pair of suede shoes and a coathanger. He takes off his jacket, waistcoat and shoes. He bangs the jacket, waistcoat and tie on the hanger and, there being nowhere else, bangs it on the mikestand. The same burst of music.* DOUGLAS *looks towards it, then put on the sweater and suedes. He looks at himself in the mirror. He ruffles his hair.*
    Enter, right, KEITH, *a teenager in a collarless Beatle jacket. He's about to speak when* DOUGLAS, *who hasn't noticed him, pulls a face in the mirror, and flops his body about, as if to affirm his liberation from the suited attire.*
    KEITH, *stopped in his tracks, waits a moment, uncertain. Then, feeling the need to advertise his presence, if only to save future embarrassment, he coughs.*

KEITH. Erm . . .

    DOUGLAS *turns.*

    Erm . . .

DOUGLAS (*not embarrassed by the interruption of his ritual*). Yes?

KEITH. Erm . . . Our mike.

    DOUGLAS *doesn't understand.* KEITH *points at the mike and the drums.*

    Our mike, and our drums. Our group.

DOUGLAS. Oh, yes.

    DOUGLAS *takes the suit from the mike stand, with a slightly theatrical gesture.*

KEITH. Ta.

*KEITH takes the mikestand, and, with some difficulty, picks
up the drum and cymbal as well, shakes his head at DOUGLAS's
gesture of help, and goes out right. DOUGLAS, left holding the
coathanger with nowhere to hang it, goes out. "Dizzy Miss
Lizzy" bursts out again. Goes on a little longer, but still peters
out. Enter BRENDA. She's 33, with a slight Yorkshire accent.
She notices DOUGLAS's luggage. Calls.*

BRENDA. Hugo? Duggie? Who is it?

Re-enter DOUGLAS, hangerless.

DOUGLAS. Brenda. I'm the first?

BRENDA. Duggie. More or less. 'Cept for Zimmerman.

DOUGLAS. Zimmerman?

BRENDA. In the basement. Playing with his skooba box.

DOUGLAS. What in God's name is a skooba box?

BRENDA. Not easy to divine. Empirically, it's a large, black
wooden box, with lights inside which flash on and off when you
sit in it. Essentially, I gather it's more to do with meditation,
mind expansion, and the hidden breathing one-ness of the
cosmos. The discovery thereof. He calls it an environment.

DOUGLAS. Ah. Reich.

BRENDA. Third?

DOUGLAS. No. Wilhelm.

BRENDA. Doubtless. D'you want some —

DOUGLAS. Artists.

BRENDA. Eh?

DOUGLAS (*going to shut his case*). You try to escape, move to the
East End, somewhere on the nether reaches of the District Line,
beyond the writ of civilization, and what happens? Artists,
they're there before you.

BRENDA. Yuh.

Pause. They smile at each other. Doorbell rings.

I'll go.

*Exit BRENDA left. "Dizzy Miss Lizzy" once more. This time,
however, only a bar before chaos. Almost immediately, enter
KEITH, who, seeing DOUGLAS, treats him with some*

nervousness.

DOUGLAS. Problems?

KEITH. Eh?

DOUGLAS. The song. You sound like you got problems.

KEITH. Erm, yuh. Only, a. Fuse gone. Won't take a second to, um.

He is looking around. He spots the screwdriver on the floor, picks it up with some relief, as BRENDA *enters.*

BRENDA. Oh, Keith. There's a lady, lots of luggage. Would you be a love?

KEITH. Beg pardon? Be a what?

BRENDA. Give her a hand.

KEITH *looks towards the group, then shrugs.*

KEITH. Oh, yuh, sure. Why not.

KEITH *goes out left, pocketing the screwdriver.*

DOUGLAS *turns to* BRENDA.

DOUGLAS. Is Eddie coming?

BRENDA. Eddie? Oh. Don't know.

Slight pause.

Apparently, last heard of, doing something counter-cultural in Madison, Wisconsin.

DOUGLAS. Doing it to whom?

BRENDA. He didn't say.

Enter KEITH *with a suitcase and portable typewriter. He puts them down.*

KEITH. Well. Here we —

BRENDA. Upstairs? First on left?

KEITH (*picks up the luggage*). First on. The left.

He goes up the stairs. Enter MARY. *She's 42, dressed in a nursing sister's uniform, her hair neatly pinned up. She carries a small suitcase and a vanity case.*

MARY. Duggie.

DOUGLAS. Hallo love.

MARY. Where am I?

BRENDA. Show you.

Bell rings. DOUGLAS *exits left.* MARY *follows* BRENDA *towards the stairs. Then* KEITH *appears.*

BRENDA. Thanks, Keith.

MARY. Oh, yes. Thank you.

KEITH. Not at all.

MARY *and* BRENDA *go upstairs.* KEITH *going out right, when* DOUGLAS *enters with* HUGO. HUGO *is in his late-30s. He too wears a suit.*

HUGO. Good afternoon.

KEITH. Good . . . Hi.

Exit KEITH *quickly.* HUGO *looks at* DOUGLAS.

HUGO. Who?

DOUGLAS. The local Beatle-boys.

HUGO. I see.

BRENDA *appears.*

BRENDA. They come in every week to practise.

DOUGLAS. Need to.

BRENDA. Hasn't been established, now we're —

HUGO. We ought to keep as many local links as —

BRENDA. Otherwise, what is the point of moving here.

DOUGLAS. Exactly.

Slight pause.

BRENDA. Moving to somewhere, where the people work. Work with their hands.

HUGO *and* DOUGLAS *look at* BRENDA.

Where mental pain and suffering is not a pastime for the middle classes.

Where people's heads are fucked up by the way they're forced to live their lives.

Round here.

HUGO. Is everything all right?

BRENDA. Well, more or less. I've even got the central heating kind of working.

HUGO. Kind of?

BRENDA. Only kind of central heating.

Pause. The THREE *look at each other.*

Well.

HUGO. Well, here we are.

DOUGLAS. Lease signed.

BRENDA. Our occupancy —

DOUGLAS. Staked.

HUGO. Our place.

BRENDA. Our liberated zone.

A VOICE (*off*). Aha!

DOUGLAS. Eh?

Enter ZIMMERMAN. *He is in his 20s. He wears his hair long for 1965. He is dressed in an old sweater, corduroy trousers, sandles and elastoplasted spectacles. A row of fairy lights hangs round his neck. He carries a lead.*

ZIMMERMAN. Discovered. A cell of mad psychiatrists.

BRENDA. I beg your pardon?

ZIMMERMAN. What would you say, assemblage? As in school of porpoises or pride of lions. Cell's not right. Um — ego? P'raps an anal? No, I have it. Trauma. I have stumbled on a trauma of psychiatrists.

DOUGLAS. You what?

ZIMMERMAN. I need a screwdriver. My environment has just shortcircuited. You don't, on any of your persons . . . ?

DOUGLAS. Try the pop group.

ZIMMERMAN. Fine.

Exit ZIMMERMAN.

BRENDA. Zimmerman.

DOUGLAS. What a pretty name.

HUGO. He changed it, by deed poll, from Dylan Roberts. So he claims. He couldn't stand the strain.

DOUGLAS. The strain of what?

BRENDA. I'll put the kettle on.

Exit BRENDA *left.*

HUGO. We should meet and eat in here. I mean, every night. We

must avoid hierarchies, chains of authority, unspoken rules. Or
we should at least speak our unspoken rules.

Re-enter ZIMMERMAN *with the screwdriver.*

DOUGLAS. Successful?

ZIMMERMAN. Very odd.

HUGO. What way?

ZIMMERMAN. Well, I went in, and, I thought quite politely,
asked if they had such a thing as a screwdriver. Dead silence. So
I asked again, d'you have a screwdriver, cos I seem to have a
short in my environment. Another silence, and then one of
them just thrusts this at me, almost desperately, saying, take it,
have it, please don't fag returning it, it's yours.

MARY *comes down the stairs.*

Well, I ask you. Barmy. Got to be.

He sits and unscrews the plug from the socket.

MARY. Hallo, Doctor.

HUGO. Oh, hallo. I didn't know you'd come.

MARY. Oh, I arrived a short time previously.

She sits.

HUGO. Are you still working at the hospital?

MARY. I am. But I'm applying for a nearer job. To save on
travelling.

HUGO. That's good.

Enter KEITH.

MARY. Yes? Can we help you?

KEITH. Erm . . .

Sees ZIMMERMAN.

Oh. uh . . .

Thinks of an alternative question. To MARY:

Wondered if us, the group, I mean, if we could come here, now
you've, erm . . .

Vague gesture at ZIMMERMAN, *who looks up from his work
and smiles pleasantly.*

You've moved your people in.

BRENDA *enters with mugs of tea, a bottle of milk and a bag of sugar on a tray, as:*

MARY. That's fine by me.

KEITH. Oh, ta –

MARY. But you must ask Dr Walker.

KEITH *looks round, trying to work out which is* DR WALKER.

KEITH (*to* HUGO). Erm –

DOUGLAS. Yes, it's fine. Come in whenever you want.

KEITH. Oh. Ta.

MARY. Brenda, jug.

BRENDA. I'm sorry?

MARY. You should use a jug, for milk, and sugar in a bowl, not
    just a scrappy paper bag.

BRENDA. I –

MARY. Now I want, please, to discuss my place here.
    Pause. KEITH *stays, watching.*

HUGO (*sits*). Go on.

MARY. You see, I feel that all this must be sorted out. Regarding,
    in particular, finance. You see, I need to know how all of you,
    this place, is situated. I would say, for instance, I earn now
    about one thousand and four hundred pounds, you see. And I'd
    suggest that I receive, say twenty pounds a week, of which I'd
    pay some rent, five pounds, with fifteen net. But there is also
    my expense account.

HUGO. Yuh.

MARY. Well, often, you see, need to, in my room, my kind of
    office, need to entertain, professionals, buy wine, cigars, and
    also in the room that's next to mine, I'd like to keep, for
    guests, e.g. my father if he came to work about the house, in
    my capacity, if anyone was ill, a patient in the house, I'd have
    them to my room and give them, tablets or hot milk or
    penicillin, as the need arose, and sleep, they'd sleep there, in my
    room or in my bed, you see, and . . .
    Pause.

    Trust all that is satisfactory.

BRENDA. Sure. D'you want some tea?

MARY. No, Brenda, tea is wrong.

HUGO. All right. You needn't have it.

Pause.

MARY. Now I have a study to complete. Case study, to complete this evening. You'll forgive me.

MARY *stands and goes up the stairs, and into her room.*

KEITH. Eh. She's looney.

HUGO. Yes, that's right.

KEITH. But she —

HUGO. She doesn't —

KEITH. Doesn't?

HUGO. Know. She doesn't know —

KEITH. She doesn't know?

HUGO. She's —

KEITH. Looney. Doesn't know she's looney.

HUGO. Yes. Precisely.

KEITH. Ah. Oh. Right.

Exit KEITH.

DOUGLAS. Should she?

HUGO. Should she?

DOUGLAS. Know.

HUGO. Yes. Yes, she should.

DOUGLAS *drains his tea, stands and goes up the stairs. Pause.*

HUGO. A Nato officer was on a naval exercise. Polaris. He refused to press the button. Said that no man should be so commanded. Diagnosed as schizophrenic, put in mental hospital.

BRENDA. Whereas the person, President, Prime Minister, controls the bomb, for real, and threatens to explode it, he is obviously sane.

ZIMMERMAN (*stands*). That's it. Loose wire. I think I'll chance it, plug it in.

ZIMMERMAN *plugs his lead into a wall-plug. The fairy-lights come on as the lights cross-fade to the upper area.*

Scene Two

Upper area. MARY *sits at a table, typing. On the table, a picture of a nun.* DOUGLAS *stands, smoking.*

DOUGLAS. What you doing?

MARY. Oh, I'm working on a study. For the *Nursing Times*.

DOUGLAS. Oh, good.

MARY. I've got to get it in the post tonight.

DOUGLAS. Oh, fine.

He picks up the picture.

Who's this?

MARY. It's St Theresa. Of Lisieux.

DOUGLAS. What did she do?

MARY. She was a nun. The nineteenth century. She died at 24. TB.

DOUGLAS. Why was she made a saint?

Pause.

MARY. I had an interview, today, a nearer hospital. They said they might employ me.

DOUGLAS. Great.

MARY. This article. Must pop out to the post, tonight.

DOUGLAS. Pop out.

MARY. She was, just ordinary. Simple. Good. An ordinary, unknown girl, who happened to be good enough to be a saint. Now. if you'll forgive me . . .

DOUGLAS. Yuh.

Slight pause.

Pop out?

MARY looks at him.

Go out? Out, Mary?

Pause. MARY very still.

MARY. Duggie.

DOUGLAS. It's OK.

MARY. I've come —

DOUGLAS. Don't worry —

MARY. Come to have a breakdown.

Pause. Quickly, MARY pulls out the sheet in the typewriter, puts in another sheet, types.

Dear — Matron — Thank — you — for — the — interview — but —
now — I'm — otherwise — engaged — Yours.

She takes out the paper, signs it.

Mary Barnes.

*Pause. MARY reaches to her hair, pulls out the pins. Her hair
falls down.*

I'm cold.

*The Beatle-boys finally get Dizzy Miss Lizzy together.
DOUGLAS looks towards the sound. MARY still. BLACKOUT.*

Scene Three

In the DARKNESS, a male American VOICE.

VOICE. Hey!

Slight pause. Something falls over.

Hey! Hey!

Noise of SOMEONE moving about in an unfamiliar dark room.

Hey, anybody home?

ZIMMERMAN (*in the DARKNESS*). I'm home. You're standing
on my home.

*LIGHTS. Main area. BRENDA, in her nightclothes, has just
switched the LIGHTS on. The VOICE, EDDIE, is standing on
the mattress on which, in his sleeping bag, ZIMMERMAN was
sleeping. EDDIE is 25, BETH, another young American, stands
nearby. Luggage about the place. It was a suitcase that fell over.*

EDDIE. Brenda.

BRENDA. Ah. It's you.

EDDIE (*to ZIMMERMAN*). Hey, I'm sorry.

ZIMMERMAN (*sits up, puts on his glasses*). Don't mention it.

BRENDA. How d'you get in?

EDDIE. The window.

    BRENDA marching across the room.

BRENDA. Right. We fix the window.

EDDIE. Brenda, this is Beth.

BRENDA. Hi Beth.

EDDIE (*following BRENDA*). We met on this plane. I brought her here. Beth tells me she's a career loco and she's —

BETH. Unhappy in my work.

EDDIE. Unhappy in her —

BRENDA (*turning to* EDDIE). It is half past —

EDDIE, *suddenly, grandly, picking up a case and plonking it on the table.*

EDDIE. For we did hear it whispered, that the centre of the human consciousness was not among the mantrad mountain-peaks of Hindu Kush, nor yet amid the San Franciscan Friaries of Northern California, nor, even yetter, as one Ginsberg, Allen, paraphrenically put it, Liverpool —

BRENDA. Look. why don't you —

EDDIE (*opening his case*). But in a crumbling fortress in East London, peopled by all classes and varieties of freak and leper, most if not all described as psychotherapist, all if not most quite certifiably insane . . .

BRENDA. Look, it is very —

EDDIE. Where, we heard it whispered, secretly, whatever it is is now at. Thus we pursued it, hither, following the star, across the oceans.

BRENDA *sits.*

There being something of a shortage, in the excise-free, of frankincense and myrhh, with gifts of liquid gold.

EDDIE *takes a bottle from the case.* BETH *is checking her A to Z against a piece of paper.*

Tequila. Mexican. Distilled from cactus. Perforates the mind.

He puts the bottle on a chair.

The spikes go straight through the brain.

BRENDA *sits.* ZIMMERMAN *manages, from his sleeping bag, to get the bottle. He begins to drink it.* BETH *looks up from her A to Z.*

BETH. Hey, Eddie —

EDDIE. Yuh?

BETH. You think we hit the wrong bughouse?

HUGO *and* MARY *come down the stairs.* MARY *is in a nightie, clutching a blanket, a teddy bear, and a picture of St Theresa of Lisieux.*

HUGO. Well, hallo, doctor.

EDDIE. Hugo, hey —

HUGO. You do know Mary?

EDDIE. Yes, we met —

HUGO. She's had a nasty dream.

> *Slight pause.* BRENDA *stands.*

> She's walking down the road. Sees men in berets, in a wire compound, and they're going to test the bomb. So down she goes, this passage, deep inside, where she'll be safe.

> *Slight pause.*

> But she's not safe, because she is the passage and the bomb's inside her. She has swallowed it, can't spew it up, or shit it out. It's going to explode.

> *Slight pause.*

> And so she wants to sleep, down, in the box, so it can melt away.

EDDIE. The box?

HUGO. It's Zimmerman's invention. Womb or tomb. For when you don't know if you're coming or going.

> HUGO *takes* MARY *out left.*

EDDIE. Hey. We're right. We're here.

ZIMMERMAN (*still clutching the bottle, falling slowly back into the horizontal position*). There are no sins inside the gates of Eden.

Scene Four

Faintly, we hear music: a Gregorian chant, behind which is the whimpering of a woman's voice. A spot fades up on HUGO. *During the speech, a spot fades up on* MARY, *in the black box, lit up, clutching her teddy.*

HUGO. Mary Barnes was born in 1923. She had a brother, Simon. School, she couldn't speak. Her mother took her to the doctor. College, she was trained to be a nurse. Her brother came into her room one night, and tried to touch her body. He was diagnosed as schizophrenic, put in mental hospital. She was converted to Catholicism. Four years later, *she* was diagnosed as schizophrenic, put in mental hospital. A padded cell. Discharged, within a year. Returned to her career. But underneath it all, still crazy.

Pause. MARY *in the box.*

In 1963, she moved into a hostel. But they couldn't cope. She was obsessed with masturbation. Priest said one thing, therapist another. We told her we were setting up a new community, but she'd have to wait a year until it opened. Many times, she nearly broke down, streets and public places, but she kept herself at bay. Until she came to live in the community.

Pause. MARY, in the box, falls gently over on to her side. She lies still.

She came to live in the community. She'd been told she must stay sane. One thing and then another. She was put in mental hospital. Became a Catholic. She saw her brother put in mental hospital. She grew up silent. She was born.

Pause. The lights fade on MARY.

Without her fingernails. Feet first. She couldn't suck. Her mother's pain. No milk to give. The agony inside her. Like a bomb. The tearing pain.

Scene Five

Main area. Day. BETH sits in an armchair, reading a book. HUGO and DOUGLAS enter.

DOUGLAS. Of course she thinks she's a foetus.

HUGO. No. She *is* a foetus. That's what she's experiencing.

DOUGLAS. OK, fine –

HUGO. And foetuses don't sort of eat.

Enter EDDIE left with a clothes-line. His mouth is full of clothes-pegs. He attaches one end of the line to a book on stage left, the other to a book on the opposite side. He goes out. All this as:

DOUGLAS. That's right. The problem is, she is also a 40-year-old woman. And if 40-year-old women don't sort of eat, they do have this tendency to sort of die of starvation. So she must be fed.

EDDIE re-enters with newspapers, which he starts spreading under the clothes-line. BRENDA enters from the stairs with a basket of dirty washing. She crosses and out left.

HUGO. She wants to be. *Be* fed. She doesn't want to *eat.*

Enter ZIMMERMAN with a basket of clean washing. He dumps it and goes out. As:

DOUGLAS. Oh, yes?

HUGO. She wants a stomach tube. Fed directly like a foetus.

DOUGLAS. Highly dangerous.

HUGO. It's difficult.

DOUGLAS. It's highly dangerous.

HUGO. Not highly.

> *Enter* BRENDA *with another basket of clean washing.* BETH *puts down her book and starts to roll a joint of marijuana.*

DOUGLAS. And what happens if she dies?

> EDDIE *looks up. He's finished laying the newspaper. He stands up. He starts to hang the washing from the left end, from* ZIMMERMAN's *basket.*

> To us? To here? The medical authorities?

HUGO. Oh, of course, the –

DOUGLAS. Not to mention her?

> BRENDA *takes clothes pegs from the top of her basket, and starts hanging from the other end.* ZIMMERMAN *enters with more clothes pegs and starts hanging washing in the middle.*

BRENDA. She paints breasts on the wall. She wants the breast, milk. Doesn't she? So all we've got to do is find some way, some one, to give her milk. Yes? No?

HUGO. They're hardly pleasant breasts. They're painted with her shit. They're horrid, smelly, shitty breasts. Not nice at all.

BRENDA. She thinks they're nice. She sculpts them into figures. Little shitty babies. No?

> ` Pause.`

DOUGLAS. Cos, after all, we're not a hospital.

HUGO. Well, OK, Duggie, fine, but we should still try the tubes, cos if we don't, then the only choice, and I hope you don't mean this, Duggie, only choice is that she goes, goes into a real hospital, and gets her mind blown up with drugs and ECT.

DOUGLAS. Well, yes –

HUGO. And, yes, of course, she will feel *better*, better in the sense of feeling nothing, feeling numb, that's what they do to you, of course, the shocks, they take away the pain, and she –

DOUGLAS. Now, Hugo, as –

HUGO. But what she wants, she's asking for, is different. It is painful. And she knows it is, because it's hers, her voyage, she planned it, somewhere in there, under all the weeds and bricks and broken bottles, far from the light, there's a little rugged seedling poking up its nose, the only thing that's living, and if we don't stamp on it, there is a chance that it'll grow again. Up straight, this time. Not with our help. We leave it be. Just give it — life support. Now do you see that, Duggie?

DOUGLAS. Yes, well. As you say. We've come here to avoid the kind of mental health that gets its kicks from putting things in people.

HUGO. *Duggie* —

BRENDA. Um —

HUGO *and* DOUGLAS *turn to her.*

You know my views. About the medical authorities.

Slight pause.

And that is *why* we must protect ourselves, this place, from them, and she must eat.

HUGO. Then someone has to tell her to. And hope she will. That's all.

BRENDA. I'll tell her.

DOUGLAS. Good.

Exit DOUGLAS.

BRENDA. But I can't — she needs looking after, all of every day.

Pause.

EDDIE. I'll feed her.

HUGO. Wonderful. Thanks, Eddie.

Exit HUGO.

BRENDA (*to* EDDIE). Right.

She goes up the stairs.

EDDIE. Um . . . what have I . . .

He goes out left. ZIMMERMAN *turns from the washing.*

ZIMMERMAN. Well I dunno. They come over here, take all the houses, grab all the jobs, rape our women and abuse our national assistance, and now they're trying to hijack our lunatics. I dunno.

He notices the washing is sagging heavily in the middle. He goes and tries to pull the line tighter. It breaks and the washing falls down.

Shit.

BETH *has been revealed. She is sitting cross-legged on the armchair, the book open on her lap, the lighted joint in her hand.*

BETH. Oh little creature, formed of joy and mirth;
Go, live without the help of anything on earth.

She offers the joint to ZIMMERMAN.

That's shit.

ZIMMERMAN *takes the joint.* BETH *gestures to the book on her lap.*

That's William Blake.

ZIMMERMAN *smokes the joint, as lights transfer upstairs.*

Scene Six

MARY's *room.* MARY *lying on her mattress.* BRENDA *sits by her.*

BRENDA. Mary. Hey, Mary, do you want to eat?

MARY. Ugh, ugh.

BRENDA. Mary, you're going to have to eat.

MARY. The tubes.

BRENDA. Mary, we got to talk about the tubes.

     MARY *sits up, looks at* BRENDA, *suddenly wide awake.*

     Mary, everyone's worried, about your state of health.

MARY. Uh?

BRENDA. You haven't —

MARY (*harshly*). Tubes. TUBES. I want the TUBES, you bitch!

     Shrieks with fury.

     TUBES!

BRENDA (*calmly*). Mary, we haven't the facilities here to tube-feed you. This doesn't mean that this might not be right for you, but we can't do it, here, and we don't want you to die of malnutrition, so if you wish to stay in the community, then you must eat.

     MARY *bursts into tears.*

     Oh, Mary.

MARY. Wha've I done.

BRENDA. You haven't done anything.

MARY. Why you gone against yourself.

BRENDA. I haven't gone against myself.

MARY. You gone against my therapy. You're pun'shing me. I killed you. Wrong, wrong, wrong. I killed you.

BRENDA. Mary, look at me, you haven't killed me, Mary.

EDDIE *comes in with a bottle of milk.*

MARY (*to* BRENDA). Wrong, wrong, wrong.

EDDIE. Hey, Mary.

MARY. Eddie, Brenda wants to stop me going down.

EDDIE (*sits*). No, no-one wants to stop you going down.

MARY. Do, Eddie, do.

EDDIE. No, Mary. Nothing's wrong. It's not your fault. We just can't feed you through a tube.

MARY. I tried to kill her, Eddie.

EDDIE. Didn't, Mary. Look.

Pause. MARY *sneaks a look at* BRENDA. *Pause. Then* EDDIE *sits, on the mattress, picks up the bottle.*

EDDIE. Drink, now?

MARY. 'lright.

MARY *starts to drink.*

EDDIE. Nice?

MARY. Mm.

MARY *drinks. Then* EDDIE *turns his head, slightly to look at* BRENDA, *to acknowledge his pleasure that* MARY *is drinking. This small gesture causes* MARY *to feel very bad, and she spits the milk out, in* EDDIE's *face.*

MARY. Wrong. WRONG. Eddie!

EDDIE *himself takes a drink of the bottle, and spits it over* MARY. MARY *looks astonished. Then* EDDIE *gives the bottle to* MARY, *who drinks and spits over* EDDIE. *She begins to chuckle.* EDDIE *drinks and spits.* MARY *drinks and spits. Laughs.* EDDIE *takes the bottle, drinks and swallows.*

EDDIE. Glug-ug-ug.

MARY *looks at him. He drinks again.*

Glug-ug-ug-ug.

MARY laughs, she takes the bottle, drinks.

MARY. Glug-ug-ug-ug.

EDDIE (*takes the bottle, drinks*). Glug-ug-ug-ug.

MARY (*takes the bottle, drinks*). Glug-ug-ug-ug.

She takes the bottle from her lips. EDDIE doesn't take it back. She chuckles, repeats the noise.

Glug-ug.

EDDIE. Come on, you want to finish up?

MARY. Mm mm.

He cradles her in his arms and feeds her with the bottle. BRENDA stands.

BRENDA. Night Mary.

MARY (*whispered, through the drinking*). Night.

BRENDA. See you in the morning.

Exit BRENDA. MARY drinks.

EDDIE. That's right. Drink it up.

MARY drinks, finishes.

All gone? All gone.

MARY. Mm.

Pause. EDDIE, very gently.

Hey. Knock, knock. Who's there?

MARY. It's Mary.

EDDIE. Mary who?

MARY doesn't reply. Pause. Then EDDIE leaves her. Stands, goes to the door. Suddenly, MARY, furious, turns and shrieks at him.

MARY. Why are you so angry with me, Eddie?

EDDIE. Me?

Scene Seven

Main area. Morning. DOUGLAS sits reading and drinking coffee. EDDIE's voice, offstage, singing raucously.

EDDIE.   Little Miss Muffet

Sat on a tuffet
Eating her curds and whey
A nasty great spider
Sat down beside her
And . . . Mm?

DOUGLAS. Frightened Miss Muffet away.

EDDIE (*sings, as he goes up the stairs*). And frightened Miss Muffet
away . . .

MARY's *room. She lies asleep, on her mattress. During the
following, downstairs, BETH enters with a duster, a drying-up
cloth and a tray of cutlery. She puts the tray on the chair.
DOUGLAS nods to her and goes out. She dusts the table. And,
from off, other voices of the day: a radio somewhere, a hoover.
EDDIE comes into MARY's room. He takes from his pocket a
big black rubber spider on an elastic string. He dangles it over
MARY.*

EDDIE. Look what I got you, Mary.

MARY (*waking*). Uh . . . uh?

EDDIE. Spider, Mary.

MARY. Oh, Eddie.

EDDIE. Great big spider, come to get you.

MARY (*grabbing the spider*). Oh, EDDIE.

EDDIE. Hey, d'you want to get up?

MARY *is playing with the spider and making little noises at it.*

Come on, get up, race you down the stairs.

MARY. What? Oh, yes.

*She jumps out of bed. EDDIE finding her clothes, tossing them
to her.*

EDDIE. Come on, let's go . . .

MARY (*desperately flinging her clothes on*). Oh, Eddie, coming,
don't go, just a minute —

EDDIE. Hey, Mary, you not ready yet?

MARY. Oh, just a minute, Eddie, nearly ready —

EDDIE (*helping MARY, who's having problems with her jumper*).
Come on, arms up, that's it.

MARY's *ready.*

OK?

Suddenly, EDDIE running out of the room followed by MARY. EDDIE into main area, and down behind the table, 'shhhing' at BETH, who follows events in this sequence with ironic detachment. MARY, who's entered, looks around. At BETH. BETH shrugs.

MARY. Eddie. Eddie. Where are you, Eddie?

She senses EDDIE's somewhere round the table, goes round one side, as he crawls round the other. Then the other way round. Then she goes down on all fours.

Where — are — you?

EDDIE growls, appears under the table. BETH still trying to dust.

EDDIE. Hey, what's that? What's there?

He growls. MARY growls.

Is it a bear? Is it a tiger?

EDDIE and MARY circling each other on all fours.

MARY. It's a — crocodile.

MARY bites EDDIE. EDDIE bites MARY. They make crocodile noises at each other. During the following, at a distance, a phone rings, merging into the other domestic noises. Half a dozen rings, then stops.

EDDIE. Hey, is that all your mouth is?

MARY. Mary's got the biggest mouth.

EDDIE. No she hasn't. Eddie has.

He opens his mouth wide.

MARY (*opening her mouth very wide*). 'o 'ary 'as.

She puts her finger in her mouth to demonstrate.

'ook, 'ook, 'ary 'as.

Growling, EDDIE's fingers approach MARY's mouth. He puts his fingers in her mouth. Withdraws.

EDDIE. OK, so Mary's got the biggest mouth. But who's got the sharpest teeth?

EDDIE bites MARY. MARY bites EDDIE. Both growling, MARY is squealing with delight. EDDIE grabs a chair, still kneeling, growling through the bars. MARY does the same with another chair. Enter BRENDA.

BRENDA. Eddie, it's the London School of Economics, on the

telephone.

She goes out. BETH *starts to lay the table, polishing the cutlery with the cloth as she does so.*

EDDIE. OK, croc. You stay there, and I'll be right back.

MARY growls, EDDIE *getting up.*

That's right. You stay right there, in the river. Won't be a minute.

EDDIE *goes out.* MARY *growls. Then again, a little uncertain. Then,* BETH *looking at her, a little growl at* BETH. BETH *smiles.* MARY *is still.*

BETH. Hey, Mary, you want to help me lay the table?

MARY goes rigid, clutching the chair. BETH *takes a step towards her.*

Mm?

Another step.

Want to help me lay the knives out?

Pause. MARY *still rigid.*

OK.

BETH *turns back to the table,* MARY *throws the chair at her.*

MARY (*as she throws*). Can't go! I mustn't go away!

BETH. Oh, for Christ's sake, Mary —

Re-enter EDDIE.

Eddie, that woman just threw this chair at me.

EDDIE (*rushes to* MARY, *who's lying rigid*). Hey, what's up, Mary?

BETH. Hey, what's up, Beth? I just had a chair thrown at me.

MARY. Came in. Came in on me.

EDDIE. It's OK, Mary.

BETH. Well, it may be OK Mary —

MARY. Broken, Eddie.

BETH. She was doing the chair-tossing.

MARY. Felt splintered, exploding, Eddie —

EDDIE. Yuh.

BETH. I mean, don't get me wrong, I'm really pleased to be a part of —

EDDIE. Beth.

> BETH *looks at* EDDIE *a moment. Then carries on laying the table.* EDDIE *to* MARY.

> It's cos I went away. And you were jealous. Threw the chair cos she was coming in on you. You felt possessed. That made you angry.

MARY (*whispers*). No. Not angry with you, Eddie.

> *Exit* BETH.

EDDIE. Yuh, Mary, you were angry with me.

MARY (*whispers*). No, no.

> *Getting angry.*

> No, you know I'd not be angry with you, Eddie!

EDDIE. Mary, you *look* angry now.

MARY (*hits* EDDIE *on the chest*). No! No! No! Confuse me. No, not angry, Eddie!

EDDIE. Hey, is that all you can hit, Mary?

MARY (*hits* EDDIE). No! No! No!

EDDIE. Hey, I bet you can hit me more than that.

MARY (*grunting as she hits* EDDIE). Uh. Uh. Uh. Uh. Uh.

> *And she grabs him round the middle.*

EDDIE. Hey? What's this now?

MARY. Snake.

EDDIE. Snake? Squeezing me?

MARY. Yuh. Squeezy-snake.

EDDIE. Hey, is that all you can squeeze? Snakey? Is that all?

> MARY *squeezes as tight as she can. Then, finally, she lets go, falls back, panting, exhausted, happy.* EDDIE *breathless as well. Then he turns to* MARY.

> Mary. You bit my ear. You hit me. Yuh? And I'm still here. And I bit you. And you're fine. Anger doesn't hurt me, and it doesn't kill you either. Both OK.

> *Pause.* EDDIE *looks round. Sees the drying-up cloth. Quickly, he reaches for it, takes it, and covers* MARY's *head with it.*

MARY (*under the cloth*). Uh?

EDDIE. Hey, where's Mary Barnes?

MARY. Uh?

EDDIE. She's gone away, she's all gone away.

He stands, looks round the room.

Hey! Where's Mary? Is she gone?

MARY *pulls off the cloth, appears, grinning.*

Oh, *there* she is.

MARY *grins, puts the cloth back over her face.*

Hey, now she's gone again.

MARY *reappears.*

Nope, she's there.

MARY *puts the cloth over her face.*

Nope, she's gone.

MARY *still.*

Still gone.

MARY *still.*

Well, there we are. No Mary, any more.

Slowly, MARY *pulls the cloth off her face.*

Well. If it isn't Mary Barnes.

Pause.

See. She can go. And she comes back again. And Eddie, goes, and Eddie comes right back again.

He puts his finger in her mouth, and then takes it out.

And Eddie comes in Mary, and she isn't hurt; and Eddie goes out, and she isn't hurt.

Pause. HUGO *has appeared. Stands there.*

And the spider's outside you, Mary.

Pause.

HUGO. Mary, Mary, Quite contrary.
        How does your garden grow.

EDDIE. Slowly.

Scene Eight

Main area. The COMMUNITY *is eating dinner.* EDDIE *sits between* MARY *and* BETH.

DOUGLAS. Now, look. Let's take a man who's frightened, says he's petrified. That's fine. However, a man who says that he's a stone, is liable to get locked up. The point is, that to petrify means that, to turn to stone.

One might, in fact, define 'delusion' as a real idea a person holds, but which a psychiatrist deludes himself into taking literally.

ZIMMERMAN. A shrink once put his patient on a lie-detector test, and asked the question: Are you Jesus Christ? The lie-detector registered he hadn't told the truth. He'd answered 'no'.

BETH. My father is a businessman. My mother's father was a building worker. Wanted me to go to college, be an architect. I couldn't draw. Dropped out. Just sat around. They shouted at me. World of my own, they said. So took me to a doctor. Couldn't move. He said that I was catatonic.

EDDIE. Scared. Scared stiff.

MARY. Eddie, why so cold?

EDDIE. It is. The central heating's playing up.

MARY. Oh, Eddie, wha've I done.

EDDIE. You haven't. Not your fault. You don't control the central heating. It's a thing.

MARY. Oh, Eddie.

EDDIE. Come on, eat your food.

DOUGLAS. Can I give anyone some more?

Pause as he hands round seconds.

BRENDA. You see, the very word is *invalid*. Invalid. You know, in feudal times, there were no mad, or sane, defined as such. Communities supported those who couldn't work, quite automatically. But then, when people started being paid in cash, as individual workers, then the criminal, the ill, the lunatic, were separated off. Defined as 'other'. On the grounds of being unexploitable. Their *functioning* impaired.

DOUGLAS. You what?

BRENDA. It's even more. The roles of family, fixed roles as father, mother, daughter, son, are products of commodity production. People are defined by their relations to commodities. I own, therefore I am. You are, the things you buy.

DOUGLAS. And that's . . . ?

BRENDA (*impatiently*). I mean, the system, buying, selling, people viewed as things, that drives them mad.

DOUGLAS. You mean . . . The capitalist system.

BRENDA (*firmly*). That's right.

DOUGLAS. I see.

Pause.

EDDIE. Last century, the Southern States, the medical profession had to classify a new disease. Occurred exclusively among black slaves. They called it drapetomania. It was manifested in the slave's desire to run away.

BETH. My parents were religious. Didn't let me stay out late or wear cosmetics. Father spoke a lot about not lying, being honest. Used to falsify his tax returns. Deceive competitors. He said so. Couldn't make it fit. I told them, once, I want to go with men. I was beside myself. I didn't mean it. Said it wasn't me.

EDDIE. They meant, you were possessed.

MARY. Oh, Eddie.

EDDIE. Yuh?

MARY. That salt. Salt on your food.

EDDIE. I like it.

MARY. Why you punishing yourself.

EDDIE. I'm not. Like salt. You don't.

MARY. Why punish me?

Slight pause. BETH *stands and goes out.*

DOUGLAS. The issue, surely, is authority.

BRENDA. The issue's state authority.

HUGO. Not all authority?

EDDIE. The issue's violence.

BRENDA. The issue is state violence.

HUGO. All violence?

EDDIE. The violence of people to each other.

DOUGLAS. In each other. The cop that really matters is the cop inside inside your head.

BRENDA. The cop that really matters is the cop that's in the streets.

ZIMMERMAN. The revolution's fucking in the road.

BRENDA. The revolution is not fucking in the road.

HUGO. The revolution . . . Is just saying what we mean.

DOUGLAS. Who isn't?

HUGO. None of you.

    BETH *enters with pudding.*

BETH. Hey, pudding, anyone?

EDDIE. Hey, Mary, jelly?

MARY. No, not jelly.

EDDIE. Cheese?

MARY. Eddie, it seems wrong to eat.

EDDIE. OK.

MARY. But seems wrong not to eat. I feel so bad.

EDDIE. You're angry, cos I'm talking to the others, Mary, cos I
    been with you all day. OK?

MARY OK.

    EDDIE *turns to* BETH.

BETH. Also, I had this brother —

MARY. Whore.

    Slight pause.

EDDIE. Beth, ignore her, she's just mad with me.

MARY. You whore.

EDDIE. It's OK, she doesn't mean it.

MARY. Whore.

EDDIE. Just saying that, cos she's so —

MARY. WHORE.

    BETH *stands, goes to the record player, puts on a record: Hey*
    Mr Tambourine Man by the Byrds.

MARY. WHORE.

    BETH *turns up the volume.*

    WHORE.

    BETH *turns up the volume.*

    WHORE.

BETH (*turns and screams at* MARY). WHAT HAVE I DONE TO YOU?

A crash from off left, DOUGLAS *to the record player, turns it off. Crash, from the other side. Exit* DOUGLAS *and* BRENDA *left,* HUGO *right.*

MARY. Uh —

EDDIE (*quickly stands*). Come on, Mary.

MARY (*as she is gets to her feet*). Uh, Eddie, me —

EDDIE. Not you, Mary. Come on, bed.

He takes MARY *up the stairs. She's moaning. Re-enter* BRENDA.

BRENDA. They're smashing windows, all around.

ZIMMERMAN. Who?

BRENDA. How do I know? Put shit, through the letterbox.

BETH. What?

BRENDA. Shit. Splat.

Enter HUGO.

HUGO. Can't see anyone. I heard them shouting, nutters, perverts, layabouts.

ZIMMERMAN. Who?

HUGO (*quietly*). The working class. With Morris Minors, television sets. Sucked in.

BRENDA (*angry*). Sucked in to what?

HUGO. Sucked into nutters, perverts, layabouts.

Slight pause.

ZIMMERMAN. Three people. One says he's Marx, and with enough to follow him, he'll change the world. Another says he's Jesus Christ, and with enough to follow him, he'll change the world. The third, who is a doctor of psychiatry, he thinks he'll change the world on his own. So which of them's the most deranged, then think ye?

Enter DOUGLAS.

DOUGLAS. I've just called the police.

BRENDA. You've what?

DOUGLAS. You heard.

ZIMMERMAN. Out of whose head?

Another crash and BLACKOUT. *In the darkness, the Beatles'*
Why Don't We Do It In The Road.

Scene Nine

Early morning. Main area. HUGO *sits.* DOUGLAS *and* BRENDA
stand. ZIMMERMAN *lies on the table, amid the debris.* KEITH
stands stage left.

KEITH. They, see . . . I mean, they're up at six or half past, lots of
them. Your bedtime, just before them getting up.

Slight pause.

I mean, they're not that keen. Asylum, in the street. Can
understand. Your, style of life.

Slight pause.

I'm sorry. Got to get to work.

Exit KEITH. *Pause.*

ZIMMERMAN. Outside, above those rows of lego houses, there's a
great fat grinning greasy fried egg of a sun.

He sits up.

They're soapboxes. They let the wind in. Only thing to do, is
stand on them and shout.

HUGO. They don't.

DOUGLAS. Perhaps they're frightened they'll fall off.

HUGO. The vertigo of freedom.

Pause.

Minute to minute. White rabbits. Need to stop the ticking,
listen to the heartbeat.

Slight pause.

Dali only melted clocks. We need to wrench their precious
little coggy innards out, and stop them telling us their time.

ZIMMERMAN *finds a bottle, pours a drink.*

Who else? But mad psychiatrists. And lunatics and layabouts
and perverts. And where else but here. Are we to find our
timeless time?

ZIMMERMAN (*drinks*). It's enough to drive you sane.

BLACKOUT *and another burst of Why Don't We Do It In The
Road.*

Scene Ten

Immediately, in the DARKNESS.

MARY. Eddie! No, Eddie! No, no, no . . .

> LIGHTS. *Main area.* EDDIE *enters, from the stairs, in a suit. He carries a briefcase, and is drinking a cup of coffee, and he's late. He puts down the cup as enter* MARY *behind him.*

MARY. No, Eddie —

EDDIE. Mary, I told you. I am going to the Clinic. For three hours. I'll be back.

> *He turns to go.* MARY *grabs him round the middle.*

MARY. No, no, Eddie. You don't mean it.

EDDIE (*pulling himself free*). Mary, I do mean it, I am going out, I'm late.

MARY (*grabbing him again*). Wha've I done. Oh, wha've I done.

EDDIE (*pulling himself free again*). Mary, stop it.

> MARY *whines.*

Mary, stop that noise.

> MARY *drops to the floor, whining.*

Mary, I am going to the clinic, now.

> *He turns to go.*

MARY. Eddie?

EDDIE (*turns back*). Yes?

MARY. Eddie, must tell you . . .

EDDIE. Come on, spit it out.

MARY. That if you go 'way, I'll run into the street, tear off my clothes, and scream out Take Me To A Mental Hospital.

> EDDIE *shuts his eyes.*

EDDIE. What?

MARY. You heard me.

> EDDIE *takes a decision. He turns to go.* MARY *to her feet, rushes, grabs him, pulls him round, screams.*

MARY. TAKE ME TO A MENTAL —

> EDDIE *punches* MARY *in the face. She staggers back.*

EDDIE. Oh, no.

MARY's *hands go to her face.*

Oh, Mary, why do you make me . . .

MARY's *hands are covered in blood from her bleeding nose.*

Oh Christ.

MARY. Blood. My blood.

She turns round.

EDDIE. Hey, now, Mary . . .

MARY. Hugo! Brenda! Duggie! Look, my blood!

She runs up the stairs.

EDDIE. Mary —

BETH *enters from the kitchen, eating a bowl of cornflakes.*

BETH. What?

EDDIE. Hit Mary.

BETH. Oh. Hit Mary.

She wanders across.

EDDIE. Hit my patient.

BETH. Eddie.

Taps her head.

Doc inside your head.

She goes out right as DOUGLAS *comes down the stairs.*

EDDIE. Duggie, I —

DOUGLAS. I know. She seems delighted.

EDDIE. What?

DOUGLAS. She says you brought her badness out. Her badness, bomb, all down her nose it came.

Pause. EDDIE *to the stairs, shouts up.*

EDDIE. Knock knock! Who's there?

MARY (*off*). It's Mary!

EDDIE. Mary who?

Pause. EDDIE *turns back.*

Oh, sure. Delighted.

He looks at his watch. He shakes his head in fury, goes out left. Then BLACKOUT *downstairs and* LIGHTS *on* MARY's *room.*

She sits on her mattress, blood pouring down her face.

MARY. This is my body. This is my blood. This is Mary Barnes.

Fade to Blackout.

Act Two

Scene One

Downstage, in the main area. MARY sitting on the floor. EDDIE appears behind her. He carries a brightly wrapped parcel.

EDDIE. Mary.

MARY. Eddie.

EDDIE. Present for you.

MARY. What?

   He tosses her the parcel.

   Oh, Eddie.

   MARY *opens the parcel. It contains a pad of drawing paper and an old tin.*

   Uh?

   She opens the tin. It contains crayons.

EDDIE. Crayons.

MARY. Uh?

EDDIE. And paper.

MARY. (*realising*) Oh . . .

EDDIE. No need to paint with shit. No need to smear on walls.

MARY. Oh, oh . . .

EDDIE. Now go on, monster. Draw.

   MARY *looking at the paper and the crayons. She sneaks a look at* EDDIE. *She looks back at the paper.* EDDIE *realises she's not going to do anything while he's there, so he goes out.* MARY *checks* EDDIE *has gone. She picks up a crayon. She begins to draw. Lights fade.*

Scene Two

Main area. Now we see MARY's *early drawings and paintings put up round the house. On her chair, her crayons, brushes, pots of paint and cloths.*

   LAURENCE, *a man in his late 30s, at the record player. He is watching a record go round on the turntable. A few moments. Then he puts the record on. It's Paint it Black by the Rolling*

Stones, but we only hear the intro, for LAURENCE *takes off the needle just before the lyrics start.*
    Enter HUGO *right, followed by* BRENDA.

BRENDA. Hugo, are you shopping?

HUGO. Shopping? No. Why?

BRENDA. Because it's your turn. There's no food in the house. The only thing in the kitchen is a cluster of thirty dirty milk-bottles and while you're out you might return them.

HUGO. Thursday. Zimmerman's turn.

BRENDA. I don't know where he is. I think he's gone.

HUGO. Gone? Why?

    Enter MARY *carrying a rolled-up canvas.*

BRENDA. Dunno. Perhaps we disagreed with him.

HUGO. Can't you . . . Oh, all right.

    HUGO *goes out.*

MARY (*to* BRENDA, *explaining the painting*). The Temptations of Christ. The Devil comes on, horrible, cos God made him come bad. But now the temple, gold. The mountain, every colour. Christ is silver, cool.

    BRENDA *smiles at* MARY.

I'll hang it up.

    MARY *goes out.* LAURENCE *puts on the record again. The same ritual, playing the intro.* BRENDA *looks on.* LAURENCE *takes off the needle, watches the record going round. Enter* DOUGLAS *with a piece of paper.*

DOUGLAS. Brenda, what is this?

    He gives her the paper.

BRENDA. I don't know. It's a group of artists. They want to stage an event.

DOUGLAS. Brenda, I'm a bit concerned —

BRENDA. Mm?

DOUGLAS. That we're being kind of taken over —

BRENDA. Well —

DOUGLAS. By freaks, and you know —

BRENDA. Freaks?

    DOUGLAS *takes the paper back.*

DOUGLAS. I mean.

He reads, as MARY enters with a painting on hardboard.

"Eeevent. We shall stop show stop bits of people cut off cut
up cut together question mark. The porpoise only is relieved in
T.I.M.E. stop. England E.S.P. ects that every man will groove
his beauty, and achieve a state of stroke ultimate hydraulic
maya that maybe semi-colon. Please bring offall dash."

It's very hard to follow. It's erratically punctuated. I am not
100 percent convinced, in fact, that it means anything at all.

BRENDA *shrugs, exit.*

MARY (*to DOUGLAS, explaining the painting*). Disintegration.
Devil's clawing bits of people he has broken, but he can't engulf
them, cos St Michael spears his heart.

DOUGLAS *smiles at MARY.*

I'll nail it up.

*Exit MARY. LAURENCE repeats his ritual with the record.
Enter HUGO carrying a large number of empty milk bottles.*

DOUGLAS (*stands*). Ah, Hugo —

HUGO *drops one of the milk bottles. It smashes. Pause.*

HUGO. Did you know that people's bodies, in America, are so
irradiated, that it's illegal to transport mother's milk across state
lines? Except, of course, in the original containers.

DOUGLAS. No, I didn't know that.

*Pause. HUGO indicates he can't do anything about the bottle
he's smashed without risking dropping the others. DOUGLAS
goes out. Enter MARY with another painting. DOUGLAS re-
enters with a dustpan and brush, sweeps up the broken bottle,
as MARY explains her painting to HUGO.*

MARY. God's Mother. 'Fore the world, bordered in gold. The
breasts are revealed. They succour men.

HUGO *smiles, goes out.*

I'll put it in the Games Room.

*Exit MARY. Exit DOUGLAS with the dustpan. LAURENCE
goes and upends the chair with MARY's things. He sits on the
chair. MARY re-enters.*

MARY. Laurence.

LAURENCE. Yes.

MARY. My chair.

LAURENCE. It is.

MARY. My things.

LAURENCE. They are.

MARY. Laurence, get off my chair.

LAURENCE. Gimme a reason.

MARY. No!

LAURENCE. Then no.

> MARY *attacks* LAURENCE. *They fight, rolling across the floor, like children, having fun, shouting and biting, knocking over chairs.* BRENDA, DOUGLAS *and* BETH *enter.* MARY *and* LAURENCE *become aware of their presence, stop fighting.*

BETH. What a shit-heap.

BRENDA. Yes. Laurence, Mary, you must tidy up.

> MARY *and* LAURENCE *stand up sheepishly.*

BETH. All these things.

BRENDA. Yes. Mary, you must move your things.

MARY. Don't —

BRENDA. What?

MARY. Don't boss me.

BRENDA. Other people keep things in their room.

MARY. Don't tell me what to do.

BRENDA (*picks up a chair*). Now, come on, Mary love, let's get this —

MARY. Do what EDDIE says.

DOUGLAS (*sits*). Yes. Eddie.

> *Pause.* MARY *knocks over a chair.* LAURENCE *picks it up. Picks up another.* MARY *knocks over another chair.* LAURENCE *sits at the record player, watches the record go round. Pause. A door slam.* EDDIE, *briskly, comes in, throws a cardboard file on the table, sits, puts his feet up. He looks at the* OTHERS *and then explains.*

EDDIE. I have just been to a committee meeting of an organization of radical therapists entitled Shrinks for Socialism.

> *Slight pause.*

They are planning a conference on the Gestalt Road to
Revolution that will form, I gather, the first step in a plan to
take over the world on strict Marxist-Jungian lines. In the land of
the mind, the slogan runs, the One-Id man is King.

Slight pause.

Sadly, we didn't get that far. We were only, in fact, on Matters
Arising when the Treasurer accused the Chairman of a conscious
strategy of maternal double-bind and thereupon freaked out.
She's very highly strung, I was informed. She should be, I replied.

Slight pause. To BETH, grossly.

Hey, Beth, why not just lie down and do the first thing that
comes into my head?

Pauses. Senses the atmosphere, stands.

Well, then, I'll just go and —

MARY. Eddie.

EDDIE. Hallo, Mary. How's your day.

MARY. Eddie, please tell them.

EDDIE. Tell them what?

MARY. About the Games Room.

EDDIE. Oh, the Games Room.

Pause. Looking at the OTHERS.

Now?

MARY. Yes, now.

Pause.

DOUGLAS. Well?

EDDIE. Uh, well. Mary wants to paint the Games Room. If that,
meets with —

BRENDA. In the Games Room?

EDDIE. More like, on it. S'wall. A kind of — mural. Painting. On
the wall.

Pause.

DOUGLAS. Last week, I remember, she did just that. With chalk.
All over, walls and chairs, the billiard table. Criss-cross spider's
web all over. Quite a mess.

EDDIE. She cleaned it up.

BRENDA. You cleaned it up.

Enter HUGO, *unnoticed, with bags of shopping.*

EDDIE. Connections. Everyone connected to each other.

BETH. What?

HUGO. That's what she meant.

Pause.

DOUGLAS. There is an awful lot of Mary Barnes around this house. It is, in fact, quite difficult, avoiding it.

HUGO. Right. Bread and wine. I shall, at last, make supper.

Exit HUGO. MARY, *quite suddenly.*

MARY. My mother said — don't paint outside the lines. I sploshed about, I shouldn't paint outside the lines. My mother was a spider. You are like a Mother to me, Brenda.

LAURENCE *puts on his Stones record. He lets it run. It covers the change.*

Scene Three

Dinner. The COMMUNITY, *except for* ZIMMERMAN, *sit round the table. The evocations of the tableau rather stronger than before.*

HUGO. A story. Back ward of a Glasgow bughouse. Jockie lies there, screaming, getaway ya buggers, getaway. To quieten him, the surgeon decides to perform a transorbital lobotomy. And it's a great success, for after it, old Jockie is heard screaming, Canna hear the buggas, canna hear the buggas now no more.

DOUGLAS. Well, that's most affecting. Anyone here in favour of transorbital lobotomies?

HUGO. Another story. Woman had a phobia about Group Therapy. For which, she'd been prescribed. The day it came, she tried to run away. They rugby-tackled her, injected tranquillizer, dragged her to the room. And if they hadn't, so the doctor said, she would have missed her therapy.

DOUGLAS. That's very salutory. Wonder if there's anybody here would want to do that kind of thing?

EDDIE. It isn't mad to want to paint on walls. Leonardo painted things on walls.

DOUGLAS. Oh, Jesus.

HUGO. You musn't talk to yourself, Duggie. You'll get locked up in mental hospital.

BRENDA. Anyone? Some wine?

BRENDA *pours wine.*

Mary, love, eat.

MARY *still.*

BETH. You don't eat up, you won't get your dessert.

EDDIE. Leave her alone.

BETH. Well, should she? Laurence eats all of his.

EDDIE. Well, Laurence isn't —

MARY *suddenly starts eating, very quickly.*

LAURENCE. S'good for you. The greens.

DOUGLAS. All right. Shall we stop pretending?

HUGO. Yes, let's stop pretending. Stop pretending what?

DOUGLAS. Well, for a start, let's drop this crap about no rules.

HUGO. Go on.

DOUGLAS. I will. Rule one. There are no rules. Rule two. It is against the rules to question rule one. Rule three. It is against the rules to acknowledge the existence of rules one and two.

BRENDA. What are you suggesting, Duggie?

DOUGLAS. I'm suggesting that we are pretending not to have rules, and we should admit that we have rules, and people who break them persistently should leave the community. I am suggesting that we are pretending not to be doctors and we are doctors and we can in the context of a non-coercive environment, without drugs or shocks, admit to so being. I am suggesting that the community is falling apart because of its childlike faith that if you scatter sick seed on the ground and neither prune nor tend nor water it then by a process of immaculate semination it will mend and heal and grow.

BRENDA. What are you suggesting.

DOUGLAS. A medical director of the community. Rules on admittance and dismissal from the community. Regular, compulsory meetings of the community to discuss —

HUGO. When you say dismissal, did you have anyone in mind?

DOUGLAS *cuts a piece of bread.* MARY *is making terrible noises.*

DOUGLAS. You said it.

He hands the piece of bread to HUGO.

HUGO. No thank you. Anyone want a piece of bread?

No-one answers. With some grace, HUGO stands and collects the plates.

BRENDA. Mary, don't gobble.

MARY. Uh?

BETH. That awful noise.

Slight pause. MARY finishes her last mouthful, quietly.

HUGO (*collecting the plates*). You finished, Laurence?

LAURENCE. Yuh. Don't want no more.

MARY looks up as HUGO takes LAURENCE's half-eaten plateful of food. MARY hands her empty plate to HUGO pointedly. HUGO goes out, re-enters during:

EDDIE. I was once in a hospital in New York, where they had a ward, a dehierarchised ward, you know, own clothes and get up when you want, and every day they had this group discussion. And there was this girl, this pretty Puerto Rican girl. And one day, at group discussion, she was standing, swaying gently to the rhythm of the voices, when the Chief Psychiatrist made a reference to her, her case, her mental state. And she heard this, or anyway, reacted to it, cos she suddenly began to dance, dance with a deal of energy, and grace, that, well, lit up that dusty, sweaty room. And everyone, the patients and the nurses, just sat back, enjoyed the show. And no harm done, of course, no harm to anyone. And then the Chief Psychiatrist said, Miss Rivera, you're disturbing us, the meeting, would you please sit down. She didn't listen. Miss Rivera, don't you hear us? We, the meeting, are asking you to stop. She didn't seem to hear. Look, Miss Rivera, if you don't sit down, the group is going to send you to your room. And still she kept on dancing. So the Chief Psychiatrist called up two aides and said, the group's decided Miss Rivera mustn't be allowed to carry on disrupting our discussion. Will you please escort her to her room. They did. She put up quite a fight.

Pause. He looks at DOUGLAS.

Nothing succeeds like duress.

DOUGLAS. Eddie, would you like some cheese?

HUGO (*translates*). Eddie, shut up.

DOUGLAS. That was a very interesting story.

HUGO (*translates*). That wasn't a very relevant story.

DOUGLAS. Do tell me, what was your reaction? Did you clout him one?

EDDIE. Duggie, you're getting ever so slightly right up my nose —

DOUGLAS. Oh, come on, now, you're only saying that.

HUGO. You know, the only conceivable explanation of the Passion Story is that Judas thought there'd been some ghastly theological mistake, and he was the Messiah. Which, I'm sure, was quite an understandable delusion. Happens all the time.

Pleasantly, to DOUGLAS.

Another piece of bread?

EDDIE. Mary, want cheese?

MARY. No, no.

EDDIE. OK.

LAURENCE. That's cos you gobbled.

BRENDA. Beth, some cheese?

BETH *shakes her head.*

Laurence?

LAURENCE. Please.

MARY. Hey.

BRENDA. What?

MARY. He didn't finish.

BRENDA. Don't be silly, Mary.

MARY. Don't be silly? Don't be silly? Didn't finish.

EDDIE. Actually, in fact, she's right.

BRENDA. Oh, Eddie, please. Encourage them.

MARY. Laurence didn't finish. Didn't *finish.*

BRENDA. All right. Laurence didn't finish.

Pause. Hiatus.

DOUGLAS. It is, of course, for everyone. But it's principally for the sake of people going down. Who need support. Need structure and security. Need to be clear.

HUGO. So give me rules. Make me feel cosy.

DOUGLAS. Hugo, please.

HUGO. Behold, I have set before thee an open door, and no man can shut it. No, however much you're terrified of what's beyond.

DOUGLAS (*to* BRENDA). What do you think?

BRENDA shrugs.

HUGO (*to* BRENDA). What do you think.

BRENDA. I think this house is getting quite unpleasant as a place to live in. And I think I'll go and make some coffee.

She stands.

HUGO. No do *not* go and make some coffee.

BRENDA (*sits*). And I think I won't go and make some coffee.

DOUGLAS. Rule four. That Brenda is allowed not to react to me. Rule Five. That Brenda is not allowed, however, to ignore Hugo. Rule Six —

HUGO. Duggie, just tell me, what can I do to make you really loath me?

DOUGLAS. Um . . . Can I have notice of that question?

BRENDA (*stands*). COFFEE.

Slight pause.

Laurence, could you give me —

MARY (*suddenly violently*). Laurence takes people's letters hides them. Peed in the Games Room. Put blood on my painting. Don't keep rules. Don't finish. Simon he said bloody had to have his mouth washed out with soap and water —

BETH. Who the fuck's Simon?

MARY (*stands*). Paintings must *stay up.* They're mine.

LAURENCE stands. He's shaking. He goes out quickly.

EDDIE. Sit down, Mary. Please.

MARY throws herself into her chair. DOUGLAS smiling, playing with a fork.

Duggie, you crow once more, you crow one time too often.

DOUGLAS. Now what have I done?

Pause.

BRENDA. Um . . . Shouldn't someone see what . . .

She's going out when LAURENCE comes back in. He has a

*number of canvases, pieces of paper, hardboards. He's taken
them down. He drops them on the floor.* BRENDA *sits.*

LAURENCE. They said, the people said the paintings should come
down. Douglas and everyone.

Slight pause.

You got inside me. Hurt my head. Made it my fault that you're
ill.

MARY *throws herself at* LAURENCE. *She hits him, bites him.*
HUGO *and* EDDIE *pulling her off.*

MARY. Betraying me. You are betraying me.

HUGO. Come on, love —

MARY. Denying me. You are denying me.

EDDIE. Mary, get off him —

MARY *is pulled off,* HUGO *sits,* EDDIE *lets her go. She runs
to the table, throws a loaf of bread at* DOUGLAS *and a glass
of wine at* HUGO.

MARY. THIS is my body. THIS is my blood. You're betraying me.

She stands there, shaking with fury.

DOUGLAS. Well. That is exactly what I mean. We have to talk
about the future of this house.

BETH. Think she should go. She screams at people. Think she
should go.

HUGO *is wiping the wine off his hands with a cloth.*

DOUGLAS. We've got to sort this out.

MARY *rushes up the stairs.* EDDIE *stands to follow her.*

LAURENCE. You said they should come down.

DOUGLAS. No, Eddie, no.

EDDIE *turns back.*

If you want Mary, take her, live with her, and have your house
covered in her paintings and her shit and have her scream at you,
assault you, and that's fine. Or give her rules, and keep her in
control, and keep her here, and that too is all fine. But she is
taking over.

EDDIE. Well, that's great. You haven't got a cop inside your head.
You got a whole division.

Pause.

DOUGLAS. Well. Now, I think I'm going to the pub.

He stands.

I think, that is in order. Anyone —

BETH. So'm I.

She stands.

HUGO (*slowly gets up*). Why not.

DOUGLAS. Um, Laurence, want to —

LAURENCE. I'm all right.

Slight pause.

You said they should come down.

He goes up the stairs.

DOUGLAS. Right, then.

To EDDIE.

They're on me.

DOUGLAS *and* BETH *go out. As* HUGO *follows them.*

EDDIE. Hey. Supershrink.

HUGO *gives a clenched-fist sign and winks at EDDIE. He goes out. EDDIE and BRENDA are left there. BRENDA half-smiles at EDDIE, picks up some of the debris from the table, goes out to the kitchen. EDDIE throws himself into a chair.*

EDDIE. Oh bloody Mary.

Scene Four

MARY's *room.* MARY *kneels, head down, on the mattress. Knock at the door. Another knock. Then the door opens, and* LAURENCE *comes in.* MARY *kneels up. She looks at* LAURENCE. *She's frightened.*

LAURENCE. I have come. I have come to say I'm sorry.

Pause. MARY *frozen with fear.*

I've come to say I'm sorry 'bout the paintings.

Pause. MARY *looks at him.*

Come to make it up with you.

He goes to MARY, and rather clumsily, puts his arms round her and kisses her on the cheek.

There.

MARY *suddenly pushes at him.*

MARY. You *can't* do that.

LAURENCE. What?

MARY. Not children any more!

LAURENCE. Uh, came to —

MARY (*quite viciously, crowing*). He says he wants to come to bed with me. He came into my room. We got to tell the doctor.

LAURENCE. Uh?

MARY. I mean, we're just not children *any more.*

LAURENCE. I only . . .

Upset, LAURENCE *stands and goes to the door, turns back.*

Came to say . . .

He turns and goes out, slams the door, MARY *lies back, rather self-confident.*

MARY. I mean. I mean to say.

Slight pause.

I had to lock the door, you were away. I had to lock the door.

Slight pause.

Quite a relief, they came, in their white coats, with jacket, for you, long white jacket, with long arms and bits of string. A great relief.

Pause.

And so you went inside.

Slight pause.

You've gone inside.

In great pain.

And you won't melt inside.

Scene Five

Main area. BRENDA *enters with cups of coffee. Puts them down.* EDDIE *stands, goes and starts rolling up the canvases on the floor.*

BRENDA. D'you want some coffee?

Pause. BRENDA *goes and helps* EDDIE.

We can put some up again. When this dies down.

Pause.

Don't worry 'bout it.

EDDIE (*busy rolling*). Of course, what she is saying, through her pictures, something on the lines of, love me, love my paintings. Please. If it's no trouble.

BRENDA. Yuh.

EDDIE. She is saying things that she can't find the words for. Take them down, and you have struck her dumb.

BRENDA. Oh, sure.

> EDDIE *looks at* BRENDA. *Then he picks up the rolled canvases, piled them on a chair.*

> Of course, what she is doing is invading people, through her pictures. Something on the lines of, taking over. So the argument would run.

EDDIE. She has been stigmatized.

BRENDA. Yuh, sure.

EDDIE. By all of you.

> *Pause.* BRENDA *a slight laugh.*

> What's funny.

BRENDA. This is funny. This place. Our, unsacred family.

EDDIE. Our what?

BRENDA. With its rules and hierarchies. Rituals and scapegoats and taboos. Its Holy Fathers and its Mothers of Invention. Brother hoods and sisters of wild mercy. Its involuntary incest and its unforbidden fruits. And acid will be taken on the terrace after dinner. And the child-like will be heard but never seen.

EDDIE. You what?

BRENDA. I just, just sometimes, wonder if it's possible at all. Do you?

EDDIE. Well, certainly, this nuthouse isn't big enough for . . .

BRENDA. No.

> *She turns to the stairs.* MARY *stands there, naked, covered from head to foot in her own shit.*

> Uh . . .

> *She turns back.* EDDIE *hasn't noticed.*

Uh, Eddie . . .

EDDIE. What?

BRENDA. It's Mary.

EDDIE turns. Sees MARY.

EDDIE. Oh, yuh. So it is.

BRENDA. Um, she's . . .

EDDIE. Oh, yuh. She's covered in her shit. No, doubt about it. Shit, is it. Could tell a mile off.

Pause. He looks at his watch.

Yup. That's the stuff she's covered in. Well, now, it's ten of ten, I think I'll just go . . . Yuh.

He walks to the exit.

MARY. Eddie.

EDDIE stops, doesn't turn.

Eddie.

Pause.

You are my goodness, Eddie.

Pause.

EDDIE (*not turning*). Oh my Mary.

He walks out left. BRENDA doesn't know what to do. MARY stands. Pause. EDDIE comes back in with half an onion and a pot of honey and a spoon. He thrusts the onion at MARY.

EDDIE. OK, monster, put that in your mouth.

MARY puts the onion in her mouth.

OK, now, creature. Spit it out.

MARY spits it out. EDDIE spoons a spoonful of honey.

Now that is badness coming out. And this —

He puts the spoon in MARY's mouth.

Is goodness going in.

MARY stands there, the spoon in her mouth.

That's better? Good. Now, monster, creature from the black lagoon . . .

MARY a slight smile behind the spoon.

We better clean you up.

BLACKOUT.

Scene Six

Immediately, in the DARKNESS, *a mantra is sung.* LIGHTS.
Main area. Mantra goes on. Enter DOUGLAS. *He carries a suit
jacket, waistcoat, and tie on a hanger, a pair of black shoes and a
suitcase. The mantra stops. He looks off right. Then he takes off
his sweater and suede shoes. He is putting on his tie as* BRENDA
enters, with three fresh bottles of milk. He looks at BRENDA.
He finishes his tie, puts on his waistcoat, jacket and shoes. BRENDA
goes out. The mantra restarts. DOUGLAS *looks off right.*
DOUGLAS *puts the sweater, suedes and hanger in the suitcase,
picks it up and goes out.* BLACKOUT *and the mantra goes on.*

Scene Seven

Main area. BETH *enters, sits, reads.* BRENDA *enters with a suitcase.
She puts it on the table and ties the straps. Upstairs,* EDDIE *enters
with a suitcase, puts it down outside* MARY's *room, goes into*
MARY's *room, where* MARY *is lying huddled under the blankets.*
EDDIE *sits on* MARY's *bed.*

BETH. Hey, did she eat today?

BRENDA. She drank some water.

BETH. Yuh. D'you think she —

BRENDA. Very thin.

BETH. Sure is.

    Pause. BETH *looks at her watch, stands.*

    Well, have lots of fun. I have to go into my trance right now.

    Exit BETH *up the stairs, meeting* EDDIE *who comes out of*
    MARY's *room, picks up his case, and comes down into the
    main area.*

BRENDA. All right?

EDDIE. So-so. She kind of waved.

BRENDA. It's only for three weeks.

EDDIE. It's only for three weeks.

BRENDA. I've called a cab.

EDDIE. Oh, thanks.

BRENDA *goes out to the front door.* EDDIE *has a last-minute check of his plane-ticket and passport, as* HUGO *enters, from the kitchen, in a pinny.*

HUGO. You on your way?

EDDIE. Yuh —

HUGO. Everything in order?

EDDIE. (*pockets passport*). Yuh. Look, Hugo —

HUGO. No.

He goes to shake EDDIE's *hand.*

It's bitter, acrid, tastes like piss, but she has got to drink it. From the inside, roll away the stone.

Slight pause. EDDIE *picks up his case.*

EDDIE. Oh me of little faith.

EDDIE *goes out.* HUGO *turns to go too, sees* BETH, *standing at the top of the stairs.*

BETH. I give you the end of a golden string
Only wind it into a ball
It will lead you in at Heaven's Gate
Built in Jerusalem's wall.

HUGO *smiles at* BETH. *They go out as the lights transfer into* MARY's *room.*

Scene Eight

Gregorian chant. MARY *moves.* MARY *gets up, slowly. She goes to the door of her room. She opens it carefully, and looks out. No one there. She goes out, goes down the stairs. Checks round the main area. No one there. She goes to a secret place and pulls out a big roll of paper. She unrolls the paper, near her pots of paint. She kneels on the paper near the pots of paint. She looks at the paper. She breathes deeply. She speaks.*

MARY. Remember, as a child, strange feelings. Feel apart. Not here, not anywhere, a thing. All clumpy, weary. Head all big and fuzzy. Bits of me.

Pause. She dips her hand in the paint. She starts to paint with her hands on the paper. Then she suddenly starts talking, playing people in the painting.

Hey. You.
Hey, get a move on.

Heavy.
Hey, you, come on. Move.
It's heavy, clumping up the hill. Like feet in treacle. Mustn't fall.
Come on. Don't whine. We haven't got all day.
Clump clump. Clump clump. We're there.
The top. The silver sky.

All right then, pass the hammer.
One. Two. THREE.

Dead thing. The dead don't feel.

Long pause. MARY still.

I'm blown apart. There's bits of me.
All floating to the other side. A leg, an arm. I'm on the moon.
Another.

Pause. She starts to paint again.

Hey, you.
Who, me?
You don't know what you're doing.
Listen, what he says. We don't know what we're doing!
Hur hur hur.
Hey, you.
Who me?
I'm telling you. Today, you're going to heaven. One of you,
Oh, yuh? Big deal. Which one? Hur hur.
Hey, you.
Who, me?
I'm thirsty.

Drink it up, then. Like a good boy.
Drink it up.

No, no. The sky's gone crimson.
God oh God why have you . . .

Long pause. MARY still.

And the urge to spew it out, the bomb. But more you tear at it, the more it seems to cling, to stick inside you. Got to lie with it, and work it through.

Pause. She starts to draw again.

Hey, you!
You up there. Come down.
If you're so great, so clever, come on down.
He can't.
Well, ask him why. Can whisper.

Can't. Can't talk.
He's sulking, in a paddy. Cos he can't come down.
I won't.
I won't come down.
Stay in the dark.

Pause.

Be empty. Nothing. Void. Hang on.

Pause. Then HUGO *appears.*

HUGO. Petrifying.

Pause.

'Mean, so bloody thin.
Just on the edge.

Pause. HUGO *goes to* MARY.

Oh, Mary, must you suffer so.

Pause. MARY *looks up, to* HUGO. *In some surprise, she realizes.*

MARY. No. Wrong. Not suffering.
No more. It's you who's suffering.
Not me. It's you who's stretched and bleeding, up against the
golden sky.

Pause. HUGO *goes out.* MARY *is alone.*

Not finished. Not alone.
You're not the only one.

Pause.

Not on my own.

Lights fade to Blackout.

Act Three

Scene One

MARY *sitting in the same place as she was at the beginning of Act Two. But now she is not still and childlike; she is busy, writing in a book. Suddenly, there is a crash of the front door. MARY looks up. A moment, then ANGIE runs into the room. She is twenty, wears jeans, a sweater, and carries a placard with the slogan U.S. Out. She throws down the placard.*

ANGIE. Hey. Hey. LBJ.

She sits on the edge of a chair, takes off her shoes, and throws them across the room, as:

Ho. Ho. Ho Chi Minh.

Pause. She breathes deeply. MARY watching. ANGIE shuts her eyes. She opens her eyes, stands, and speaks.

Angie came to the house, in 1968. She'd known some people, round the place. Then she'd freaked out in, of all places, the Sudan, which can be rather dodgy. So someone flew out, to bring her back. She was really smashed. Angie's father was a Brigadier-General. Her brother was a stockbroker. Her mother was a Justice of the Peace. Her lover was a Maoist. It did not make for a stable and happy home environment. Bit of a cliché, really: straight family with radical chick. What wasn't a cliché was that background-versus-boyfriend was driving her right out of the little her breeding had left of her mind.

She sits.

If you say to someone, often, dear you don't mean that, eventually they're going to believe it. Become drained. If you say to someone, frequently, that what they do is not their nature, then their nature gets a mite confused. Remade. Becomes a second nature. Whose am I. If you say these things to someone, constantly, they end up living in response to other people, all the time.

She lights a cigarette.

When she was 14, her mother bought her a blouse. It was three sizes too big. It was extremely ugly. She couldn't change it. She wore it, and she felt ashamed. The blouse demonstrated how ugly she was. It showed that her bosom was too small. She didn't fit the blouse. When she was 16, told her father she believed in free abortion on demand. This shocked him rigid. Sanctity of life. He was a General. A fucking Army General. His *job*, desanctifying life.

When she was 21, Paul — the Maoist lover — told her that she'd never be a real Communist because of her conditioning. He told her that she'd never be a real revolutionary cos of something — which he called the Roedean Factor — which would stop her really hating those from whence she came. To really, hate, her mother. And he told her, that as soon as they returned from Africa, he was going to ditch her for some soft-Trot proletarian in Sunderland or Leeds and settle down.

Pause. She stubs out her cigarette.

If you take someone's thoughts and feelings away, bit by bit, consistently, then they have nothing left, except some gritty, gnawing, shitty little instinct, down there, somewhere, worming round the gut, but so far down, so hidden, it's impossible to find.

Longer pause.

Imagine, if you will, a worldwide conspiracy to deny the existence of the colour yellow. And whenever you saw yellow, they told you, no, that isn't yellow, what the fuck's yellow? Eventually, whenever you saw yellow, you would say: that isn't yellow, course it isn't, blue or green or purple, or . . . You'd say it, yes it is, it's yellow, and become increasingly hysterical, and then go quite beserk.

There's an awful lot of sand in the Sudan.

ANGIE *stands there.* MARY *stands, goes to her, still holding her book.* MARY *takes* ANGIE *by the hand and leads her upstairs, into her room.*

Scene Two

MARY's *room.* MARY *sits on her bed.* ANGIE *sits on a chair, her head down. Beside her, on the floor, a pile of academic books, a pen, a ringfile. Silence a few moments.*

MARY. Hey, Angie. Angie.

ANGIE. (*looks up*). Yuh?

MARY. I got a book. My stories. Want to read?

ANGIE *nods.* MARY *gives her the made-up book.* ANGIE *looks at it a moment. Then she tosses it back on the bed. Head down. Pause.*

MARY. Hey, Angie, want to lie down?

ANGIE. No.

MARY. OK.

Pause. Then ANGIE *looks up.*

ANGIE. Hey, Mary? Could you kill your mother?

MARY. I did, in my heart.

ANGIE. Yuh, no, I mean really. Blow her up. One afternoon. At tea. Bits of mother, floating in the milk-jug, dribbling down the wall.

Slight pause.

It'd be like suicide.

MARY. I know.

ANGIE. Be like you killed yourself.

MARY. I've felt that too.

Pause.

ANGIE. I was born with a Caesarian. From my mother's womb untimely ripped. Hail Caesar. Ha!

Pause. She breathes deeply. Gets herself together.

Now, Mary, got to read. I got to write this essay.

MARY. Angie, no.

ANGIE (*picking up a book*). The daily tasks, we must complete.

MARY. No, Angie.

ANGIE. Hey, don't you bug me, Mary, now, OK? I gotta read.

She picks up the ringfile and a pen to take notes. She opens the book and reads a bit. Then she lights a cigarette. Reads some more.

Hey. Cop a load of this. "I is another. I am present at the flowering of my own ideas. I watch them, listen to them, it is wrong to say I think, I ought to say, I Am Being Thought". The poet Rimbaud. Rather good.

Pause. She takes a drag. Then her head whips down and the book and the ring-file fall. Pause.

What did you do?

MARY. Went down.

ANGIE. Like how?

MARY. When I was frightened that I'd kill myself, I'd lie down, in the dark, for weeks, see no-one. Hold the anger in myself. Like as if cross-legged, or something. Hold yourself in pain.

ANGIE (*head up*). Oh. Kind of yoga.

MARY. All religions.

ANGIE. Opiate. Um.

> *Pause.*

> In Africa, I thought I was giving birth to baby Jesus. Quite impossible, of course, because I'm barren. Cunt is like a dust-bowl. Running sore.

> *Pause. She stubs the cigarette out in the wastepaper basket.*

> I am alienated from my means of reproduction. Ha!

> *Pause.*

> I wanna be in the dark. Put ashes on myself.

MARY. I know. I felt that too.

> *Pause.*

ANGIE. Look, Mary, I ought to go ring Max. Tell him, come over.

MARY. Oh, Angie, why?

ANGIE. We're working on this pamphlet. It consists, you will be staggered to gather, of a critique of the capitalist system.

MARY. Oh, Angie, no.

ANGIE. Also, I usually take a little sexual intercourse at this hour. Ha!

MARY (*whispers*). No.

ANGIE. A fucking sandpit.

> *Pause.*

> What's that? That noise?

MARY. It's just the dustbinmen.

ANGIE. They're emptying my cunt.

MARY. You feel that they're inside you.

ANGIE. Yuh.

MARY. I felt that too. I felt that everything was me. And nothing. Eddie, me. And Eddie went away, I went away. The only thing to do was lie down with my anger, keep quite still, and it dissolves.

ANGIE. It does?

MARY. Eventually.

ANGIE. I feel that everything, is going on inside my head. A thousand armies, are manoeuvring, around my brain.

Pause. She goes and sits on the mattress next to MARY.

A hundred thousand little yellow men. Manoeuvring.

Slight pause.

I wish they'd melt away.

Suddenly, she picks up the waste-paper basket and empties it over her head. Lots of nasties. Pause.

Should I have done that?

MARY. Yes, you should.

Pause. ANGIE *rubs the stuff in her face. She picks a cigarette butt out of her hair. She eats it. Pause.*

ANGIE. Eaten it.

MARY. I understand that.

ANGIE. Do you?

MARY. Course. I felt like that. I used to eat my shits.

ANGIE. Wow. What d'it taste like?

MARY. Just like shit.

Pause.

ANGIE. Mary, I gotta go ring Max.

MARY. No, mustn't go.

ANGIE. Look, Mary, not just Max. The fucking revolution.

MARY. No, that's not the real thing. You must go down.

ANGIE. Go down.

Long pause.

Hey, Mary.

MARY. Yes?

ANGIE. Gimme your rosary. I want to hold it.

MARY *gives* ANGIE *her rosary.* MARY *cradles* ANGIE. *Long pause.*

MARY. This is the important thing.

ANGIE *suddenly tightens. She pushes* MARY *away.*

Angie?

ANGIE. No. No. No.

ANGIE *up, to the washbasin, splashes water over her face.*

MARY. Angie . . .

ANGIE, *her face still dripping, finds a comb, and, combing her hair, runs out.* MARY *up.*

Oh . . . Oh, *no.*

MARY *leaves her room after* ANGIE. ANGIE *then enters down the stairs, and runs across. She bumps into* EDDIE *who enters left eating a sandwich.*

EDDIE. Hey, Angie, how's it go?

ANGIE. I gotta PHONE.

She runs out left.

EDDIE. You gotta phone.

MARY *down the stairs. To* EDDIE.

MARY. Eddie, quick —

EDDIE. Hey, hey, what goes on?

MARY (*trying to pull* EDDIE *towards the left*). It's Angie, she's trying to phone —

EDDIE. Why shouldn't she?

MARY (*still pulling*). Oh, cos she's got to go down Eddie —

EDDIE. Mary. Stop that.

Pause. MARY *lets* EDDIE *go.*

MARY. But —

EDDIE. Listen. P'raps you're right. But mustn't force her, do what you did. What she wants. OK?

Slight pause.

Just let her, what she wants to. Different from you.

ANGIE *has reappeared from left.*

ANGIE. Now that is true. I'm definitely different.

Pause. She walks up the stairs.

MARY *looks at* EDDIE, *who makes a vague, non-committal gesture.* MARY *runs out after* ANGIE. EDDIE *goes out.* ANGIE *comes into* MARY's *room. Enter* MARY *behind her.* ANGIE *sits on the bed. She puts the rosary round her neck.*

ANGIE. So did you really feel like me?

MARY. I did.

   MARY *sits on the bed.*

ANGIE. It's awful.

MARY. Yes, it is.

ANGIE. I rang my mother.

MARY. Did you?

ANGIE (*crying*) Cos I fucking love her, don't I? Motherfucking mother. Hurt my mother, she hurts me.

MARY. I don't.

ANGIE. You don't . . .

MARY. Don't hurt you.

   ANGIE *looks at* MARY. *She's stopped crying.*

ANGIE. Oh, I like it here.

MARY. You do?

ANGIE. Yuh. Do.

   Pause.

   Gimme your tit.

   MARY *gives* ANGIE *her breast, cradling her in her arms.*

   You are my mother, Mary.

   Long pause. ANGIE *down, lets* MARY's *breast go.* MARY *sits there, looking at* ANGIE.

MARY. I wrote this story once. About a tree. Which felt all sad and lonely, for her trunk was hollow, and her head was lost in mist.

And to the other trees, she seemed quite strong, but really she was lonely, and she grew so tired of standing, that she was relieved when one day a great storm blew up, and threw her to the ground.

The tree was split, her branches scattered, and her roots torn up. And all the other trees looked down, and gasped, and didn't quite know what to do or say. And there the dead tree was, all bare, and open to the wind and sun, and rain.

But then, one day, the wetness of the rain, the tree put down new roots. And with the sun she stretched, and grew again. And in the wind her branches bent to other trees, and she felt loved again, and lived, and laughed with life.

ANGIE *looks up. She smiles.*

ANGIE. Oh, yuh?

MARY. I am. I am your Mother Mary.

Lights fade.

Scene Three

In the darkness, we hear PEOPLE *singing.*

Happy Birthday to you
Happy birthday to you
Happy birthday dear (Angie
                              (Angela
Happy birthday to you.

LIGHTS. *The* PEOPLE *are applauding. They are* HUGO, BRENDA, ANGIE's MOTHER *and* BROTHER, *standing either side of* ANGIE, *who sits in front of a small table with a birthday cake on it. She is eating a piece of cake. The* OTHERS *have pieces of cake or cups of tea.*

MOTHER. Your father was so sorry he couldn't be here.

ANGIE. Oh. Yuh.

MOTHER. But he sends you lots of love.

ANGIE. Oh, thank him, please.

MOTHER. Of course.

Slight pause. The MOTHER *gestures at the* BROTHER, *who queries, realizes and goes out. Pause.*

Lovely cake.

ANGIE. It's smashing. Brenda made it.

MOTHER. I must get the recipe.

Pause.

This is your main living area, is it?

BRENDA. Yes, that's right. We eat, and things, in here.

MOTHER. It's good and spacey.

BRENDA. Yup.

Re-enter the BROTHER *with a parcelled present.*

MOTHER. Ah. Here we are.

ANGIE. Oh. Me?

MOTHER (*smiles*). Who else?

ANGIE *smiles. She takes the parcel, opens it. It's a print dress. It is obviously highly fashionable, expensive and much to* ANGIE's *taste.*

ANGIE. Oh, it's lovely.

MOTHER. Do you like it?

ANGIE. Oh, that's really nice. Hey, can I try it on?

MOTHER. Of course you can.

ANGIE *gets up, shows the dress to* HUGO *and* BRENDA.

Hey, look at this.

BRENDA. It's very pretty.

ANGIE. Oh, I must . . . Hold on a minute.

She's going to the stairs exit.

MOTHER. Darling, I'll come with you.

ANGIE. Fine.

MOTHER. So, while we're at it, we can get you packed.

Pause.

Your things.

HUGO. Um —

ANGIE. Don't want to go.

MOTHER. Darling, that's not true.

ANGIE. Don't want to be with you.

MOTHER. Now, Angela, you don't mean that.

ANGIE. I do, I hate it, being with you.

MOTHER. Look, darling, I don't mind it when you say that, cos I know that you can't help it.

ANGIE. I can help it.

MOTHER. If I thought that you weren't ill, I'd be so angry.

Pause.

We only came because you asked us to.

Pause. ANGIE *shrugs. Exit* ANGIE *and her* MOTHER. *The* BROTHER *doesn't look at* HUGO *or* BRENDA.

HUGO. Where were you thinking of taking her?

BROTHER. She rang my mother up.

HUGO. That doesn't quite answer the question.

Pause.

BROTHER. I imagine she strikes you as something of a paradigm, my mum. Bit of a classic, really. She will wear those hats. She will get so up-tight when people cut her off from her own daughter. She will get so upset when people say that Angie's illness is her fault. That she has driven her own daughter to distraction.

BRENDA. Well, that isn't —

BROTHER. Isn't it? You tell her that.

Pause.

It's obvious that Angela's in pain. She's suffering. The treatment stops the suffering.

HUGO. Now, look —

ANGIE *and her* MOTHER *come in.* ANGIE *wears an expensive overcoat that doesn't go with her sweater and jeans. Her* MOTHER *carries her suitcase.*

BROTHER. So where's the dress?

MOTHER. She decided not to wear it, for the drive.

BROTHER. Oh, yes.

HUGO. Um —

MOTHER *turns to* HUGO.

I'd like to ask you to leave Angie with us, for a while.

Slight pause.

I would really like you to consider that possibility.

MOTHER. You'll upset her.

HUGO. *We'll* upset her?

MOTHER. Angela is ill. Needs curing.

HUGO. Look, curing, with respect, is what one does to bacon.

MOTHER. Bacon?

HUGO. Not to human beings.

Pause.

MOTHER. She's been eating cigarettes.

Pause.

Now, shall we, please —

ANGIE. Where's Mary?

MOTHER. Mary?

BRENDA. Mary's out.

MOTHER. Who's Mary?

ANGIE. Mary . . . lives here, in the house.

Pause. The BROTHER *picks up the luggage.*

BROTHER. I'll go and load the car.

He goes to the door, but decides to wait as ANGIE, *after a pause, goes to* BRENDA, *kisses her. She goes to* HUGO, *kisses him. Then she notices she's still wearing the rosary. She takes it off and gives it to* HUGO.

ANGIE. There's rosary. That's for remembrance.

She laughs. Then stops. Then, with an odd little clenched fist sign, she walks out.

Ho. Ho. Ho.

She goes, followed by her BROTHER. *The* MOTHER *smiles at* HUGO *and* BRENDA, *as if* ANGIE's *odd behaviour confirmed her view. She makes to go.*

BRENDA (*suddenly, a step forward*). First break two dozen eggs —

MOTHER *turns back, interrupts, quite genuine.*

MOTHER. No, please. It's hard enough. Please don't.

She goes out. Pause.

BRENDA. Come the great day, she will be the first.

Suddenly, HUGO *runs out right.*

Hugo?

No reply. A moment, then re-enter HUGO. *He's pulling on a pair of black shoes, and fastening a tie.*

BRENDA. What you doing?

HUGO. Going after.

BRENDA. Where?

HUGO. The hospital. Only one of three.

BRENDA. To get her back?

HUGO's running to the door.

HUGO. To try and get her back.

He's gone.

Scene Four

Main area. EDDIE stands looking at the debris of the tea party. He can't work it out. Door slam and enter MARY.

EDDIE. Well, hallo, horror.

MARY. Hey, guess who?

EDDIE. I can't.

Enter ZIMMERMAN.

Hey, Zimmerman —

MARY. And guess *what* —

EDDIE. I can't. Hey, Zimmer-

MARY. GUESS.

EDDIE. You've been elected Pope.

MARY. No, no!

EDDIE. I've been elected Pope.

MARY. Oh, Eddie.

To ZIMMERMAN.

You tell him.

ZIMMERMAN. Who me?

MARY (*going up the stairs*). Yes, you!

EDDIE. Well?

ZIMMERMAN. Glad tidings of great joy. Having made one of herself for so long, Miss Barnes has now got herself an exhibition.

EDDIE. What?

ZIMMERMAN (*takes a letter from his pocket*). A one-loon show. Peruse.

He gives the letter to EDDIE, who reads it.

EDDIE. That's wonderful.

Enter MARY, carrying a large number of canvases and bits of paper. She drops them on the table.

MARY. Right now. This is some of them.

ZIMMERMAN. Hey, Mary —

MARY. Mean, for a start.

ZIMMERMAN. Um, a gallery. Small gallery. Not Wembley Stadium.

MARY. The triptych! Eddie, come on, give a hand.

ZIMMERMAN has picked up a painting on a plank of wood.

ZIMMERMAN. Now, how do I frame that?

MARY has noticed HUGO, who has entered left. She's about to go and tell him her news, but his face stops her. HUGO takes off his tie. EDDIE and ZIMMERMAN still looking at the paintings.

EDDIE. Hey, this one has to go.

ZIMMERMAN. Which is that?

HUGO goes to MARY and gives her the rosary. The OTHERS notice, and look at MARY and HUGO.

HUGO. Our family, was not quite strong enough. Compete against the family that's in her head, her family.

Pause.

MARY. Oh, Hugo, why did —

HUGO. She was growing up again, but they couldn't stand the sight of her, the colour of her leaves, the way she tossed her branches in the wind.

Slight pause.

And so they cut her down.

HUGO goes out. LAURENCE wanders in to the record player.

MARY. Eddie.

EDDIE. Mm?

MARY. I want to —

EDDIE. Mm?

MARY. Please, Eddie, find my brother. Want to be here, with my brother. Want to have him grow up too.

LAURENCE puts on a record. It is Julie Driscoll's 'Colours'. Lights fade as ZIMMERMAN and EDDIE take out the paintings . . .

Scene Five

*The music continues. Suddenly, the bang of the front door. HUGO,
BRENDA, ZIMMERMAN, EDDIE and MARY come in. They have
come from the exhibition and everyone is in their best gear. MARY
looks radiant, and clutches a bouquet of flowers. LAURENCE
enters, as MARY jabbers to ZIMMERMAN, and BRENDA switches
off the record player.*

MARY. And did you hear the lady. Lady from *The Times?* You
heard what *she* told Zimmerman?

EDDIE. (*to* HUGO). The best thing since sliced bread.

MARY (*thrusts the flowers at* EDDIE). In water.

EDDIE. Water. Sure.

> EDDIE *takes the flowers out.* HUGO *and* ZIMMERMAN *finding
> a bottle of wine.*

BRENDA. Hi, Laurence.

MARY (*rushing to him*). Oh, Oh, Laurence.

LAURENCE (*a learnt question*). Did It Go All Right?

MARY. Oh, let me *tell* you . . .

> MARY *takes* LAURENCE *by the arm.*

HUGO (*to* ZIMMERMAN). What did the lady say?

ZIMMERMAN (*shrugs*). The best since sliced . . .

> *Waving the bottle.*

> Another?

HUGO. Well. Why not.

> MARY *whispering to* LAURENCE. *But* BRENDA *near enough
> to hear.*

MARY. I saw my brother. Simon came. Thought it was wonderful.
He's coming here.

BRENDA. He's coming here to visit, Mary. For an afternoon. Not
going to stay.

MARY (*as if that mattered, running upstairs*). He's coming here to
visit me.

> *The* OTHERS *look at* LAURENCE. *He goes and puts the record
> player back on.*

Scene Six

MARY's *room. Tea is laid out, with a pot, cups and cakes.* EDDIE *sits on a cushion on the floor.* MARY *sits on her mattress.* SIMON *sits on the only chair. The* MEN *drink tea,* MARY *drinks milk. Pause.*

MARY. Would you like a cake?

SIMON. No thank you. I have a meal back at the hostel.

MARY. How is the hostel?

SIMON. It is very pleasant. I have my own room.

MARY. Not in the chronic ward, no more.

SIMON. No, not in the chronic ward. But still, they give me my depixol.

Slight pause.

MARY. Just depixol?

SIMON. And the disipal. To counter-act the tremors. And the mogadon, to make me sleep.

He sips his tea. MARY *a desperate look at* EDDIE. EDDIE, *to stop* MARY *saying anything.*

EDDIE. Are you working, Mr Barnes?

SIMON. Yes, I'm working in a factory.

EDDIE. What doing?

SIMON. Oh, I cut up bits of metal to make coils.

MARY. Kind of electrical.

SIMON. That's right.

Pause. SIMON *sips his tea.*

It's better than my last job.

Slight pause.

EDDIE. What was —

MARY. Simon — Eddie, Hugo, everybody here, they could look after you.

Slight pause.

They did for me. They saved me. They could do the same.

Slight pause.

Simon, we're from the same womb. We got all twisted up

together. But things can get untwisted. Really.

Slight pause. More desperately.

Simon, was a girl, here, in the house, was getting better, really better, and they came and took her to the hospital and smashed her up like . . .

She breaks.

Simon, come and stay here. PLEASE. Why won't you understand what's best for you?

Pause.

SIMON. Is there a lavatory?

MARY. Yes, across the corridor. I'll show you.

SIMON *puts down his cup,* MARY *gets up, takes* SIMON *out. A moment.* EDDIE *puts his cup down, stands.* MARY *enters, in some passion, and bashes* EDDIE *on the chest.*

EDDIE. Hey, what's that for?

MARY. Eddie, Simon's cutting up bits of metal. It's not making him better, he's still on drugs, why don't you make him come here.

EDDIE. Make him?

MARY. He looks like wax, a robot. Disappearing. Make him stop. Make him go down.

EDDIE. Can't make him.

MARY. Why not?

EDDIE. Cos he may not want to.

Pause.

You do what you want to.

MARY. Oh, I do so want him to be better.

EDDIE. You're greedy for him to be better. You want to eat him being better.

MARY. Oh, Eddie, why d'I feel so bad.

EDDIE. Because you're angry with me and you want to kill me because I won't make Simon be like you.

MARY. Not angry with you, Eddie.

EDDIE. Aren't you?

Pause.

MARY. I want him to become himself.

EDDIE. Who's that?

MARY turns away. Pause.

Hey, Mary.

MARY. Mm?

EDDIE. You know, I said you're greedy. But you're not the greediest.

MARY. Mm? What?

EDDIE. There's someone who's much greedier than you.

MARY. Yuh? Who?

EDDIE. That's me. That's Eddie. I'm the one that's greedier than you.

Pause. MARY smiles.
Then SIMON comes in. EDDIE stands.

EDDIE. Right, I think I ought to go.

SIMON. I must go soon, too. Ten minutes.

EDDIE. Good to see you. Hope you come again.

EDDIE and SIMON shake hands. Exit EDDIE. SIMON sits.

MARY. I'm glad you like the hostel.

SIMON. Mm.

MARY. I'm sorry, shouted.

SIMON. Mm.

MARY. I hope you'll come and visit me again.

SIMON. I shall.

Pause.

MARY. I've changed. You see that?

SIMON. Yes, you've changed.

Pause.

I've no foundation.

MARY. But you, but you could . . .

She stops herself. Pause.

SIMON. In fact. In fact. I've given in my notice.

MARY. Oh, Simon, have you?

SIMON. Yes. In fact, I'm thinking about changing my accommodation. Can't eat meat. I want a place where I can make my own food.

MARY. Oh, Simon, you can do that . . .

Slight pause.

Cook my own food here.

SIMON. You do?

MARY *nods slowly.*

I will think about it, moving here. If I fit in.

He stands, notices there's paint on his coat.

I've something on my coat.

MARY *jumps up.*

MARY. Oh, that it's paint, it must have come off . . . Look, I'll find some turps . . .

SIMON. It's on my coat.

MARY *rushes round, finds turps and a cloth, dabs SIMON's coat.*

MARY. It's coming off.

As she works, a little laugh.

My room's an awful mess. I don't know how it gets this way, however much I . . . There, it's gone.

MARY *stands.*

SIMON. I think it's gone.

MARY. Your own room wouldn't be like that, of course. That would be tidy, as you like.

SIMON *stands there. Pause.*

SIMON. I. Used to paint. Before my illness. Haven't done so much, since then.

Pause.

Mary, when I came into your room, that night, before I went away, I wasn't going to have sex with you. I just wanted to touch you, that's all.

He picks up his scarf, puts on his coat.

I'll have to get a certificate. I'll need it, for the people, if I'm coming here.

He goes out.

Scene Seven

Main area, on the record-player. It's night. LAURENCE sits in front of the record player, he's playing a record: Helter Skelter by the Beatles. He turns it up louder. He shakes about. He turns it up louder. SIMON appears, in a dressing-gown and slippers over pyjamas buttoned up to the neck. He watches LAURENCE. LAURENCE turns the music louder. SIMON puts his hand to his head. LAURENCE turns the music even louder. SIMON turns, walks out. LAURENCE turns the music even louder. BLACKOUT. Music on a few moments, very loud, then an awful scratching noise as if the record is ripped off, followed by smashing metal and wood, followed by the broken record-player being thrown on the floor.

Scene Eight

LAURENCE *stands downstage. The broken bits of the record player are at his feet.* BRENDA *and* MARY *stand.* HUGO, EDDIE *and* ZIMMERMAN *sitting.*

LAURENCE. I'm sorry.

BRENDA. Not your fault.

LAURENCE. I made him go away. Too noisy.

HUGO. Not your fault.

   LAURENCE *kicks the record-player bits.*

LAURENCE. I like the noise. He couldn't stand it. Sorry.

   Exit LAURENCE *right. Pause.*

MARY. He just, wanted to be left alone. Be quiet, to make his food, and eat it, do the things he does, precisely, organize his day. He wasn't taking tablets any more. He wasn't taking drugs.

HUGO. He'll come back.

MARY. Gone. This is the END.

HUGO. It's not the end.

MARY. He'll be destroyed.

BRENDA. Mary, Simon's different, he hasn't got your painting and your writing —

MARY. Painting? Writing? That's not important. What's important is my brother. And you helping.

   She shouts at the OTHERS.

   You know him better than he knows himself!

EDDIE. You know that isn't true.

MARY. It's just the same as Angie. You just let them go.

HUGO. Oh, shut up, Mary.

MARY. The lot of you. You're therapists, aren't you? You're
healers, aren't you? Well, then, do your job. And CURE HIM.

EDDIE. Oh, for Christ's sake, Mary . . .

MARY. Oh, I'm so angry with you, Eddie —

EDDIE. Are you? Are you angry?

MARY. Yes!

EDDIE. Then say it —

MARY. I am angry —

EDDIE. Once again —

MARY. I am very angry with you, Eddie —

EDDIE. Knock, who's there —

MARY. It's MARY —

EDDIE. Mary who —

MARY. IT'S MARY BARNES!

Pause.

EDDIE. That's good.

MARY. Oh, I'm so *angry* with you, Eddie!

MARY *storms out. The* OTHERS *smile.*

EDDIE. Very good indeed . . .

Pause.

ZIMMERMAN. Will her brother come back?

EDDIE. May do. It's not for long.

ZIMMERMAN. Why not?

BRENDA. We're moving out. The lease expires.

ZIMMERMAN. Can't you extend?

HUGO. The worthy burghers wouldn't wear it.

ZIMMERMAN. What'll happen?

EDDIE. Simon will stay in mental hospital. Why not? It's his
career. His job. His place in life.

Pause.

ZIMMERMAN. Mary once told me a long a rather rambling tale about her masturbating. One would say without fear of contradiction that her clitoral attitude was ambivalent. This seemed partly due to the fact that, before she came here, she was going to the shrink on Monday, told her it was fine, you carry on, and then on Tuesday, to confession, where they told her she was in a state of mortal sin.

EDDIE. And so?

ZIMMERMAN. I just wondered, what you thought, on opening her soul, to find the Catholic cross still etched across her heart. That's all.

Pause.

EDDIE. That's how she is. That is her journey. That is real and right and true for her. That's all.

Slight pause.

She's better than she was. And she is better without shocks or drugs or anything. That's all.

Slight pause.

It's possible. That's all.

Slight pause.

It's not my job, my place, to tell her how to run her life. Or anyone.

Exit EDDIE. Pause.

ZIMMERMAN. I liked it when the students went to Washington, and hummed a mantra, tried to levitate the Pentagon. Good image. Liked it when we dropped a little acid, and convinced ourselves the secret sacred gardens in our heads were somehow blooming across the cosmos. A nice, analogy.

HUGO *stands.*

HUGO (*with a little smile*). I think I liked it, very much, when Lyndon Johnson went on television, and announced he'd not seek re-election. Liked it very much when all the wretched of the earth, the great unwashed, made LBJ give up his second seal for peace. I liked that, metaphor. I think, I think it was the very best. You know.

He goes out.

ZIMMERMAN. When do you leave?

BRENDA. First week in May.

ZIMMERMAN. What do you think will happen?

BRENDA. I don't know.

> ZIMMERMAN *says nothing.*

> I know . . . I think I know . . .

> *Pause.*

> For me, it was best of all . . . Just see ourselves, each other, all our, lumpy nakedness. To hear our voices, all their, I don't know, their rasping melody.

> Capture our lives in their, messy majesty.

> You see?

ZIMMERMAN. Of course I see.

BRENDA. We didn't build the future. But we are no longer, other, to ourselves.

> *Pause. With a smile.*

> We've closed the door behind us. And, who knows, what lies beyond, the point, beyond the pale.

> *She goes out, up the stairs.* ZIMMERMAN *stays there. He sees* SIMON, *standing with his suitcase, having entered from the street.*

ZIMMERMAN. Ah. Hallo.

> *Pause.*

> Hey, Mary! Mary!

MARY (*from off, tetchy*). Yes?

ZIMMERMAN. Someone to see you!

> *Slight pause.*

> Mary!

> MARY *appears, down the stairs.*

MARY (*still tetchily*): Who?

> ZIMMERMAN *nods to* SIMON. MARY *turns to* SIMON. *Pause.*

> BLACKOUT. *During the change. No More Heroes, by the Stranglers. Dust sheets are thrown over the furniture in the room.*

Scene Nine

Then, in the darkness, a crash, of glass and breaking wood. A shaft of LIGHT *on the empty stage. It is some years later. Enter*

KEITH *and* ANGIE. *They have just broken in.* ANGIE, *who is dressed rather formally, brushes herself down.* KEITH *is in contemporary clothes.*

KEITH. Well, this is it.

Pause.

We used to play, our group, we used to play through there, along the corridor.

ANGIE *looks round.*

Mean anything?

ANGIE *shakes her head.*

ANGIE. Don't think so.

KEITH. Don't think so.

Slight pause.

Look, you did live here?

ANGIE. Yes, I'm sure. I had this pocket book, you see, with lots of names, addresses, and afterwards I couldn't quite remember them, and so I went round, looking, trying to reconstruct it, bit by bit.

KEITH. You found the people?

ANGIE. No. They'd moved on, all of them.

KEITH. Except this place.

ANGIE. That's right.

Pause.

KEITH. They must have wiped you out.

ANGIE. They did.

Pause.

The shocks. You see, it's like a photograph. Before, it's there, and then you look again, it's faded. Just a blur. It's odd, you feel much better.

KEITH. Better?

ANGIE. Lets you forget, the things that hurt you, I suppose. It takes you back. Back to the comfort that you knew before.

Slight pause.

Better get back. My mother will expect me.

Pause. KEITH *shrugs, as if to apologise for* ANGIE's *not remembering the place.*

Thank you so much for showing me. It's tricky on the A to Z. The streets don't quite look, how they are.

KEITH. Well, things have changed, round here. They're changing all the time. Most of the places that were here, not any more.

ANGIE. Except this place?

KEITH. That's right.

ANGIE smiles. She makes to go.

You know, the people round here, us, so frightened of the people in this place. They threatened us. Disrupted our, uncomfortable security.

ANGIE. I'm sorry?

KEITH. Know, my sister, got three kids like other people got the measles, and gets through the day clogged up on valium, cos she's so petrified of what she'd feel if she woke up.

ANGIE. I beg your pardon?

KEITH. Can't, you can't forget the pain for ever. Can you? Can't, forever, stop the clock, and go back where you were before?

ANGIE. Don't know.

ANGIE has found a hardboard painting leaning against the wall. She looks at it. To KEITH.

Who's that?

KEITH doesn't follow.

Whose? There?

KEITH goes and looks at the painting.

KEITH. That's Mary.

ANGIE. Mary who?

KEITH. That's Mary Barnes.

Pause.

ANGIE. Hey --

Slight pause.

Hey —

Slight pause. She doesn't remember. With a shrug.

Hey-ho.

And she turns from the picture and goes and sits down. And KEITH stands there.
LIGHTS *fade.*

Saigon Rose

SAIGON ROSE was first presented at the Traverse Theatre, Edinburgh, in July 1976, with the following cast:

VICKY	Tammy Ustinov
CLAYMORE	Martin Black
HEATHER/NURSE	Juliet Cadzow
CLIVE	Mark Penfold
McLUSKY	Roy Hanlon
MO	Tricia Scott
DOCTOR	Godfrey Jackman
MAN ON BEACH	Ronnie Letham

Directed by Chris Parr
Set designed by Tot Brill
Costumes by Prudence von Rohrbach
Lighting by Alastair McArthur

The play was subsequently broadcast on Radio 3 on 3 April 1979, with the following cast:

VICKY	Alison Steadman
CLAYMORE	Blain Fairman
HEATHER	Miriam Margolyes
CLIVE	Peter Pacey
McLUSKY	Bill Patterson
MO	Patti Love
DOCTOR	Geoffrey Matthews
MAN ON BEACH	Stephen Yardley

Produced by Michael Rolfe

Characters

VICKY *is in her mid-20s, English, middle-class.*
CLAYMORE *is a little over 30. Soft American accent.*
HEATHER *is 30, from the Borders, wears trouser-suits.*
CLIVE *is in his late 20s, English, middle-class.*
McCLUSKY *is over 35, from Glasgow.*
MO *is 19, from Aberdeenshire.*
THE DOCTOR *is middle-aged, English.*
THE NURSE *is a little younger, Scottish.*
THE MAN ON THE BEACH *is in his late 20s, cockney, dressed in
    a combat jacket and jeans.*

HEATHER *or* VICKY *could play the* NURSE.
CLAYMORE *can double the* MAN.

The play is set in the capital of Scotland, except for Act Two,
Scene Two, which is set on the beach at Peterhead.

It is the mid-1970s.

Act One

The colours in this act are rich, bright and mixed. While the audience are coming in, Bob Dylan's 'Tangled Up in Blue' plays.

Scene One

Music fades and lights come up on the empty stage. Enter CLAYMORE followed by VICKY. CLAYMORE looks round. VICKY stands, fiddling with the door keys. CLAYMORE turns to VICKY, smiles. VICKY indecisive. She puts the keys in her bag, tosses it on a chair. CLAYMORE takes a step towards her, she sniffs, picks up her bag, fumbles for a handkerchief. He converts his step towards her into another look at his surroundings. VICKY wipes her nose, puts her hanky away, looks at CLAYMORE, who's looking elsewhere. He turns to her, she smiles, nervously, takes a step towards him. This time he turns, moves. Then stops, turns back to her. They look at each other. She takes a step towards him. He takes a step towards her. Pause. Then she half-shrugs, half-smiles, goes to him, puts her arms round his neck and they kiss.

CLAYMORE. Right, then.

VICKY. Right — then.

Snap blackout. Music: The opening phrase of side two of the Electric Light Orchestra's 'On the Third Day'.
Then a spot lights up HEATHER. VICKY and CLAYMORE have gone.

HEATHER. Where had it started? She'd often asked herself. Where do things start? Which is the first spoke in the wheel, the first daisy in the chain.

Not that it mattered. All that mattered was that it hadn't started here, in this room, here in her city, her place. It was an invader, an uninvited guest, a tourist, that had come with the other tourists, the ones that actually enjoyed the hills and steps, and learnt to ask for pints of heavy, and brought the little plastic kilted ladies on the Royal Mile.

It had started, in so far as it did start, years before, and thousands of miles away; travelling quietly, persistently, unheralded, unknown, across the lands and seas and oceans, the awful consequence, the dreadful side-effect; the poisoned flower, the slug beneath the sepulchre.

Reaching a man and a woman in a room in her city.

A burst of Electric Light Orchestra. Blackout. Exit HEATHER. Lights.

Enter CLAYMORE. *He is doing up his shirt. He sits, at the table. He finishes his shirt. He waits. Enter* VICKY *in a dressing-gown, with a tray, on it a bowl of cornflakes and two cups of coffee. She puts them on the table.*

VICKY. Cornflakes all right?

CLAYMORE. Wonderful (*He starts to eat.*) You not having any?

VICKY. No, I don't.

CLAYMORE. Right.

CLAYMORE *eats.* VICKY *looking at him, concentrating.* CLAYMORE *attempting to concentrate on his cornflakes.*

VICKY. Don't tell me, let me guess.

CLAYMORE *looks up.*

CLAYMORE. Right.

Pause.

VICKY. University?

CLAYMORE. No.

VICKY. London?

CLAYMORE. No.

VICKY. Isle of Wight?

CLAYMORE. Isle of Wight?

Slight pause.

VICKY. Don't tell me.

CLAYMORE. I wouldn't dream of it.

VICKY. I know the face.

CLAYMORE *smiles as he eats. Pause.*

Sorry. Give up.

Slight pause.

You're going to have to help me.

Slight pause.

It's not going to come.

CLAYMORE. As the peanut farmer said to the Daughter of the Revolution.

He finishes his cornflakes. Wiping his mouth.

I crashed with you. Some pad in the New Town. Round about 1968. I was having fire-resistance problems with a draft-card.

VICKY. Oh, *yes.*

Slight pause.

When you say with me?

CLAYMORE. On your settee.

VICKY. That's what I thought.

CLAYMORE. Sorry?

VICKY. I mean, I'm sure I would have remembered, if it hadn't been.

Pause.

Did they get you?

CLAYMORE. Who?

VICKY. The draft people.

CLAYMORE. I didn't go back to get got. Canada.

VICKY. Now.

CLAYMORE. Canada. England.

VICKY. Both?

CLAYMORE. I commute.

VICKY. Jesus Christ. Doing?

CLAYMORE. The same.

VICKY. Which is?

CLAYMORE. I take photographs.

Pause.

VICKY. My husband's in papers.

CLAYMORE. I'm in magazines.

Pause.

(*Matter-of-factly.*) You're married?

VICKY *waves her wedding ring.*

I didn't spot it.

VICKY. You haven't aged.

CLAYMORE. You're too kind.

VICKY. No, I mean, Clive, my husband, says the definition of approaching middle-age is when you start looking at people's third fingers as a matter of course.

CLAYMORE. How old is he, for Christ's sake?

VICKY. As he puts it, the wrong side of 29½.

CLAYMORE. Which is?

VICKY. 29¾.

CLAYMORE *smiles. Then he stands.*

CLAYMORE. Well, I'd —

VICKY (*quickly*). Have you had enough to eat?

CLAYMORE. I certainly have.

Slight pause.

And had a lovely time:

VICKY (*slightly acid note*). Oh, good.

CLAYMORE. I'm sorry?

VICKY. What for?

CLAYMORE. What's the —

VICKY. Nothing. I just, think you ought to know, I don't make a habit of it. That's all.

Slight pause.

CLAYMORE. Habit of what?

VICKY *gestures vaguely.*

CLAYMORE. (*Enjoying the word.*) Oh. A-dult-er-y.

VICKY *looks embarrassed.*

CLAYMORE. I'd better go.

VICKY (*stands*). Did I give you the number?

CLAYMORE. You did.

VICKY. You're in town?

CLAYMORE. For a while. Where's Clive?

VICKY. Dumfries. Some scoop.

CLAYMORE. See you, then.

Pause. He goes and kisses her. Then he goes to the exit.

VICKY. I remember.

CLAYMORE *turns back.*

You had this magazine. For Americans in England. You did the graphics. I bought it. Every issue. After you stayed. Screw the Flag.

CLAYMORE. Right. Ciao.

Exit CLAYMORE.

VICKY. Ciao.

Pause. She goes and picks up the tray.

Bugger.

She goes out as blackout. Spot lights up HEATHER.

HEATHER. It was 16.37, West Coast time, the 27th April 1975. The big Boeing troop-carrier circled over the Airforce base somewhere in upstate California. Inside the plane, the men showed no emotion at their homecoming. There'd be no crowds to welcome them, just the private, tearful faces of the ones they'd left behind. They weren't coming home with victory, or even peace with honour, but at least the boys were coming home.

The wife took her seat in the smoking sector of the DC9. She checked her forty dollar coiffure, and fixed her seatbelt, then relaxed. Four days, she thought, four days away from — well. What was he? A national hero, or just another tired and tiring vet without a job. Anyway, four days. She'd never been to Miami and she was sure as hell going to enjoy it.

Well, at least it wasn't raining. The Florida sun beat down on the guy in the bleached sneakers and the light-blue baseball cap. The trip wasn't going too well. He'd hoped to make Louisville in two days. Still, he'd enjoyed that extra night in Miami. And if he'd not been thinking quite so hard about that night, the blue-rinsed Californian at the barbecue, he would have looked back to the Tallahasee exit, seen the battered Buick make a right towards him.

The girl was tired. She hadn't, after all, had that much sleep. She parked the 1966 olive-green Buick convertible in the parking lot and walked down to the beach. This morning she'd been — where? Columbus? Louisville? No, Louisville was Wednesday. Last night was Columbus and today was Interstate 24, Detroit, the border and Toronto. Jesus, what a drive. The girl looked out, across Lake Erie, thought about the easy rider in the baseball cap, and wondered if she'd ever see the guy again. She knew, whatever, hell as right, that she'd remember him. She didn't know, however, quite how hell as right she was.

It was 8.03, Greenwich Mean Time. The Air Canada Tristar from Toronto taxied to a halt outside Terminal Three at London's Heathrow Airport. The young man waited till the other passengers had bustled off the plane, and when he did move, caught the cute come-hither of the well-stacked hostess at the cabin door. Twenty-four hours later, he left the buxom redhead sleeping in the bedroom of the Putney penthouse, caught a cab, and made the Scottish pullman just in time.

Blackout and Music: John Lennon, 'Jealous Guy', covers the change.

Scene Two

Lights. An open suitcase, on the table. Enter VICKY, *with another suitcase, a few clothes over her arm. She puts down the suitcase, and is putting the clothes in the open one as* CLIVE *enters, aggressively brisk, with a bag of dirty washing. She turns, stops what she's doing.* CLIVE *empties the bag into the open suitcase, exit.* VICKY *begins to sort out the mess, a moment or two. Re-enter* CLIVE *with a pile of gramaphone records. He goes through them, dumping* VICKY's *in the open suitcase, and his own on the table.*

CLIVE. Meum, teum, meum, meum, teum, meum, (*With distaste:*) Teum, teum — what's the Latin for 'ours'?

VICKY. I don't know, Clive.

He drops the record from its sleeve, breaks it in half, tossing half into the suitcase and half on to his pile.

CLIVE. Teum, meum,

Last record.

Meum.

Exit CLIVE *with his pile.* VICKY *looks at all the stuff. She goes out, re-entering with a carrier bag. She packs some of the things into the carrier bag.* CLIVE *comes in again with a tray of foodstuffs, tins, jars, even bags and fresh vegetables, and pours them into* VICKY's *suitcase, then turns and goes.*

VICKY. Clive, there really isn't any —

He's gone. Pause. VICKY *looks at her watch, exits, returning with a telephone on a long lead. She sits and dials.*

VICKY. Hullo? Me. No, I haven't. I'll be late. Yes, we're being a bit melo —

She's cut off.

Hullo?

Realising what's happened, she takes the receiver from her ear.

Dramatic.

Enter CLIVE with the end of the lead, which he's pulled out of the socket. He dangles it at VICKY. She replaces the receiver. He drops the lead.

CLIVE. Right. That's the sounds all sorted.

VICKY. Mm.

CLIVE. I decided to go halves on Wagner. You can have *Die Walküre.*

VICKY. Yes. Fine.

CLIVE. But there's some further items. That I think you've ripped off.

VICKY. Come again?

CLIVE. For a start, I seem to be short of one Snoopy and the Red Baron bathtowel.

She finds the towel in her suitcase and gives it to CLIVE.

And my Killer of the Deep t-shirt.

VICKY. *Your* Killer of the Deep t-shirt?

CLIVE. My Killer of the Deep t-shirt.

Slight pause. VICKY opens the case, finds the t-shirt, shuts the case.

And a bottle of yellow shampoo.

VICKY. Oh, Clive . . .

CLIVE. And there's also Volume Three of the Deutscher Trotsky biography, which I'm particularly keen to repossess, as I've just finished Vol Two and I'm eager to find out who did it.

VICKY. Clive, you know I haven't got your Deutscher. I haven't heard of Deutscher. I'm not too sure I've heard of Trotsky. As you've so often said, I wouldn't say I was dumb, but I do think that comintern is the Russian for gang-bang.

Pause.

CLIVE. I don't get it.

VICKY. Oh, blimey --

CLIVE. And my key.

VICKY (*finding it*). With pleasure. I'm really not likely to need it.

CLIVE. Likely?

VICKY. Going to.

CLIVE *takes the key.*

CLIVE. No?

Pause. CLIVE is trying to formulate a question. The words won't come. He gestures vaguely. He's almost in pain. Finally, he darts at VICKY, who recoils, and draws a question mark on her forehead with his finger.

VICKY. I said. I'm bored.

CLIVE. Did I ever tell you, when I was at University, I once shared a room with a bloke who was positively boring. I mean, actually positive. His dullness beamed out of him, in great concentric circles of tedium, like radar waves. I would walk into the room, and if he wasn't there, I could work out precisely how long he'd been absent by how bored I felt.

Slight pause.

VICKY. You're being rather tortuous.

CLIVE. I'm feeling rather tortured.

VICKY. It's not the first time in history.

CLIVE. I suppose that's the point.

Pause.

I had a very odd experience the other day, I meant to tell you. I met an old, extremely close acquaintance, chap I knew back when. We had a pint, old times, and fell to chatting, as one does, affairs of state, and he said, suddenly, that he was thinking of emigrating. Where? I said. New Zealand. Why? I said. Because this country's being taken over. By whom? I said. The wogs and communists. I mean, this guy had been — well, I'd assumed, one does, that everyone, albeit quietly, is more or less, to use a naffish phrase, on the side of life . . . I mean, this guy's a Tory. And my shock at that was only just outweighed by his when I confessed my view of things. He looked at me, as if I came from outer space. I looked at him, as if he came from outer space. We sat there, goggling at each other, like two extras from *Startrek*. And I thought, I'll ask him round to dinner. Just the three of us. I thought you'd like to meet him. Have a naff laff.

VICKY. You're being left, Clive.

CLIVE. Sorry?

VICKY. In the sense of gone from.

Pause.

CLIVE. Who was that on the phone? Your draft-dodging friend?

VICKY (*suddenly angry*). Clive, I have already said. I have
  already been through the whole thing. I have described him,
  our meeting, and our stolen night of bliss in graphic, one
  might say morbid detail. I've done the lot. I have repeated
  dialogue and simulated action. I have provided character notes
  and hints on staging. I have drawn little diagrams with
  coloured pens on overlayed sheets of Cellophane. But, if you
  insist, once more: I am not leaving you for him. It was fun,
  very fun, but it was a one-off, I'm not seeing him again, and I
  don't even know his name.

CLIVE. You must know his name. You put him up. Twice.

VICKY. I don't know his name.

CLIVE. Vicky, it's a ridiculous cliché to sleep with people and
  not find out who they are. People don't do it any more. It's
  such a, self-consciously Roundhouse thing to do.

VICKY. I'm going now.

CLIVE. Where?

VICKY. Friends.

CLIVE. Who?

VICKY. I'm not going to tell you.

CLIVE. What if —?

VICKY. Ring me at the school.

CLIVE. D'you want a bite of breakfast?

VICKY. No.

CLIVE. Not just a little hash muesli and home-turned yoghurt?

VICKY. CLIVE.

Pause. VICKY in tears.

CLIVE. Oh blimey. As someone said.

Pause.

VICKY. Clive, I told you. There isn't anyone . . .

CLIVE. Comes close to you.

VICKY. I mean, come on . . .

CLIVE. Dry your —

VICKY. You can't say —

CLIVE. We never tried. Jagger Richard. RSR 1973.

   Pause.

VICKY. I mean, love, please do try and —

CLIVE. See it my way.

VICKY. I mean, do I have to . . .

CLIVE. Keep on talking till.

VICKY. I can't go on.

CLIVE. Lennon McCartney. Decca. Circa 1966.

   Pause.

VICKY. It's just that something . . .

CLIVE. Inside has died.

VICKY. I've . . .

CLIVE. Tried but I . . .

VICKY. Just can't . . .

CLIVE. Fake it. King. A & M Autumn '71.

   Pause.

VICKY (*suddenly*). What?

CLIVE. Have you?

VICKY. What.

CLIVE. Been faking it. During coitus. Let us take, for example, last night's coitus.

VICKY. What do you want me to say?

   Slight pause.

   Because anything I say — yes, no, or indifferent, anything I say'll make you . . .

CLIVE. Knots. R.D. Laing. Tavistock 1970, subsequently Penguin.

VICKY. What?

CLIVE. Knots. K.N.O.T.S. As in tie.

   VICKY *picks up her bags, goes to the door, opens it.*

VICKY. Cut.

CLIVE. Y'what?

VICKY. C.U.T. Cut. As in ties.

Exit VICKY. CLIVE notices that she's left the carrier bag. He sits on the edge of the table, waits. Door bell. CLIVE stands, picks up the carrier bag and exits. Enter VICKY, followed by CLIVE who's holding the bag away from her. VICKY looking round, turns to CLIVE, who produces the bag. She grabs it and exits. Pause. CLIVE goes, picks up the telephone lead, exits, re-enters, to telephone, dials.

CLIVE (*asking for an extension*). McLusky.

Pause.

Hello, McLusky? Brent. Can you say I shan't be in.

Pause.

Oh a touch of something. A touch of grief.

Pause.

G.R.I. . . . No, terrible line. Tell them flu, or bronchitis, or the clap or something. Ciao.

He puts the phone down. Pause.

Gracelessly vacating your cloud.

Blackout.
Then spot lights up HEATHER.

HEATHER. I was in the office, brewing up my morning caffeine fix, when the broad blew in. I'd had a heavy evening and the LSO were playing Mahler on my frontal lobes, but this chick was the kind that makes the morning after feel just like the night before. She had that shade of vivid red hair that makes you want to check if it's genuine, and, I wouldn't say she was well-stacked, but the British Museum could have picked up hints from her shelving. I retrieved my pupils from her cleavage and directed her to lay it on the line.

'They sent me here,' she whispered, in that type of percolator voice that doctors tell you to avoid. 'They said I ought to see you. It's about this guy.'

Well, I won't say I welcomed this new element in the plot, I'd got the script all planned out, and what I had in mind was essentially a duologue, with the accent on the do. But I hid my feelings underneath the desk, and told her to proceed.

'It was several weeks ago. I haven't seen him since. I don't know where he lives or what he does. I can't remember what he looks like and I never got his name. They said you ought to find him soon. It sounds as if it might be difficult.'

The kid was right, but I didn't like to tell her. Tell a dame she's right, and next thing you know, she's making up your laundry list.

'Look kid,' I said, 'as far as I'm concerned, running a case is like making love. It's a lot easier when it's hard. Look on the bright side. We know he's a guy. That narrows it right down to 30 million.'

She didn't laugh, in fact she burst into tears. I didn't have a hanky, so I lent her my shoulder. She said she'd do anything for me if I'd help her, so when I'd got that signed and witnessed, I said I'd take my time, two Alka-seltzer, and the case.

Blackout and music: John Lennon, 'How do you sleep', covers the change.

Scene Three

Full lights. Three chairs at the table. At one of them sits McLUSKY. He looks ill at ease. Pause.

McLUSKY (*calls*). Hey!

Pause.

Hey, Clivey!

Pause.

Hey, Clivey, are you getting us a beer?

CLIVE *enters with a tray, on it two plates of cold food, cutlery, and two mugs of tea.*

CLIVE (*unloading the tray*). There isn't any beer, McLusky.

McLUSKY. No?

CLIVE. No.

McLUSKY. No beer.

CLIVE *begins to eat.* McLUSKY *investigates his plate with a fork.*

Uh, Clivey —

CLIVE (*mouth full*). Mm?

McLUSKY. Where's the meat, Clivey?

CLIVE. Meat?

McLUSKY. I canna find the meat, Clivey.

Slight pause.

CLIVE. I don't think there is any meat, McLusky. It's a vegetarian restaurant. They don't have meat. It's their thing. Like Jews and bacon.

McLUSKY. Ah.

CLIVE *eats.* McLUSKY *looks at his mug of tea.*

Uh, Clivey —

CLIVE (*mouth full*). Mm?

McLUSKY. What's this?

CLIVE. It's a mug of tea, McLusky.

McLUSKY. Clivey, I don't want to alarm you, but this tea is not as tea should be.

CLIVE. In what way?

McLUSKY. It's bright green.

Slight pause.

CLIVE. It's supposed to be that colour, McLusky. It's called bancha. It's the same as ordinary tea, it's just drunk at a different stage of development. The leaves are still alive.

McLUSKY. Ah.

CLIVE *eats.* McLUSKY *pauses.*

Uh, Clivey —

CLIVE (*drinking*). Mm?

McLUSKY. What the fuck are we doing here, Clivey?

Pause.

CLIVE. We're here, McLusky, because it's the only place in the city we can guarantee not to fall over my wife.

McLUSKY. That's absurd. This place is right up her street.

CLIVE. Exactly. She knows that, and, more to the point, she knows that I know that.

McLUSKY. You're becoming paranoid, Clivey —

CLIVE. What you call paranoia, McLusky, I call a cool and considered evaluation of the facts.

McLUSKY (*waving a forkfull of food at* CLIVE). This tastes like fucking seaweed, Clivey —

They are interrupted by the entrance of MO, a waitress, although dressed in mufti. She picks up the empty tray and exits the other side, as McLUSKY realises what she is.

McLUSKY. Hey!

CLIVE. McLusky —

McLUSKY. Hey! You! You!

Re-enter MO with a couple of dirty crocks on the tray.

MO. What seems to be the bother?

McLUSKY. Hey. Are you a waitress?

MO. And what's that to you?

McLUSKY. Are you an employee of this luncheonette?

MO. And wha'f I am?

McLUSKY. Do you have some ministerial relationship with this hashhouse?

MO. Aye, pal, d'you want to make something of it?

Slight pause. MO starts to go out.

McLUSKY. So what the hell's this?

MO (*looks*). Hiziki.

McLUSKY. What's hiziki?

MO. Fucking seaweed.

Exit MO. CLIVE scratches his ear. McLUSKY sniffs. The two men begin to eat.

McLUSKY. We're going to be late back.

CLIVE. Bugger it. We're on a feature.

McLUSKY. We are?

CLIVE. We are. On the *reductio ad absurdum* of the counter-culture to plates of fucking seaweed.

McLUSKY. Middle-class obsession, Clivey.

CLIVE. I am. Middle-class. White. Anglo-saxon. Church of England. Male. Even heterosexual. Nothing going for me at all. A historical reject. A sociological leper.

Slight pause.

A personal reject.

Pause.

McLUSKY. D'you think she'll come back, then?

Pause. CLIVE *eats.*

Dinna you bother about it, Clivey. Commitment, what counts, not origin. The working-class movement clasps you to its bosom.

CLIVE. Well that's very kind of it. (*Slight pause.*) The answer to the question is no.

McLUSKY. Mm. (*Pause.*)

CLIVE. Well, this feature. Did you know, the whole ethos of this stuff is totally sexist?

McLUSKY. I did not.

CLIVE. It is based, you see, on the concept of yin and yang.

McLUSKY. Go on.

CLIVE. Now, yang is flesh, red, hot, sweet, active and male. Coca-Cola, for instance, is about as yang as you can get. Yin, on the other hand, is green, cool, passive and female. Pineapple is more or less that way, as is eggplant, and, apparently, you can't get yinner than yoghurt.

McLUSKY. You know a lot about it.

CLIVE. Yes, well, I read a book. One evening, some pill-in at one of Vicky's gruesome friends', they were all rapping on of this and that -- homeopathy, the biosphere, how together China was, dianetics, all that sort of thing, and I just sat in the corner, getting into the bookshelf, you know, as one often does, and there was this very badly bound American paperback called *Zen and the Art of Aubergine Par-Boiling* and I . . .

McLUSKY. Mm?

CLIVE. And while they rapped . . . I read.

Pause. MO *approaches with a tray.*

MO. You done.

CLIVE. Yes, thanks.

MO *starts piling plates on the tray.*

McLUSKY. Hey.

MO. Aye?

McLUSKY. Why aren't you *dressed* as a waitress then?

MO. We don't.

McLUSKY. Why not?

MO. It's considered demeaning.

McLUSKY. What of?

MO. Us.

CLIVE (*helpfully*). The menial implications, of little white aprons and short black skirts.

MO. Aye.

McLUSKY. It doesna change what you do.

CLIVE. I think that's what we professionals call a contradiction.

MO. Right. (*Picks up tray.*) Oh, by the way, what's the time?

CLIVE. Um . . .

McLUSKY. Five-past three.

MO. Good.

> MO *drops her tray on the floor. She sits down with* CLIVE *and* McLUSKY *and lights a cigarette. She smokes her cigarette.*

CLIVE (*scratching his head*). Um . . .

MO. That's my notice.

> *Slight pause.*

My notice expired at three.

> *Slight pause.* CLIVE *is looking at the tray of broken crockery.*

I'm no longer employed by this establishment.

> *Slight pause.*

And if you want my opinion, anyone who pays 85p for a plate of seaweed needs his head looking at.

CLIVE. Um . . .

> CLIVE *stands and goes and picks up the tray in an offhand sort of way.*

McLUSKY. Clive, what are you doing?

CLIVE. Oh, just . . . tidy up . . .

McLUSKY. Clivey that stays right where it is —

CLIVE. You know how it is, I always . . .

> McLUSKY *stands, goes to* CLIVE *who stands with the tray.*

McLUSKY. Clivey, take that tray out, and you are guilty of a direct and conscious act of class betrayal.

CLIVE. Um . . .

CLIVE *turns and quickly exits with the tray.* McLUSKY *back to the table, sits, talking excitedly.*

McLUSKY. You see, all the same. Oh, they're fine, up to their noses in tracts, slaving over a hot concept, but you confront them with the need for direct action, and what happens? Acute embarrassment. You know, come the great day, the streets are running with beer and blood, the ruling class swinging from the lamp posts, you'll get Clivey and his ilk saying, I mean, right on, comrades, but isn't the whole thing ever so slightly unnecessarily impolite . . .

CLIVE *has reappeared.*

CLIVE (*sitting*). McLusky —

McLUSKY (*still to* MO). It is rumoured, indeed, that Clivey's only regular, conscious contribution to the class struggle is confined to using the toilet while the train is still standing at the platform. And even then, he waits till it's moved off to flush.

CLIVE. McLusky —

McLUSKY. It's not true, however, that he has not, in the past, albeit dim and distant, made sacrifices in the cause of the revolution, indeed, sustained personal injury. One thinks of the occasion when, during some fracas in Grosvenor Square, concerned with some South-East Asian conflict or another, he was witness to a particularly brutal assault by the forces of law and order on a small and defenceless group of young ladies from a provincial college of education. Clivey, noting this, turned, ran, and fell right over a police horse.

CLIVE. McLusky, you know full well, I was a committed pacifist at the time. My actions were completely in accord with the cowardice of my own convictions.

MO. What the hell are you on about?

McLUSKY. Ah. Now, you hear that, Clivey. Now, there's you, a rigorous intellectual who can detect a reformist tendency at five hundred paces on a cloudy day, and here's —

MO. Mo.

McLUSKY. Mo?

MO. Short for Maureen.

McLUSKY. Maureen, who wouldna know a petit-bourgeois deviation if you served it up garnished with hiziki, but who has just delivered a blow against the ruling order, or at least that subsection of same that runs wholefood bistroteques, a blow beside which —

CLIVE. Shut up, McLusky.

McLUSKY. Class instinct, Clivey. No substitute.

CLIVE. I said shut up, McLusky.

McLUSKY. You see, Maureen, Clivey here earns his daily bread by —

CLIVE. Shut UP. Up.

Pause.

It doesn't matter what I do, at all.

Pause.

MO
McLUSKY } *(speaking simultaneously)*. Well, I think I'd best — Where you from Maureen —

MO. Go on.

McLUSKY. I was just asking where you came from, Maureen.

MO. Peterhead. (*To* CLIVE:) Just north of Aberdeen.

Pause.

McLUSKY. Why d'you come south?

MO. Och, you know.

Pause.

McLUSKY. Have you na got another job to go to?

MO. Have I fuck.

Pause.

McLUSKY. What you going to do?

MO (*shrugging her shoulders*). Something that pays me. Bit of the gravy. Why not. Something that pays me, fucking well.

CLIVE (*suddenly*). My wife has just left me, on the grounds of rigid boredom. I have a number of friends, most of them delightful in their way, but with all of whom I have relationships of grotesquely labyrinthian complexity, interpersonal cat's-cradles of resentment on the grounds of sex and race and this and class and creed and that, and while coping with radical feminist Trots and Maoist ecofreaks is, of course, all part of life's rich tapestry, where would we be without it . . . nonetheless . . . sometimes . . . when one meets someone who you only know as Mo . . . who wants a bit of the gravy . . . one wonders if, perhaps . . . she'd care to allow you to show her the Royal Mile.

MO. I've seen the Royal Mile.

CLIVE. The Forth Road Bridge?

MO. That too.

CLIVE. Or something.

Slight pause.

MO. Right. You're on.

Lights snap down to a quarter. McLUSKY exits with the table. Lights back to full. Pause. CLIVE stands, flaps about.

CLIVE. I'd put some music on, but I have neighbour problems. They are all terribly old. I'm surrounded by rejects from the Royal Infirmary's Geriatric Ward. (*Pause.*) Are you sure you don't want anything to drink?

MO. No, thank you.

CLIVE. Right. (*Pause.*) Did you enjoy Leith? (MO *nods.*) I am in no way generally distinguished, but I do have a slight claim to fame. I was once stopped for speeding in Great Junction Street. They let me off with a caution, so I have actually been dismissed by the Leith police. (*Long pause.*) I'm a bit unprepared. I usually like to plan these things down to the last soft light.

MO. I see. (*She lights a cigarette.*)

CLIVE. I'm also — always worried, I mean generally, about these one-night stands with women I don't know. Usually I make it a rule not to sleep with a woman until I know her well enough to be sure she'll get the joke. (*Slight pause.*) Or be polite enough to laugh, just the same.

Slight pause.

If she spots when it's the punchline.

Slight pause.

As it were.

Pause.

MO. Why not gimme a nudge when it comes. (*She stands and exits.*)

CLIVE (*following her out*). Now, you must stop me if you've heard this before . . .

Blackout. A spot lights up HEATHER.

HEATHER. It was the tone of voice that surprised her. 'Find the Yank.'

Before, with carriers, she'd been told to contact. See. Even, occasionally, look for. But never, with quite that quiet insistence, find.

She'd mentioned it to Hutton. Hutton had been fussing round his gas ring in the tasteless, cosy little office he always called his bloody cubby-hole. 'Tea or coffee?' he asked her.

'Coffee,' she said.

Hutton looked hurt. 'It is Earl Grey,' he said.

'I'd still like coffee,' she said.

Hutton didn't reply, but spooned out the instant granules with a kind of formal precision, and insisted on offering her the sugar though he knew she didn't take it. Then he began to talk about the Yank.

'Kicked off in S.E.A., of course, like anything that involves the bloody Yanks. Well, back to Mum it duly comes, popping up all over, and because the pill-boys didn't get its measure, thriving on everything they give it, and ping-ponging all over the Land of the Free. Only a matter of time, of course, before it jumps border into Canada. London thinks our carrier's numero uno, but of course that's pretty bloody academic now. Point is, stop the rot before it get O.O.C. Apparently, the Department's pushing too, so London's getting pretty bloody jumpy. Hence, the AI of nailing down your chap. All clear?'

And Hutton turned away from her and began to clean his nails with a straightened paperclip, a gesture which always meant, to her at least, that the audience was over.

She found him easily. Not, just this once, the vague ·rememberance, I think her hair was blonde, he may have come from Glasgow, all the clues they'd often given her. No, since the Putney red-haired girl had told her all, a lot of all, this one was like a dream. Because, apparently, according to the dusty fellow in the camera shop, there really weren't that many youngish Yank photographers engaged in magazine work in Midlothian at any one specific time.

And it wasn't 'whether' any more, but just 'how long'.

Blackout and Don Mclean's 'American Pie' covers the change.

Scene Four

The music continues. Spotlights come up on MO. She is sitting on a beanbag, with a glass of wine in her hand. Elsewhere on the set are an ice-bucket with wine, another glass, a telephone and a screen. We are in fact in a rented photographer's studio, but we don't realise this yet. MO sips her wine. Then she calls:

MO. Nice place!

Pause.

Nice place, nice wine!

Pause.

Nice music!

Blackout and the music grinds to a halt.

Or, um – was.

A different configuration of lights comes up. What's happening is that the photographer is working out how an offstage switchboard connects to the spotlights in the studio, but, again, we're not yet aware of this.

Aha.

Pause. MO finishes her wine.

Do you do this often? I mean, with lots of people? I mean, do you do this kind of thing with – lots of people – lots? Or, even, often?

As there is no reply, she shrugs, and crawls across to the bucket, to refill her wine glass. As she gets there, most of the lights snap out, and then a new configuration snaps up. She looks up at this before pouring.

Well, it's a funny old business, life. I mean, here's me, wandering up Chambers Street, sunk in gloomy speculation as to how the fuck I'm going to make ends meet . . .

She's crawling back to her beanbag, has a second thought, returns for the bottle and takes that too.

And passing by the Clytemnestra Bookshop, specialists in left-wing literature, high-class pornography and the occult . . .

She's back at the beanbag.

Not I have to tell you the sort of place I'd ordinarily frequent, but then it's not in all respects been an ordinary sort of week.

Another light change.

And then, on a noticeboard called LINKS, discreetly nestling between rebirthing classes, meetings of the Workers' League of Scotland (Marxist-Leninist), shiatsu, primal screaming, Third Girl

sought for Morningside collective living situation waterbed
provided water sign preferred . . .

Blackout.

Well, it's comforting to know you've got all this together.

Lights snap up and out again.

I mean, if there's one thing sets a person's mind at rest, it's
knowing they're involved in something that's been planned down
to the —

Light change.

— last —

Light change.

— soft light.

Enter CLAYMORE. *He is festooned with camera equipment. He
could be carrying a tripod, which he could set up during the
following. The cameras finally confirm that we are in a studio and
that* CLAYMORE *has been assembling the lighting state he wants
to photograph* MO.

CLAYMORE. I'm sorry?

MO. Sorry?

CLAYMORE. I'm not sure I caught all that.

MO. Well, I just wanted to — make clear . . .

   CLAYMORE *is fiddling around, so, a little offhand:*

CLAYMORE. Yuh? What?

MO. That — that I'm not, not usually . . .

CLAYMORE. Mm? Yuh?

MO. That sort of girl.

   CLAYMORE *looks at* MO.

CLAYMORE. You mean . . .

MO. I mean, the sort . . .

CLAYMORE. . . . that does the sort of thing you're doing now. I
see.

He picks up the bottle from MO *and pours himself a glass.*

I chose the hippy bookstore because there are people who regard
the free expression of their sexuality as a revolutionary statement
of itself.

MO. There are?

CLAYMORE. Surely. 'Do your own thing.' 'Let it all hang out.'
'Why don't we do it in the road.'

MO. I can think of many reasons. Most of them hygienic.

CLAYMORE. Or climatic.

MO. Certainly round here.

CLAYMORE. In February 1974, at the height of your wonderful
general election campaign – the miners' strike, the three day week,
civilisation as we know it threatened to its basis – our equally
wonderful Suzi Quatro's 'Devil Gate Ride' was at number one in
the pop charts for two weeks. And she's reputed to have promised
that if it stayed at number one a third week, she would appear
stark naked on a live TV rock show to sing it.

MO. So what happened?

CLAYMORE. It fell to number two. But then, so did the
Government.

Pause. It's clear that CLAYMORE's *preparations are more or less
complete.*

MO. Um – do I –

CLAYMORE. So, what *is* your sign.

MO. You first.

CLAYMORE. I'm Sagittarius. We most of us have body odour and
you shouldn't lend us money.

MO. Uh?

CLAYMORE. And we're into incest in a big way. You?

MO. I'm Pisces. We . . . have an unhealthy interest in fish.

CLAYMORE. Well, thank goodness you're not Taurus. Or Cancer,
for that matter.

MO. Pardon?

CLAYMORE. Bulls and Crabs.

MO. I think – I'd like to do this now.

CLAYMORE. Would you prefer, behind the screen?

MO. Why not.

She goes behind the screen to undress. CLAYMORE *removing the
bucket and other detritus.* MO *calls:*

I mean, the way I look at it is this. I have a soul. I have a body. And if keeping them together implies keeping them apart –

CLAYMORE. Exactly so.

A long, single telephone ring.

MO (*in panic*). What's that?

CLAYMORE. It's nothing. Just the phone.

As CLAYMORE reaches for the phone, blackout, and, hugely, the ELO phrase from the beginning of the play. A spot finds HEATHER at the side of the stage. MO and CLAYMORE have gone. The ELO phrase fades.

HEATHER. Right. Let me explain. You see, the problem is, with this disease, that the germ is building up resistance to the penicillin that we've used to treat it. One example, perhaps the most well known, occurred in Vietnam, where prostitutes were found to treat themselves with insufficient dosages and thus became, ironically, walking cultures of mutating gonococci. This resistant strain of gonorrhoea is known colloquially as Vietnam, or Saigon Rose. It came back with the troops. There is a race, between it and the chemists, to effect a cure. And there are signs that it's the chemists that are losing, and the thing is spreading, now, around the world.

A spot comes up on CLAYMORE.

CLAYMORE. Why tell all this to me?

HEATHER. Because you've got it. You've got Saigon Rose. You gave it to the girl in Putney. By the time her boyfriend realised he'd got it, you were up here, spreading it around.

Pause.

I'm sorry.

Spot on VICKY.

Sorry.

Spot on CLIVE.

Sorry.

Quick fade to blackout, as the Electric Light Orchestra comes up again, this time playing on into the interval.

ACT TWO

Scene One

The set is white. Three chairs, one side of the stage. At the other, a table, two chairs and a white screen. In the darkness:

NURSE. 4597!

   Lights, CLIVE *sitting on one of the chairs. The* NURSE, *near the table, has just called him. The* DOCTOR *sits at the table.* CLIVE *checks a card, stands, goes through to the* DOCTOR. *The* NURSE *stands in attendance.*

DOCTOR. Well, hallo.

CLIVE. Hallo.

DOCTOR. Do sit.

CLIVE (*sitting*). Thank you.

DOCTOR. Now.

CLIVE. I was contacted.

DOCTOR (*looking at a file*). Yes. Your wife.

CLIVE. My ex-wife.

DOCTOR. Who picked it up from an American.

CLIVE. Yes.

DOCTOR. Well, isn't that a lesson to us all. Had any symptoms?

CLIVE. I've had a discharge. I think.

DOCTOR. You think. Found any? On your pants, pyjamas, sheets?

CLIVE. No.

DOCTOR. Well, then?

   Pause.

CLIVE. On my cock. End of it.

DOCTOR. What were you doing when you noticed it?

   Pause.

CLIVE. Using the john.

DOCTOR (*writing*). Pus on, tip of, tool. Anything else?

CLIVE. Bit of pain, urinating?

DOCTOR. Pissing razor blades. (*He writes.*) Partners?

CLIVE. Just my wife. And this one other girl.

DOCTOR. Know her?

CLIVE. Yes.

DOCTOR (*writing*). Any men or boys at all?

CLIVE. I beg your pardon?

DOCTOR. It does happen.

CLIVE. No. As it happens.

DOCTOR (*writing*). Good boy. (*To* NURSE:) Blood test?

CLIVE. Yes.

NURSE. Aye.

DOCTOR (*writing*). Aye.

  To CLIVE:

  Right. Let's have a butchers.

  CLIVE *stands, lowers his trousers and his pants. The* DOCTOR
  inspects him.

  Mm.

  The DOCTOR *turns to write something.* CLIVE *pulling himself
  up.*

  Sorry, not yet.

  CLIVE *stands there, the* DOCTOR *writing.*

  Now I'm going to have a little poke about with my dipstick.
  Nothing to get fussed about.

CLIVE. It's not your cock.

DOCTOR (*finding the swab*). Beg pardon?

  CLIVE *says nothing. The* DOCTOR *swabs* CLIVE.

CLIVE. Uh –

DOCTOR. Brave boy. All over.

  *He wipes the swab on a small piece of glass. Then he places a
  urine sample jar in front of* CLIVE.

  Now, if you'd be so kind . . .

  CLIVE *is about to pee into the jar, when the* DOCTOR
  intervenes.

  Behind the screen. You'll embarrass Miss Montrose.

  CLIVE *picks up the jar and clutches his lower garments to
  himself.*

  Not to mention me.

  CLIVE *hobbles behind the screen. The sound of peeing. The*
  DOCTOR *takes off his glove and puts the specimen under a
  microscope and looks at it.* CLIVE *re-enters, still with his trousers*

half down, not wishing to be caught with his pants up. He hands the sample to the DOCTOR, *who holds it up to the light.*

What a nice big one.

He hands the sample to the NURSE, *who takes it out.*

You can put it away now. Don't want it to catch anything. Else, that is.

The DOCTOR *laughs.* CLIVE *laughs.* CLIVE *dresses as the* DOCTOR *takes off the glove and puts the specimen under a microscope and looks at it.*

Sit, sit.

CLIVE *sits.* DOCTOR *turns from the microscope.*

Subject to contract, as the estate agents say, you have gonorrhoea. According to what we found in your wife, rather a virulent variety. Superclap.

He laughs. CLIVE *laughs.*

Adaptable little buggers. Are you allergic to penicillin?

CLIVE. No.

DOCTOR (*writing a prescription*). Good, because I'm giving you rather a lot of it.

He's finished.

Are you going to tell the girl?

Slight pause.

CLIVE. Yes.

DOCTOR. Tell us when you've done it. Or we'll have to. And we'll see you in a couple of days.

Hands over the prescription. CLIVE *stands.*

Look, old son, I know sheaths are a godawful bore, washing your feet with your socks on and all that, but I really would advise, if you think it's a dodgy one . . . Mm?

He starts indexing the specimen.

CLIVE (*almost blurted out*). I used to be able to do it with one hand.

DOCTOR. Beg pardon?

CLIVE. Open a durex, in the dark, in the old days, with one hand. Even the Cellophane on the packet. That's the pity, isn't it, with our increasingly technological universe, you lose these old skills.

DOCTOR *looks at him.*

DOCTOR. You get the pills from the dispensary. No drinking, screwing or wanking for six weeks.

He writes. CLIVE *looks at the prescription.*

CLIVE. I do have a name.

DOCTOR (*not listening*). Mm?

Blackout and music: Rolling Stones, 'We Love You'.

Scene Two

Lights as music fades. Bright sun. We're on a beach. White Rocks. CLIVE and MO, who carries a bag, and a coat. She puts down her bag and coat on a rock.

MO. Well, here we are. Away from sight and sound. The sunbeams dancing on the shimmering sea. (*Slight pause.*) You wanna build a sandcastle?

CLIVE. No thanks.

MO. No thanks. (*Pause.*) Well, nice to see you once again.

CLIVE. And you.

MO. You could have waited, though. I'm going south this afternoon.

CLIVE. I couldn't wait to see you.

MO. And I can't wait, to get away. (*Slight pause.*)

CLIVE. Why, what's the matter?

MO. Och, nothing. Just a wee bit of personal embarrassment. Family matter. Things which we ought not to have done, and there is no health in us. You know. (*Slight pause.*)

CLIVE. They know?

MO. They do.

CLIVE. But how?

MO. Well, they –

CLIVE. You told them?

MO. Did I fuck.

CLIVE. Then how –

MO. Look, Clive –

CLIVE. I didn't know you knew.

MO. Neither did I. I think we're talking at cross-purposes.

CLIVE. I think we are.

MO. Let's start again. D'you wanna build a sandcastle?

CLIVE. Mo. I've –

MO. Or, better, have a glance at the matter in hand.

She takes a glossy sex-mag from her bag, delicately, with finger and thumb, and gives it to CLIVE.

CLIVE. What's this?

MO. Have a flip through.

CLIVE. Well, I'd –

MO. Go on.

CLIVE. Really rather not.

MO. Will you look at it.

Slight pause.

CLIVE. Why?

MO. Clivey, do as I say.

CLIVE (*turning the pages rapidly*). I don't like dirty magazines.

MO. No more do I, but it's a living.

CLIVE *looks at her. She turns the magazine a couple of pages back.*

There you are. A three-page spread of Technicolor gravy.

CLIVE *looks at the pictures.*

There's a couple I'm quite pleased with. That one I dinna like 'cos I'm looking at lens but that's apparently market demand. Now this one I do think's good, I mean, it's basically a crutch shot but we think it has a definite spry charm.

Slight pause.

Do you na think?

CLIVE. Oddly enough, I thought the body looked familiar, but I didn't spot the face.

MO. Now isn't that funny, cos with my bro it was exactly the other way round.

CLIVE. Your brother?

MO. You see, as you doubtless know, the north-east of Scotland has something of a reputation for a rather fundamentalist attitude to matters sexual. I mean, up here they think that Calvin was basically sound but just a wee bit high church. And therefore, in the past, it has been reasonable to assume that the stench of big city vice will not be smelt in small-town Peterhead. However, with the arrival of Messrs Gulf, BP and Texaco, all that's changed. Take the Crosse and Blackwell factory, that's over there, where the walls are but festooned with crumpet of all class and creed and hue. My God, said bro, I didna ken the rest of it, but I couldna miss the face. (*Pause.*) I dinna think I'm exaggerating when I say it didna go down too well. (*Pause.*)

CLIVE. No.

MO. Och, well, it canna be helped. Cut your ties and hit the road. So here I am.

CLIVE. Yuh.

MO. So what's the fuss with you.

CLIVE. Well . . . (*Embarrassed.*) Well . . . you know, uh . . .

MO. Gimme a clue. Are the words 'sexual' or 'object' on the card?

CLIVE. If you like. (*Pause.*)

MO. Aye. And – brother, double standard of. And father, equally, no doubt. Who comes home every day, expects his tea there on the table, and has na done the washing up since 1959. (*Pause. Brightly:*) Well? Why d'you come and see me?

CLIVE. Did you sleep with the photographer?

MO. No.

CLIVE. Or anyone since me?

MO. It's no concern of yours, but no.

CLIVE. Good.

MO. Why?

CLIVE. I've given you a dose.

MO. Eh?

CLIVE. I've given you VD.

MO. You've what?

CLIVE. You've probably, almost certainly, got VD.

MO. What VD?

CLIVE. Venereal disease.

MO. I mean, which.

CLIVE. Gonorrhoea. Apparently –

MO. Well, that's a relief.

CLIVE. Why?

MO. Syphilis gives you a face-rash. The clap's much more interior altogether.

CLIVE *moves away. She calls after him.*

What d'you do?

CLIVE. What?

MO. For a living? D'you remember? You went all coy about it.

CLIVE. I'm a journalist.

MO. Left or right handed?

CLIVE. Ambidextrous.

MO *to* CLIVE, *grasps both his wrists.*

MO. Then how would you like me to break your fingers, one by one.

Pause. She lets him go.

No more do I want blemishes disfiguring my flesh.

Pause.

CLIVE. I'm looking at your town. From this scrubby apologia for a beach. I'm looking at those ulcerations of the ends of your bay. Those cranes and tanks and greasy cables. I'm listening, and I hear the humming of machinery, and, yes, the warble of a helicopter, but I don't hear any birds.

Slight pause.

MO. Och, well, it's brought a lot to the place. Just shut your eyes, and listen to the cash-till. Lie back and think about the balance of payments. Just how fastidious you can afford to be.

Long pause.

CLIVE. I went to a party on the 30th of April 1975.

MO. That's nice.

CLIVE. Yes, and I met a lot of people I knew.

MO. One does.

CLIVE. And all of them – us – had reason to view that date with some – involvement, personal attachment. If you like, a kind of celebration.

MO. What?

CLIVE. One chap, for instance, who had been involved in all the stuff that we were celebrating, had recently returned from Portugal. Much impressed, he'd been, although he had, as it fell out, been in Oporto when it was all happening in Lisbon and in Lisbon when they were getting it all together in Oporto, but there

we are, and anyway it didn't matter 'cos his thesis was on Sexual
Discourse in the Later Thomas Hardy and he knew Wessex like
the back of his hand.

MO. What?

CLIVE. Another was a woman from a different tradition, she was
much more on the San Franciscan wing of things, the horticultural
persuasion, you know, give a pig a dahlia and you're bound to
free his head, and she'd been into counter-journalism, cut-ups,
page on page of jolly turn-on stuff you couldn't read because of
massive transfer overlay, but does it matter, and she's now the
really rather well-off owner of a periodical devoted to the martial
arts of, well, to do her justice, North Korea.

MO. What?

CLIVE. And the third was a Marxist working for a group of
economic forecasters. You know, a City firm. A kind of Red in
Residence, their pet Trot, he was, they often have one, just the
one, they find them useful, partly as they're often rather right, and
he works down among the company reports and Extel cards, as
happy as the day is long, exploring all the veins and arteries of
capital, like looking at the inside of a watch, and finding how it
ticks, and if, or when, it's likely to stop ticking.

MO. What?

CLIVE. And there were other, old campaigners, veterans of various
domestic wars, the Piccadilly squat, the Springbok tour, oh happy
days, de-schoolers, counter-culturalists, free-lawyers and anti-
psychiatrists, some who were worried about copping out and
many who couldn't recall ever quite copping in —

MO. WHAT?

CLIVE. And we few, we happy few, we band of brothers, who
doubtless, back before your time and out of mine, believed with
all sincerity that every joint was stubbed out in the very navel of
the body politic, became grotesquely merry, merrily grotesque,
and reminisced and showed our scars and raised our glasses, if
you please, to several thousand little yellow people who were at
that very moment driving tanks into the centre of Saigon. (*Slight
pause.*)

MO. What?

CLIVE. There is, apparently, a variety of carp that lives in Lake Erie,
an otherwise dead environment. The reason they survive is that
they've mutated sufficiently to live off the poison in the water.
(*Pause.*)

MO. Is that the end?

CLIVE. Well, no, not quite, for on that very evening, I was walking home, and I got myself attacked. By a particularly nasty, ugly, vicious gang of Hibs fans, ranging through their streets, and finding me. Got beaten up quite badly. Mugged, in fact. Lost £40, a bank card, and my Omega. And all my efforts to remind myself that property is theft just somehow didn't quite convince me, as I crawled across the street, dropping teeth yardly, to find a broken phone. I mean, it's funny. Actually, it's very, very funny. (*Pause.*)

MO. I'm sorry. I couldna give a shit. I'm lonely and I'm ill.

MO exits quickly. CLIVE stands, as if to follow. Then he sits again. Blackout.
Almost immediately, lights. Low, golden, early evening. CLIVE still there. A MAN stands on the other side of the stage. CLIVE notices him, then looks away again. The MAN walks to CLIVE.

MAN. Good afternoon.

CLIVE. Good afternoon?

MAN. And welcome to Peterhead Bay.

CLIVE. Well, thank you very . . .

MAN. Situated 28 miles north of Aberdeen, and serviced by good 'A' roads.

CLIVE. You what?

MAN. Once no more than a fishing village, the borough of Peterhead has become, in the wake of North Sea oil and gas discoveries, a thriving, lively community, replete with points of interest.

CLIVE. Yes, well . . .

MAN. From the vantage of the beach, one can view, on the left, the Peterhead B.O.C. supply base, complete with bustling heliport, and, on the right, the South Bay base of the Aberdeen Service Company. The bases are sited, it can be seen, at either end of the Harbour of Refuge, constructed by inmates of Peterhead Prison, the grim and forbidding exterior of which one cannot fail to notice, on one's right, as one drives into the town.

CLIVE. Look I –

MAN. On your left, you'll note my home. (*Pause. He laughs.*) I mean, it is. Did you see them? Those huts. Chalets. Dozen men to each. Spaniards, Germans, Irish, English. A truly international community. Where I live. (*Laughs.*)

CLIVE. You work on the oil?

MAN. Gas. The St Fergus Depot. I'm a guest construction worker. D'you mind me talking to you?

CLIVE. Not at all.

MAN. What d'you do, then?

CLIVE. I'm a journalist.

MAN. That's lucky.

CLIVE. Why?

MAN. 'Cos you could do a story on me. (*Pause. Laughs.*) Couldn't you? Eh? (*Pause.*)

CLIVE. Go on.

MAN. My life. Up here.

CLIVE. Go on.

MAN. I told you about the huts.

CLIVE. Yuh.

MAN. And the overtime.

CLIVE. No.

MAN. Well, that's the point. I mean, the money isn't in fact that good, at base, but there are ample opportunities for extensive and compulsory overtime.

CLIVE. How much d'you –

MAN. Twelve to fourteen hours a day.

CLIVE. For how –

MAN. For twenty days.

CLIVE. And then you –

MAN. Five days leave. With two days travel pay. Then back again.

CLIVE. You don't have unions?

MAN. Oh yes. Got unions. (*Pause. Laughs.*) Though better off without them. Self-employed. And who knows where you're going? (*Pause.*)

CLIVE. What do you do, for leave?

MAN. Wander around.

CLIVE. You don't go home.

MAN. I used to. (*Pause. Laughs.*) I think the phrase used for a place like this is a combination of conspicuous consumption with a grossly inadequate social infrastructure. No houses. That people can afford. Yank goods in all the shops. No one but us and the Yanks the cash to buy them. (*Pause. Laughs.*) Eh? (*Pause.*)

CLIVE. Saigonization.

MAN. What?

CLIVE. What they did in Saigon.

MAN. Oh, yuh.

Pause.

Bit of a cock-up, really. Actually, I jumped. Mid-month. She'd been saying long enough, she either wanted me, at home, you know, for ever, or her independence. Well, my daughter's born. So off I go, break contract, hitch down to Reading, nineteen sodding hours it takes me. But she doesn't want to know. No more. She said she couldn't cope, with marriage to a fucking mercenary. So I said – well, I'm home for ever now. And she said – bugger you – I've learnt to live without you, mate. I don't need you no more.

Pause.

Your home's a kind of refuge. Need it. Really. Shelter from the storm.

Pause.

Now everyone I talk to's either paying me or being paid by people paying me. (*He laughs.*) 'Cept you. (*He notices the magazine. Picks it up.*) D'you mind?

CLIVE. No, go ahead.

MAN. They say it's the Asia-Pacific basin next. Who knows. Might even go. (*He laughs. Turns to* CLIVE:)

That's good. Saigon has risen on the shores of the North Sea. (*He turns the page. Comes to the pictorial.*) Bloody hell.

CLIVE *looks away on the other side of the stage.*

Snap blackout. Music: The Rolling Stones: 'We Love You'.

Scene Three

Lights. The three chairs of scene one. However, where the DOCTOR's desk was is now a white couch, in front of, and parallel to, the screen. At one end of the couch two arms are fixed, going up at an angle to support two foot-long metal half-cylinder leg-rests, about nine inches above the couch. These can be adjusted for someone lying on the couch, resting their legs in the leg-rests below the knee. Also fixed to the couch, an anglepoise lamp. At this end, a low stool and a small table, on it, a tray of instruments. MO sits on the couch, in a white operating gown, holding a full

urine sample jar. Next to her, on the couch, her clothes, higgledy-piggledy.
Enter the NURSE *from behind the screen. She carries a large piece of paper. She takes the sample, puts it on the instrument table.*

NURSE. Pants off?

> MO *picks up her knickers to demonstrate. The* NURSE *goes and dumps* MO's *clothes on the chair.*

Stand up, please.

> MO *stands. The* NURSE *lays the sheet of paper on the couch.*

Lie down, please.

> *She lies down. The* NURSE *standing downstage of the leg-rest end of the couch.*

And put your feet in the stirrups.

MO. Eh?

> *The* NURSE *taps the leg-rests.* MO *puts her legs in them. The* NURSE *adjusts them a little wider. Then she leans over, switches on the anglepoise, angles it between* MO's *legs.*

NURSE. Right.

> *Pause.* MO *is lying with her hands behind her head, looking up.*

MO. What happens now?

NURSE. Wait for the doctor.

> *A very long pause.* MO *looks around above her. The* NURSE, *for something to do, adjusts one of the leg-rests slightly. Then she stands, leaning on the couch. More pause. Then the* DOCTOR *comes in, from behind the screen, to the head of the couch.*

DOCTOR. Well, hallo.

MO. 'Lo.

DOCTOR. This won't take a moment. (*He goes to the low stool, sits, lays his file open on the instrument table, puts on a disposable glove, as:*) Been waiting long?

> *Pause.*

NURSE (*to* MO, *who assumed the question was directed at the* NURSE). Have we been waiting long?

MO. Oh. No, not long.

DOCTOR. Bit of a busy time. Always snowed under, after the hols. Right. I'm going to have a little feel. (*He inspects* MO.) Good. Had any pain?

MO. No pain.

DOCTOR. Not been conscious of any inflammation, at the mouth of the womb?

MO. No.

DOCTOR. And no discharge, that you're aware of?

MO. Eh?

NURSE. Any fluid coming out.

MO. Oh, no.

DOCTOR. Or pain, during intercourse.

MO. I've had na intercourse.

   DOCTOR *checks his file.*

DOCTOR. Oh, no. Right. Now, I'm just popping in to have a little look. (*He picks up a scissor-like instrument, about four inches long, to insert and expand the vagina.*) Just relax. (*He tries to insert it.*) Sorry, you're not relaxing.

MO. Uh?

DOCTOR. Unless you relax, I'm afraid it'll hurt.

   MO *turns her head away.* DOCTOR *puts down the instrument and stands.*

   You're not from this neck of the woods, are you?

MO. No. I'm from –

DOCTOR. Don't tell me. Aberdeenshire.

MO. That's right.

DOCTOR. Clever me. Why did you come south?

   Pause. MO *turns her head again.*

MO. For work.

DOCTOR. Yes.

   He picks up the instrument, tries again. Looks up at the NURSE, *shrugs.* MO *winces.*

   There we are. All in. (*He takes a swab, puts it on a glass, removes the instrument.*) There we are. All over. You can get up now.

   MO *takes her legs out of the stirrups. She sits on the edge of the couch. The* NURSE *takes out the sample and the specimen. The* DOCTOR *takes off his glove. Then he stands.*

Right. If you could just hang on for twenty minutes or so,
Maureen, we can give you the results.

MO looks up at him, suddenly.

Then, if it's positive, it's just a matter of –

MO. Eh.

DOCTOR. Yes?

MO. Should you –

DOCTOR. Yes?

Slight pause.

MO. Nothing.

DOCTOR. *(looking at the file).* Then it's just a matter of some pills,
and keeping off the booze and the boys for a few weeks. The
nurse'll explain.

Smiles at MO, who's still staring at him.

Bye for now.

*Exit. The NURSE enters, picks up the instrument tray, notices
that MO is still sitting there.*

NURSE. You can get dressed.

The NURSE makes to go, when:

MO. What a fucking job.

NURSE *(turns back).* What?

MO *(to the NURSE, violently).* Poking up people's fucking cunts all
day.

Pause. The NURSE goes out. MO does not move.

He shouldna know my name.

She does not move.
Music: Brian Ferry's 'It's My Party'.

Scene Four

*The chairs and table set as for CLIVE's flat, Act One. The
CHARACTERS are either in party clothes, or rather self-consciously
not. MO and CLAYMORE are dressed in particularly beautiful,
complementary costumes. Lights on VICKY and CLAYMORE.*

CLAYMORE. Vicky.

VICKY. Claymore.

CLAYMORE. You know my name, at last.

VICKY. The people told me.

CLAYMORE. Well, isn't this a gas. (*Pause.*)

VICKY. Who else is here?

CLAYMORE. We were the first.

VICKY. Who's the other half of we?

CLAYMORE. Mo. A girl I'm working with. With whom, I gather, your husband . . .

VICKY. Ah. (*Pause.*) I can't make up my mind whether this thing is funny or ghoulish. In that respect, it's a bit like a Hammer film. Before or after Clive?

CLAYMORE. We met independently.

VICKY. Full circle.

CLAYMORE. No. Not with a model. A breach of etiquette. Also, it's inclined to upset your hand-held work.

VICKY. When you say model?

CLAYMORE. Well . . .

VICKY. Oh, yes, I see. I didn't realise. (*Pause.*) I don't think I've ever met a –

Enter MO.

CLAYMORE. Ah. Vicky, this is Mo. Mo, Vicky is a teacher, an old friend of mine, a warm and wonderful human being, and your ex-lover's ex-wife.

VICKY. Hullo.

MO smiles and sits.

CLAYMORE. Mo wasn't sure she wanted to come. I said I thought it was a splendid idea. She's been talking to our host.

VICKY. Yes, where is Clive?

CLAYMORE. I think he's in the kitchen, filling the vol-au-vents.

Slight pause.

I'd forgotten. How delightful this apartment is.

VICKY. Yes.

CLAYMORE. I must say, I really like these tenement buildings. There's such a feeling of community.

VICKY. Yes. Clive likes them too.

Enter CLIVE with two plates of crisps. He is wearing a Donny Osmond t-shirt.

He doesn't ever actually speak to his neighbours of course, but he nonetheless just adores feeling the community.

CLIVE. Crisp. Ss.

He puts the crisps down as VICKY *turns.*

VICKY. Clive.

CLIVE. Vicky.

VICKY. How are you?

CLIVE. Fine. How are you?

VICKY. Fine. Are you going to explain the t-shirt now, or do we have to wait for a full house?

CLIVE. What? Oh, yes. No, it's just that I'm into pre-puberty. I think it's really groovy. I can't be doing with all these snobs who despise them for gaining a mass, popular audience. I'd have them rather than Jefferson Aeroplane any day. It's like Rollerball, which I know everyone's very snotty about, but I thought was a wizard yarn.

VICKY. I see.

Doorbell rings.

That's the doorbell, Clive.

CLIVE. So it is. Claymore, would you and Mo like to go and answer the door?

CLAYMORE. Of course.

He signals to MO, *who gets up and follows him out. Slight pause.*

CLIVE. To see you, nice.

VICKY. And you.

CLIVE. I'm sorry about the way, you know –

VICKY. Doesn't matter. After all, I've reason to apologise.

CLIVE. Oh, no. After all, now there's always something there to remind me.

VICKY. I hope not. Well?

CLIVE. Bacharach/David, 60-ish, recorded by Sandie Shaw in 64 on Pye.

VICKY. You're unbelievable.

Pause.

CLIVE. One day, who knows, we might, um . . . get together and, mingle a microbe.

VICKY. Well. Perhaps. Who knows.

CLIVE (*kissing her quickly*). You burn me up inside.

Exit CLIVE. VICKY *smiles. Enter* CLAYMORE *and* McLUSKY, *followed by* MO, *who sits.*

VICKY. Andrew.

McLUSKY. Hallo, Mrs B. Long time.

VICKY. Yes.

McLUSKY. Where's Clivey?

VICKY. Getting into bubblerock. Have you been introduced? This is Andrew McLusky. He's Clive's best pal. It's very touching. They make David and Jonathon look like vague acquaintances, and when they get into their act, they're such fun to be with.

McLUSKY. Good to see you, Mrs B.

VICKY (*Scots*). And you, Andrew.

Enter CLIVE *with a tray of glasses and a jug of orange juice.*

CLIVE. Drinky-time. (*He puts the tray on the table, starts pouring.*) It's a piquant little number, from the sunny side of the grove, slightly gauche, perhaps, but I think one laughs with it rather than at it. Here you are, Vicky. McLusky. It's orange juice, McLusky. (CLIVE *passes on.*)

McLUSKY (*confidentially*). Uh, Mrs B, why are we drinking orange juice?

VICKY. Because we've all got gonorrhoea, Andrew.

McLUSKY. Oh. Aye. Sorry.

VICKY. Think nothing of it.

CLIVE (*handing round*). Claymore. Mo.

A thought strikes McLUSKY.

McLUSKY. Uh, Mrs B. I havena got gonorrhoea.

VICKY. Pour encourager les autres, Andrew.

McLUSKY. Oh, aye?

CLIVE (*pouring his own*). You know, in the bad old days, they used to make infected women wear yellow skirts, even sometimes branded them. Now we're much more civilised. We set the diseased apart from the whole by the simple expedient of forcing them to survive for six weeks on Britvic.

McLUSKY (*unhappily*). Cheers.

CLIVE (*merrily*). Cheers.

Doorbell.

VICKY. Yet more?

CLIVE. The guest of honour.

Exit CLIVE.

McLUSKY. What the fuck's he playing at?

VICKY. Well, I've no idea. Just enjoy the fun.

McLUSKY *looks into his orange juice for the fun.*

CLAYMORE. I think it's a splendid idea.

VICKY. Yes, I imagine you –

Enter CLIVE *and* HEATHER.

Jesus.

CLAYMORE. Uh?

CLIVE. Everybody, I'd like those of you who haven't already to meet and greet Heather McIntyre. Heather is a friend of mine – of ours – who does an unpleasant and difficult job, often under extremely trying circumstances. When I asked her to come along, she was concerned about the ethical implications. I pointed out, however, that she is, strictly speaking, a social worker, and that Hippocratic Oaths and the like do not apply. Vicky, Claymore, you know, this is Mo, this is McLusky, and can I interest you in a glass of orange juice?

HEATHER. How do you do.

MO *stands, making to go.*

CLIVE. Ah, Mo, while you're up, please give that to Heather.

MO *gives the glass of orange juice to* HEATHER.

HEATHER. Oh, thank you.

Pause.

McLUSKY. 'Pour encourager les autres.' They've all got gonorrhoea.

VICKY. She knows that, Andrew. She told us.

McLUSKY. Oh.

VICKY. Yes.

CLAYMORE. Well –

CLIVE. Right.

McLUSKY. Um –

HEATHER (*laughs girlishly. Slight pause*). I'm really looking
forward to this evening.

*Blackout. A few more phrases of Bryan Ferry's 'It's My Party'.
Then lights. MO, CLAYMORE, McLUSKY, VICKY sitting.
HEATHER is pouring herself the last of the orange juice.*

HEATHER. I mean, we're pretty sure that Mussolini had both
gonorrhoea and syphilis, Hitler had gonorrhoea, Lord Randolph
Churchill, of course, was syphilitic, as was Henry VIII, Ivan the
Terrible, Napoleon, Catherine the Great, Louis XV . . .

The loud buzz of an electric liquidizer interrupts.

And there's the artists, Wilde, of course, Van Gogh, Strindberg,
Gauguin, even Keats, certainly Schubert and Schopenhauer,
Goya . . .

Liquidizer again.

And during the great outbreak of the 1490s and 1500s, of course,
you couldn't move for them.

Enter CLIVE with a jug of pineapple juice.

Charles VIII and Francis I of France, Erasmus, Benvenuto Cellini,
Dürer, at least three Popes –

CLIVE. I'm very interested in Botticelli.

McLUSKY. Botticelli?

VICKY. It's an amazingly complicated and rather silly game which
allows Clive to show off how many people he's heard of.

CLAYMORE. I thought Clive meant he'd had it.

CLIVE. Actually, quite precisely not. Anyone want a pineapple
juice? Claymore?

CLAYMORE (*hands over glass*). Never mix, never worry.

McLUSKY. What about fucking Botticelli?

CLIVE. Right. Help yourselves.

*He bounces out. They help themselves during the following
dialogue.*

VICKY. Where were we?

CLAYMORE. Heather was just telling us that Hitler had
gonorrhoea and what good company we're in.

VICKY. Oh, yes. I'm sorry about Clive, Heather. He always gets
over-excited at party-time. Sooner or later he'll be sick.

HEATHER (*sitting*). Well, I was only –

Enter CLIVE excitedly with an open art book.

CLIVE. Yes. I was right. Primavera, 1480, Birth of Venus, 1485. However . . . (*Turning pages.*) Raphael . . . Leo X, 1517, La Donna Velata, 1515, and even the Goldfinch Madonna, 1506.

McLUSKY. Point of story, Clivey.

CLIVE. Well, McLusky. Botticelli and Raphael were both wop painters –

McLUSKY (*as all his remarks, to* HEATHER). You see, I'm pig-ignorant.

CLIVE. Who painted very pretty and famous works of art.

McLUSKY. Culturally deprived.

CLIVE. They painted, however, in very different styles. Botticelli was essentially arcadian, evocative of prehistoric golden ages of lost innocence, and much admired by the more flowery Romantics of the later nineteenth century . . .

McLUSKY. I mean, I'm so thick, I think Tintoretto's an Italian aperitif.

CLIVE. Whereas Raphael was a much more urban, nay urbane phenomenon, with his painting finger very definitely on the pulse of all the latest current scientific thinking, the iron laws of human progress, all that stuff, and thus much unadmired by said Romantics, who christened themselves Pre-Raphaelites for that very reason.

McLUSKY. And that Whistler's Mother was a racehorse.

CLIVE. Now, Botticelli painted all his great works before 1494, when Raphael was just eleven years old, and hadn't got beyond the dirty doodle stage.

VICKY. Get to the point, Clive. This is getting boring.

CLIVE (*triumphantly*). Syphilis was brought to Europe by Christopher Columbus in 1494. (*He slams the book shut and then throws it on the table. Pause.*)

VICKY. Isn't that fascinating.

CLIVE. Don't you see? A world of truth and simple beauty, gentle trios of graces banging idyllically away up and down the greensward, is suddenly and irrevocably shattered. The time of man's innocence runs out. The worm in the old apple finally triumphant. Eden, R.I.P. (*To* HEATHER:) Yeah? Well?

HEATHER. Yes, well. Um, specifically, that is based on the somewhat discredited assumption that syphilis came back from

America, which is now regarded at best as lazy biology and worst as downright racialist.

CLIVE. Ah.

CLAYMORE. There you are, we get blamed for everything.

VICKY. Not you, Claymore. Heather meant the Red Indians.

CLAYMORE. I have Red Indian blood. I'm one thirty-secondth genuine Blackfoot.

VICKY. Sorry.

HEATHER. In fact, the 1490s epidemic was caused by freer travel, mobile, rootless populations, relaxation of morals and war. It's said to have started during some siege or other among mercenaries.

CLAYMORE. The blob on your knob can cost you your job. Eh?

HEATHER. I beg your pardon?

CLAYMORE. It's what they used to tell the soldiers in Vietnam.

VICKY. It didn't do much good, did it?

CLIVE. Um . . . McLusky . . .

McLUSKY. I'm thinking, Clivey . . .

VICKY. What?

CLIVE. 'Don't give a dose, to the one you love most.'

VICKY. Awfully clever.

CLIVE. 'You're not nice to be near . . .'

VICKY. 'If ya got gonorrhoea'?

CLIVE. Ah, yes, but can you *spell* it. Do come on McLusky.

McLUSKY. There . . .

CLIVE. There what?

McLUSKY. There was a young man from Torbay,
    Who thought that the syph went away.
    He believed that a chanchre
    Was only a canker
    Which healed in a week and a day.

CLAYMORE. What?

McLUSKY. It's a poem, students learn, about the symptoms of syphilis. I once had an affairette with a final year medic from Inverness who used to mumble it all the time, often at the most inopportune moments. Now how did it go. Something about . . .

HEATHER. But he's now in a terrible plight.

McLUSKY. That's it.
  But he's now in a terrible plight
  His pupils won't close in the light
  His heart is cavorting
  His wife is aborting
  As he –

HEATHER. Squints.

McLUSKY. Thank you, squints through his gun-barrel sight.
  Althralgia cuts into his slumber
  His aorta's in need of a plumber,
  Sorry –

HEATHER. And now he has tabes.

McLUSKY. And sabre-shinned babies
  And his gummas have grown beyond number.
  Um . . . don't tell me –
  His hair it is falling away
  As his . . . spirochetes increase each day
  He's developed paresis
  Has long talks with Jesus
  And thinks he's the Queen of the May.

  CLAYMORE, VICKY and CLIVE applaud.

HEATHER (pleasantly). The last verse refers to GPI, the last stage of neurosyphilis. General Paralysis of the Insane. We know quite a lot about it because of a study of 200 blacks in Alabama, who were diagnosed as syphilitics in 1932 and left to die of it over the following 40 years.

  Pause.

CLIVE. I think you have contravened the parameters of taste, McLusky.

  Slight pause.

HEATHER. Oh, I'm sorry, I didn't mean –

CLIVE. It doesn't matter. He does it all the time.

  Slight pause.

McLUSKY (scratching his ear). Watch it, Clivey.

  Pause.

CLAYMORE. I mean, the way I look at it is this. When I was a kid I had measles, mumps and whooping cough. In adolescence I had sinusitis and impacted wisdom teeth. Since then I've had conjunctivitis, several bouts of flu, and venereal disease. I mean, for Christ's sake.

VICKY (*ironically, though* CLAYMORE *unaware*). Exactly.

Blackout. Another snatch of Bryan Ferry. Then lights. CLIVE *is perambulating.* HEATHER, CLAYMORE, McLUSKY *and* MO *sitting.* MO *is reading the art book,* VICKY *still sitting on the floor.*

CLIVE. There's this little boy wandering round the Grassmarket late at night, you see, and a copper comes up to him and says, Hey, sonny, what are you doing here? And the little boy says, I'm looking for a tart. And the cop says, why are you looking for a tart? And he says, well, because I want to catch VD. And the cop says, why on earth do you want to catch VD? And the boy says, well, if I catch VD, I can give it to the au pair. And she'll give it to my dad, and my dad'll give it to my mum, and my mum'll give it to the milkman. And he's the bastard I'm really after, yesterday he trod on my tortoise.

Reaction. Pause.

VICKY. Girl comes back from a holiday in Eastern Europe. And she tells her friend, it's terrible, I think I've got a dose. And her friend says, how d'you know, have you had a check-up? And she says, no, it was a Hungarian.

Not very much reaction.

Please yourselves. I've run out. I only know one joke, and that was it.

McLUSKY. I did hear once –

CLIVE. Heather.

HEATHER. Oh, I don't –

McLUSKY. Of this Englishman –

CLIVE. Shut up, McLusky.

VICKY (*to* HEATHER). Oh, come on. You must be a one-woman anthology.

HEATHER. Oh, well . . .

McLUSKY. Who had acute –

VICKY. Fuck off, Andrew.

HEATHER. It's set in Chicago. I can't do the accent.

CLIVE. Try.

HEATHER. Well . . . Chicago Speakeasy, you know. And Bugsy comes in, and sees Big Louey at the bar and says, Hi Louey, where's the broad I saw you with last night? And Louey says, what broad, Bugsy? And Bugsy says, you know, that big blonde dame with the huge . . . you know, and Louey says, Oh, that broad. Well, it really cut me up, Bugsy, but she died. And Bugsy says, that's terrible Louey, what did she die of? And Louey says, well, Bugsy, she died of gonorrhoea. But, Louey, you can't die of gonorrhoea. You can if you give it to Louey.

Merry laughter. McLUSKY *stands.*

McLUSKY. Well, I think I might be going.

CLIVE. McLusky, why?

McLUSKY. Och, well, you see, I'm a bit out of all this, and it is —

VICKY. A quarter to ten.

McLUSKY. Precisely, and —

CLIVE. McLusky.

CLIVE *reaches behind or under something and produces a quarter bottle of whisky.*

McLUSKY. Clivey.

CLIVE *throws the bottle to* McLUSKY, *who catches it, and is opening it when he has a good thought.*

What about les autres?

CLIVE. It'll be so good for our souls.

McLUSKY *finds a glass on the table, offers bottle to* HEATHER, *who shakes her head, pours a shot, sits on edge of table and drinks.*

McLUSKY. Um, I did once have a sort of — pelvic rash.

CLIVE. A pelvic rash? Which you are claiming as an STD?

McLUSKY. A what?

HEATHER. A sexually transmitted —

McLUSKY. I thought that STD was telephones.

CLIVE. It's like the telephone.

VICKY. You can get anybody on it —

CLIVE. But it only involves two people at any one time.

VICKY. So then, McLusky's rash?

McLUSKY. Well, I was told – they said, it could have been venereally passed on.

VICKY. Well, one suspects, in your case, Andrew, that cirrhosis of the liver could be venereally passed on.

McLUSKY (*refilling his whisky*). No, I won't have this. I won't feel guilty.

CLIVE. No. But perhaps, left out. (*Slight pause.*)

McLUSKY. Beg pardon?

CLIVE. For, McLusky, I'm so sorry, naturally this breaks my heart, but there is status and degree in all things, and in the pecking order of decadent disorders, pelvic rashes are essentially bottom drawer. I mean, this doesn't make you any less of a good person, let me make this clear –

McLUSKY. Och, well, if we're talking about decadent diseases –

CLIVE. Yes, McLusky? What, if we're talking about decadence?

McLUSKY. Well, then, we might consider –

CLIVE (*suddenly threatening*). Well, indeed. (*Slight pause.*)

McLUSKY. Clivey . . .

CLIVE. For you see, Heather, McLusky, as he's about to tell you, is himself an example of conscious decadence, he does it deliberately, as his little bit for the cause. McLusky sees himself as serving the purpose of being a visible personal embodiment of the atrophy of capitalism; a kind of 'before' photograph in the advertisement of the revolution.

McLUSKY. Clivey.

CLIVE. But, in fact, of course, underneath this cosmetic lies the wizened flesh of a genuine, sturdy son of toil. If pressed, or even if not, McLusky will, a tear creeping into his eye, launch into his collected tales of Red Clydeside, all hammers and sickles up the shipyard cranes, and plaintive humming of the *Internationale* as the troops moved in.

McLUSKY. Clivey –

CLIVE. He will then proceed to jangle about his Gorbals down-bringing, which you note he wears round his neck like an Olympic medal, and the rafters will but ring with the clatter of clogs on cobblestones, and we will all relive with him the cheerful proletarian bonhomie of the warm and vibrant rat-infested tenements of his youth.

McLUSKY. Clivey.

CLIVE. And finally, we get the tales told at the knee, the General
  Strike, and how his old Dad ran —

VICKY. Shut up, Clive.

CLIVE. Why?

VICKY. You're being rather silly.

CLIVE. No, I'm not.

VICKY. You are.

  Pause.

HEATHER. Well, I —

McLUSKY (*quietly*). Clivey. There are some things.

HEATHER. Think I'll —

CLIVE. Don't.

  Slight pause.

  Right. Something else. You, me, the clap, we've done. The Black
  Death? Famine? War? Or how about, marriages, collapse of. Our
  wretched lies, deceits, inadequacies. Packaged, coped with,
  exorcised. By some means or another. With all wit, and charm,
  and grace. You see? *You* see?

VICKY. Go on.

CLIVE. Go on? All right. I will. We're comfortable, cosy. We can
  cope with anything. Our copeability and coziness just oozes from
  us, like detergent. It's the only thing we're really good at, and . . .
  (*Slight pause.*) There's people in this room, two people, only two,
  who aren't cosy. 'Cos cosiness is just what being folk like us, not
  folk like them, is all about. (*Slight pause.*) The point of story.
  Point of evening. (*Slight pause.*) So, dear Heather? Want to go?
  and miss the further cosy fun?

McLUSKY (*suddenly, forcefully*). All right. Let me ask you a
  question. Some guy rings you up, a guy you know, perhaps you
  havena seen him since University, or something, you havena been
  in touch, and he's, he needs a favour. And you owe him one. Let's
  say he once removed a splinter from your paw. And let's — let's
  also say he's been involved, you know, not active, with supplying
  something to the Angries, or the Scots Libs, or the Provos. And
  you don't approve, of course, why should you, but the guy's a pal.
  And he says, put me up. I need a place to go to. And you know
  that, you do it, and you're aiding and abetting. And you'll go to
  jail. OK, but more, you'll lose the lot. Your job, your life-style,

everything, you'll sacrifice, for that small, liberal gesture, helping out a pal. So – what d'you do?

CLIVE. Well, I –

The phone rings. VICKY *answers it.*

VICKY. Mr Brent's residence?

She hands the phone to CLIVE.

CLIVE. Hallo? Yes. No, of course. No, no problem. Be right there. OK. (*He puts the phone down.*) It's the office. Apparently, there's a meeting, assorted Rightists, Orange Lodgers, and they think some National Front. Anyway, it's being picketed, things are looking uglier by the minute and they want me down there right away. To cover it. I got the contacts, see.

CLIVE *exits. Pause.*

CLAYMORE. You know, sometimes, I don't think people realise the revolution that's taken place. I mean, you just look at the mid-60s; a complete mammary obsession. No technique, no charm, just endless acres of tit. And then, of course, you had the plastic period, everybody into Cellophane and PVC, and water, droplets on the skin, and soap, all kind of sub-Pirelli. But now it's soft and tender, filters, texture, body hair, the pores, about relationships of light and shade on flesh.

CLIVE *crosses the stage, putting on a polo-necked sweater, and exits. Pause.*

But there is an argument we've got too sophisticated. And for that reason, I'm getting back into flash. No back light. All hard edges, black shadows, set against plain drapes or seamless paper. Make it look, as far as possible, just like a polaroid family snap. Make the reader feel that he could shoot his girl just like I'm shooting mine.

CLIVE *crosses the stage again, putting on a denim jacket, with his press card in his mouth, and exits. Pause.*

HEATHER. I read somewhere of an actress who'd done a set of photographs. It was a wonderful set; it made her look so good she could hardly believe it was her. Indeed, the photographer had to swear to her that he hadn't retouched the pictures.

Enter CLIVE, *wrapping a long scarf round his neck. He stands, watching.*

And she looked, the next day, in the hard, cold light of her bathroom, at her face, and compared it with the face in the picture. And she went to a plastic surgeon, with the pictures, and said, make me look like that. And he shortened her nose, and trimmed her jaw and cheekbones, and made her look, in the hard cold light of day, just like she looked in the pictures.

McLUSKY (*to* CLIVE). You havena answered the question.

CLIVE. Well, I'm sure that in that wildly unlikely event, I'd manage to bluff my way out of it somehow. Even that. Quite sure of it.

Exit CLIVE. McLUSKY *looking out after him.* CLAYMORE *stands.*

CLAYMORE. Mo.

MO. Yes?

CLAYMORE. I've booked the studio tomorrow.

MO. Yes?

CLAYMORE. About 9.30?

Pause. MO *shrugs.*

Now dance with me.

Pause.

VICKY. Don't, Mo.

CLAYMORE. Dance with me.

Pause. MO *stands. Music is faintly growing.*

MO. It's a wonderful feeling. To free your knots. And cut your ties. With no restrictions any more. No family. No refuge. Nothing. You're completely independent. You're completely free.

She puts her arms out to CLAYMORE. *As he moves into her arms we remember* VICKY *and* CLAYMORE *at the beginning of the play. The music now full. It's 'Crazy Man Michael', Fairport Convention.* MO *and* CLAYMORE *dance together, very slowly and beautifully.* HEATHER *stands and exits. A few moments.* VICKY *stands and exits. A few moments.* McLUSKY *stands and exits. Just* MO *and* CLAYMORE *dancing. The lights fade very slowly, and the music goes on.*

O Fair Jerusalem

To Christopher Honer

O FAIR JERUSALEM was first presented at the Birmingham
Repertory Theatre Studio in May 1975, with the following cast:

SINGER	Michael Carter
WILLIAM FRANK MASTER PRIEST	James Coyle
BISHOP WOLFE BULL	Terence Davies
HAM NEVILLE LORD	Derek Fuke
ACTOR JOHN GEORGE NOBLEMAN	Geoffrey Leesley
CLERK HAMMOND BUNG	Robert O'Mahoney
LADY AGGIE	Natasha Pyne
KNIGHT HARRY 2nd PRIEST	David Quilter
HENDERSON	David Rome
MOTHER ACTRESS HILDA NOBLEWOMAN CLERK's WIFE	Gay Rose
DICCON NORMAN	Graham Watkins
READER CHILD	Peter Kershaw
BEGGARS/ACOLYTES/SOLDIERS MONKS/SEXTONS/BODIES	Glenn Cunningham Philip Grady, Martin Head

Directed by Christopher Honer
Designed by Chris Dyer
Lighting by Eric Pressley
Music compiled and directed by Michael Carter

Characters

1348
SINGER
WILLIAM
His MOTHER
LADY
CLERK
KNIGHT
DICCON
PRIEST
HAM
An ACTOR
An ACTRESS
BISHOP
A READER
JOHN
SECOND PRIEST
NOBLEMAN
NOBLEWOMAN
BULL
BUNG
MASTER of the Flagellants
LORD
A CHILD
Clerk's WIFE
Knight's DEATH
PEASANTS, MONKS, SEXTONS, SOLDIERS, BEGGARS, BODIES

1948
DR HUGH HENDERSON
HILDA
REV. JOHN HAMMOND
NORMAN
NEVILLE
HARRY
AGGIE
FRANK
EDMUND WOLFE

The play is written for a company of ten. The 1348 parts are played by nine of the 1948 characters. HENDERSON does not appear in the 1348 scenes, and the SINGER does not appear in the 1948 scenes.

Setting
The play is set in a parish church. The audience on two sides of the central, nave area. Exits to the street and into the vestry. There is a curtained recess, in addition to the usual areas, altar, pulpit, lectern, etc. The cross on the altar is made from two roof beams, nailed together.

Act One

Scene One

Easter 1348. A single light on the SINGER.

SINGER. The moon shines bright,
    And the stars give a light,
    A little before 'tis day:
    And bids us awake and pray.

    Awake, awake, good people all,
    Awake, and you shall hear,
    Our Lord our God died on the cross
    For them he loved so dear.

    So teach you well your children, men,
    The while that you are here,
    It will be better for your souls,
    When your corpse lies on the bier.

General lights come up.
The SINGER *disappears.*
*We are in a country church. In a corner, a table, representing
the interior of a peasant's cottage.*

It is very early morning, before dawn.
PEASANTS *enter the church, genuflect, kneel. They include*
WILLIAM *and his* MOTHER.
TWO MONKS, *in white habits, carry a simple wooden cross
and place it in the area concealable by a curtain.*
A THIRD MONK *brings in a white shroud, covers the cross with
it. The* MONKS *draw the curtain across. They retire.*
A FOURTH MONK, *dressed in an alb; carrying a palm, enters and
stands facing the curtain. The song ends.*
The THREE MONKS, *wearing capes and carrying censers of
incense, enter at the other end of the church.*

1 MONK. Alas, our Master he is dead,
    The innocent,
    By guilty hands his body rent,
    And murdered.

2 MONK. The evil ones spit in his face
    And split his side.
    For thus our gentle saviour died —
    Accursed race!

3 MONK. Alas, thy followers devout
    Must loathly weep:
    The shepherd stolen of his sheep
    The light snuffed out.

1 MONK. So thus we watch with prayers contrite,
    Bear costly spikenard to the font,
    The bleeding vessel to anoint
    With sacred spice.

2 MONK. But how shall we
    With women's hands
    Move the great stone that guards the sepulchre?

3 MONK. And who is he
    That proudly stands
    Afore the tomb?

4 MONK. Good Christians, tell me, what is it you seek?

1 MONK. Jesu of Nazareth, Christ crucified, O holy one.

4 MONK. Do ye so little hold his words in memory?
    Did ye not con his words in Galilee?
    That he shall on the third day rise again?

He pulls back the curtain. The cross is gone.
He lifts the shroud, shows it to them.

Seek not the living from among the dead.
He is not here, he's risen, as he said,
To conquer death,
To vanquish pain.

MONKS. The God of Gods is ris'n today!
    In vain ye seal the tomb, men of Judea!
    Sing Alleluia!
    He that was dead is resurrected here —
    And Death is conquer'd!

At the beginning of the carol, WILLIAM stood and quickly
exited. His MOTHER notices he's gone, leaves the Church.
Lights up on the cottage area. WILLIAM enters and starts
packing implements into rough cloth. Lights fade on church.
MOTHER enters to WILLIAM.

MOTHER. William. What are you doing?

WILLIAM *doesn't reply.*

Why d'you leave church?

WILLIAM *puts on a coat.*

WILLIAM. I'm going.

MOTHER. You'll be caught.

WILLIAM *shrugs.*

Why d'you want to go?

Pause.

WILLIAM. The soil's too thin. There's too many folk working it. Hardly better than dirt. And every year the Steward gives more land to pasture. Save me, you'll be all right.

MOTHER. You're bound to the land. You can't go.

WILLIAM. I don't know aught of that. I know I'm bound to be hungry, 'less I go.

MOTHER. I know men've got their freedom. Paid wages. Money.

WILLIAM. What good's money if the soil's dead from tilling?

Pause.

Aught that binds me don't reach further than that hill.

MOTHER. Why d'you think to go today?

WILLIAM. Thought it in church.

MOTHER. Don't go on a holy day.

WILLIAM. Sun's coming up.

MOTHER. Don't go on Easter Day.

WILLIAM. Best day to go.

MOTHER. Say it's to be a good summer, this year. Must be.

Pause.

WILLIAM. I can see the light on the hill.

WILLIAM *exits, quickly.*

MOTHER (*calls after him*). Where you going to go, William? Where you going to go?

The SINGER *reappears.*

SINGER. O fair O fair Jerusalem,
When shall I come to thee?
When all my grief is at an end,
Thy joy then we may see.

Scene Two

A town square. Whitsunday. Steps to a church door.
TWO BLIND BEGGARS bunched, still, holding sticks, facing
each other. WILLIAM stands looking at them.
Then WILLIAM goes and sits on the church steps.
Enter a LADY and a CLERK, who serves her husband. The
LADY is dressed in blue, white and gold. She is young, and
beautiful. The CLERK is not much older, an unbeneficed priest,
in that he wears a black priest's robe, but has no parish or church
appointment.

LADY. A Lady once, of high sanguinity
    Was wedded unto mercantile senility
    Her merchant spouse was more than generous
    Perforce, however, less than amorous
    Antiquity sits strange with gay jeunesse
    And passion unrequited seeks redress.

    They move towards the church door.
    Enter KNIGHT and DICCON. The KNIGHT is dressed in green.
    He is young. DICCON, a bowman, is probably not much older.
    He is roughly dressed, carries on his back many cans, cups,
    arrows and a longbow.

CLERK. The Merchant's nephew of great learning was
    And expert counsel gave unto his coz
    But though amored of formal disputation
    And quick to cite a text or refutation
    Still yet his *a priori* was, alas,
    Glory mundane, not *sancta spiritas.*

KNIGHT. The Knight from deadly danger puissant
    Wends home to face as bitter covenant
    A fair maid's heart to serve pursuivance
    Requires a martial perseverance
    O would his pain depart with some emollient
    Some physic, unguent or aperient!
    But still he prays for love's compleisance
    And nothing doth but pledge his full obeisance.

    A look between KNIGHT and the LADY. A PRIEST comes
    out of the church.

PRIEST. Then bells ring out and ope the portals wide
    To celebrate this feast of White-Sun-Tide.

    The LADY, the CLERK and the KNIGHT follow the PRIEST
    into the church. DICCON sits on the steps. THE BLIND
    BEGGARS suddenly begin to hit each other. They will fight,
    accidentally, bloodily, untidily and increasingly tiredly,
    throughout the scene. A few moments. Bells cease.

DICCON. A running man, are you?

WILLIAM. Eh? No.

DICCON. Tell. Wide-eyes and brown boots.

WILLIAM (*standing*). I'm a freeman.

DICCON. Poor man, either road. Sit. Sit.

> WILLIAM *sits.*
>
> (*Introducing himself*). Diccon.
>
> *Pause.*

WILLIAM. William. William of —

DICCON. No need to tell, don't want to hear.

> DICCON *takes out a loaf, offers half to* WILLIAM, *who eats eagerly. A moment or two, then* WILLIAM *realises* DICCON's *courtesy requires conversation.*

WILLIAM (*thumb to church*). He your master?

DICCON. No. I'm a free bowman. Serve any man, he serves me right. Eh, you been earning?

WILLIAM. I — no.

DICCON. How long?

WILLIAM. Thirty days.

DICCON. By all the saints and martyrs.

> *He stands, gestures* WILLIAM *up, points.*
>
> See over. On the hill. Building a new church, high as the sky. Go there.

WILLIAM. You working there?

DICCON. Me, Diccon, laying my shoulder to building a church! Damned afore.

> *Pause.*
>
> Aren't you going to ask my cause?

WILLIAM. What cause?

DICCON. Of why I'll not lay a shoulder to Bishop's stone.

WILLIAM. Ay. What cause?

> DICCON *looks round, then sits and explains, generously, as if* WILLIAM *had asked unprompted.*

DICCON. Thieves and vagabonds. To a man.

WILLIAM. The builders?

DICCON (*scornful*). No. The holy boys. The beneficed clergy. The church visible and invisible. Militant, mendicant, triumphant. Whole pack of 'em. I've seen things'd make your nose fall off your face. I have seen prebends and parishes, and not a few, taken on a dice. There's a black one here, he's paid a stipend, by the abbey. So the monks can sit bibing and gorging theyselves on their tithes and taxes, like tomorrow's the last day and they were already preening theyselves in paradise.

WILLIAM. You don't dread to be speaking such?

DICCON. No space in hell for me. It's all crammed up with popes and cardinals.

WILLIAM (*amused*). You'd bind the Devil hisself to a stone?

DICCON (*serious*). Ay. If need be. I'm a bowman.

Pause.

WILLIAM. Where you been fighting?

DICCON. Now there's a story. Say, villein, where you come from, do they speak of Jerusalem?

WILLIAM. Ay.

DICCON. And the Turkish infidel that holds the Holy City in his iron fist?

WILLIAM. That too.

DICCON. Well, there's a story.

Slight pause.

(*Generously.*) I'll tell it then. Story of a fieldman, as you, upped and off one cold dark morning, knowing he's hungry and can't be hungrier, but he could be fat as a king. And he comes to a town and there's no work, and he's no guild and served no master as apprentice. And there's thousands like him too, begging and starving, and some in cowls as well. And then he hears tell on a distant land where Jesu Christ hisself . . . And goes. Not looking after, for there's naught after, sets his eye and goes.

WILLIAM (*impressed*). You saw the Holy Sepulchre?

DICCON. No, didn't get further than Italy. Roads thronged with folk, and their childer, all bawling at every place, is this Jerusalem, is this the Holy City. But it weren't. Place called Venezia. Too many folk, all rushing as bad water, didn't know where they were or where they were going. Half way to midsummer, most of 'em. Or dying with hunger. And word comes there's work for a fighting man in France, so back up the high road I go, to beat the arse off the Frankies.

WILLIAM. That's a Holy War too?

DICCON. Some say aught's a Holy War. I say none. Didn't look holy, sat up outside Calais walls eleven month, starving poor bastards out.

WILLIAM. But Crecy. Were you at Crecy.

DICCON looks round, then proudly shows WILLIAM his longbow.

DICCON. You know what that is?

WILLIAM. It's a bow.

DICCON. Longbow. You want to pull it?

WILLIAM tries to pull the bow.

No. You're just using your arm. That's what Frankies do. Look, as me,

He demonstrates.

use the whole body. There. See? Now, loose this bow, you'll pierce an inch of armour.

He lets the string go. WILLIAM jumps.

No shaft, boy.

He drops the bow, takes an arrow.

One of these, shot of a well-held bow, knock a proud lord off his horse. A thousand, as at Crecy, wipe out the nobility of France. Not a Holy War. A bowman's war.

WILLIAM (*pauses. Suddenly, as if noticing the* BLIND BEGGARS *for the first time*). What are they doing?

DICCON. They're starving. So some bright joker, for a laugh, you know, puts 'em in a pen with a pig so they can kill it and eat.

WILLIAM. Oh.

Pause.

But they're beating theyselves.

DICCON. They're blind. So they can't see the pig. So they're beating each other. That's the point of the joke.

WILLIAM. Oh.

Pause.

But there's no pig there.

DICCON. Aye, but they don't know that, do they?

WILLIAM. Ah.

Enter PRIEST *and* KNIGHT *from the church.*

PRIEST. Then, goodly knight, your pilgrimage did not extend
Beyond the confines of the Holy See,
Unto Byzantium and the Holy Land?

LADY and CLERK enter during this speech.

KNIGHT. No, sir, but made I solemn vow
Afore this travail I emprised,
That e'er the sun a year's round spun again,
By God's good franchise,
The gates of Sion shall, I trow,
Stand wide to Christian men.

PRIEST (*who has noticed the* CLERK, *to whom he wants to
speak, out of the corner of his eye*).
A plaintive, saintly aspiration.
Pray, blessed Mother, for its ordination.

He gives a little bow. A slight hiatus. Then the KNIGHT
responds.

KNIGHT. Farewell, pastor.

PRIEST. Knight, farewell. (*To* CLERK:) Master Clerk, a word.

They go into conference. KNIGHT *to* LADY. *They know
each other.*

KNIGHT. My lady —

LADY. Sir, was France fair?

KNIGHT. Aye, lady.

LADY. Its people gentle?

KNIGHT. Aye, lady.

LADY. Yet of great discretion?

KNIGHT. Aye, lady.

LADY. Then as you, my lord.

Pause. KNIGHT *bows and withdraws a little.*

CLERK. So as the Merchant is in Flanders still,
The present off'ring to the church must be
A token of intent,
Of greater gift to come,
When commerce presently
In train is done.

He indicates a bag of money he carries.

PRIEST. Reward will come in paradise.

CLERK. Reward comes when my master is in paradise,
    But will remain on earth

PRIEST (*not understanding*). Good master —

CLERK (*pointing*). Sir, survey that monument
    To whose construction this small offering's donated.
    Its cornerstone was laid
    Before the birth of any still alive,
    Its last stone stays for days beyond our deaths.
    By us, it is immortal, and
    The contribution that we make,
    However paltry, adds to our immortality.
    You look askance.

PRIEST. Remember, sir, the parable of Babel Tower
    Where one proud prince, King Nimrod,
    Sought to build a stair to God,
    And claimed mankind to be invincible,
    Of any labour capable.
    God, wrathfully, did scotch the Man
    By visitation of a thousand tongues,
    That they could no longer understand
    Each other, thus be less inclined to wrong.

CLERK. But, certain, pastor, through our Mother Church
    All tongues are one, the babel's lost:
    Today, Priest, is the feast
    Of Pentecost.
    Our Holy Church's founders thus spoke clear
    The gift of knowledge, we'er of letters
    Or of skilful masonry
    Could never be
    A sin against the Holy Ministry.

PRIEST. Sir, make your disputation, but recall
    In wisdom's grief, Ecclesiastes tells,
    And as increases knowledge, so does sorrow.

CLERK. Sir, you omit Ecclesiastes all:
    That wisdom so far foolishness excels
    As darkness is excelled by light of morrow.

PRIEST. In chapter twenty-six of Proverbs, sir:
    There is more hope of wanton foolishness
    Than wise, conceited men.

CLERK. In chapter four of self-same Proverbs, sir:

That wisdom is a virtue to be blessed
So wisdom gain.

PRIEST. St Paul: men are puffed up by cognizance,
Love edifies the globe.

CLERK. Who darkens counsel with his ignorance?
Says Job.

Pause.

PRIEST. You are a man of learning, but beseech:
The vice of Lucifer is pride;
His jaws are open wide,
To snap you in his teeth.

CLERK (*suddenly, angrily*). No, no man is a man of learning,
Priest, while your heavy hand lies on the neck of knowledge,
which is folly only when it is dimly understood. A new
wind blows in the world, and you turn up your coat and say,
what wind? I feel it not. *Exempli gratia:* For a thousand years,
we've built up temples of wood and stone, discovering thereby
great laws, but still the temple of the Holy Ghost remains a
mystery. Still yet we comfort the infirm with swallowed
paternosters, grounded bones and muddled allegory, and still
we torture those who could unlock the secrets of our ills. A
man I knew, in Paris, not a year ago, was tried and burnt for
cutting of a corpse. Has God's church learnt no more than
this? Should it not know, as Paul teaches, that we see but as
through a darkened glass, and the hottest place in hell is kept
for those who'd keep the mist before that glass? You claim the
knowledge of the very stars, yet you know not what goes on
beneath your shirt.

PRIEST. Tomorrow, sir we may be at the gates of Sion.
And what profits it a man if he wins the world but loses his
own soul.

CLERK. Take therefore no thought for tomorrow, for tomorrow
shall take thought for the things of itself. Boast not of
tomorrow; for you know not, Priest.

He tosses the money-bag to the PRIEST.

My lady.

CLERK *and* LADY *go.*

DICCON. Eh, what does hap beneath your shirt, eh, Priest?

PRIEST. Watch — your — soul.

Disappears into the church. A pause. DICCON *and*
WILLIAM *look to the* KNIGHT, *who stands transfixed. At
last, he speaks:*

KNIGHT. Through countless moons of bitter, mortal war,
    I've worshipped in the church of *belle amor*,
    Lit tapers of deep sighs for intercession,
    To God, of love made passionate confession.
    For my unworth sung penitential psalms,
    And read synoptic gospels to her charms.
    All gall consume I gladly, that at last,
    My pain is consummated with the Host.

    Exit KNIGHT. *Pause.*

WILLIAM. I didn't catch a word of it.

DICCON. No more should. Come on.

WILLIAM. You're not to serve your master?

DICCON. No. In war he needs a rough man as me.
    In peace-time, summat sweeter.

    To the BEGGARS, *giving them bread.*

    Eh. Here, bread, in your hands, boys.

    The BEGGARS *eat.*

    What a road to earn a living, eh?

    The SINGER *appears as lights fade on* DICCON, WILLIAM
    and the BEGGARS.

SINGER. Can love be controlled by advice?
    Can madness and reason agree?
    Oh Mary, who'd ever be wise,
    If madness be loving of thee.
    Let sages pretend to despise
    The joys they want spirit to taste:
    Let us seize old Time as he flies,
    And the blessings of life while they last.

    Dull wisdom but adds to our care,
    Bright love will improve every joy;
    Too soon we may meet with grey hairs,
    Too late may repent being coy.
    Then, Mary, for what should we stay,
    Till our best blood begins to run cold?
    Our youth we can have but today,
    We may always find time to grow old.

Scene Three

A rose garden. It is Corpus Christi. SINGER *between* LADY *and*
KNIGHT.

SINGER. From white-sun unto Corpus Christi's feast
    The Knight and Lady dance at love's behest.

The first four speeches are spoken apart.

KNIGHT. The Lady wears colours of the morning
    Blue for fidelity and piety
    Colour of sapphire and the planet Jupiter,
    Colour of love;
    Yellow for her constancy
    Colour of Topaz and the glowing sun
    Colour of faith;
    White for her truth and purity
    Colour of pearl and moon's-shine,
    Colour of hope.

LADY. The Knight is dressed in verdant green, colour of faithless-
    ness and youthful passion. The Lady loves the Knight, but
    ought not. The Lady should love her lord, but cannot.

SINGER. But then her husband's from his journey come,
    And tells her, we must fly and leave our home.

KNIGHT. The lady wanders by a couch of roses
    And with her knight picks many lovely posies:
    Cutting the sanguine rose of Burgundy
    Significant of love's simplicity
    The Daily rose, that smiles on fair amor,
    And every bud that speaks of passion pure;
    Leaving to bloom untouched the Faded Rose
    Sign of a passing beauty, fleeting joys,
    The Moss Rose, surface-show alluring,
    And all that speak of love not long enduring.

LADY. The Knight picks the Lady roses, finds white virgins and
    red martyrs trapped between the thorns of cruel necessity.
    The Lady and the Knight needs must to part; she knows not
    why, and cares not where.

SINGER. She would their last hours were in passion spent
    Her love's farewell is of a stranger bent.

To each other:

KNIGHT. Madam, accept my solemn pledge and promise
    My lips shall touch not wine's becoming chalice
    Until that day our eyes lock once again
    Be I ever so thirsty;
    And take my heart's true vow and undertaking

These garments are upon my back remaining
And none shall strip them, be they ten times ten
By our sweet lady.
Whereas I break this vow,
Show no compassion,
Cause both my sufferance and pain to grow,
In your own fashion.

The LADY's *ritual responses to the* KNIGHT's *vow begin assured, but grow more strained*:

LADY. Sir, your humble supplication
    Of true temperance
    Seems to me an affectation
    And not obeisance.

KNIGHT. Whereas I break this vow
    Show me no mercy
    Cut out my tongue to make the vain heart bow
    Shower me with curses.

LADY. Sir, I despite your seemly protestation
    Make further ordinance
    Still must I ask in reparation
    A greater sufferance.

KNIGHT. Whereas I break this vow
    Show me no quarter
    Break me and fly me to the deepest slough
    There to self-slaughter.

LADY. Sir, your worthy lamentation –

KNIGHT. Whereas I break this vow
    Show me no grace
    Smite me with pestilence, I care not how,
    Tear off my face –

LADY. Sir, please –

He stops. She puts her arms out to him. He smiles. They hug each other. They break.

KNIGHT (*quickly*). Whereas I break this vow,
    Show me no ruth:
    For-ever is my pleading now
    I pledge my truth.

Exit KNIGHT. *Music stops.*

LADY (*whispers, to herself*). I'll miss you, O I'll miss you.

Enter CLERK. LADY *turns.*

CLERK. Madam, the baggage is ready, and your husband's
    waiting.

LADY. Where are we going?

CLERK. North.

LADY. Will no one tell me why?

Pause.

CLERK. Madam, your husband's waiting.

LADY. Will you not tell me?

Pause.

CLERK. Lady, your husband brought news, of a strange wind, that's blown from the east, from Sicily, and Italy, and France and Germany, and Flanders, and which, now, blows to us.

LADY. Sir, I don't understand.

CLERK. Madam, your husband.

LADY *exit, followed by* CLERK.

SINGER. In olden days, the wind might not have spread
Now every road is straight, and full, of dead.

Blackout and in the Darkness a huge sound:

CHOIR. *Dies irae*
Dies illa
Solvet saeclum
In favilla

Scene Four

Corpus Christi. An open place. At the end of the 'Dies Irae', lights snap up on a troupe of actors: HAM, ACTOR, ACTRESS.

HAM. And now, gentles, for our next performance
The which we trust will be your joy and pleasance;
A moral, muddled parable or fable,
Of temporary duration,
For your best lightenment and worthy
Edification,
On this the feast of Corpus Christi.
The goodly Jew so called it is
The story shows
The world a wicked walking-place
Wherto ye go
So comes the man, who stalks from Winchester
Unto St Albans on a summer day:
See now man's fortunes fester
Be they ever so gay.

ACTOR *as a* MERCHANT.

ACTOR. A burel, barrell man am I
    A merchant of Winchester
    To St Albans market now I hie
    For a semester.
    To buy an ox or two, perhaps a hog,
    Or a bale of grain, thus on the road I trog.
    But now my eyes are bleary
    I'll take a nap,
    Being so weary.

He sits and sleeps. ACTRESS *and* HAM, *with wooden swords, as thieves.*

ACTRESS. My name is Debt.

HAM. My name is Wedlock.

ACTRESS. My name was given in forfeiture.

HAM. Mine for my mam gave me in name
    what she could not give in nature

ACTRESS/HAM. Footpads are we
    Nefarious thieves

ACTRESS. for murther black my soul is yeller!

HAM. If's as good to be hung for a sheep as a lamb
    Why not go to hell for a feller?

Sees ACTOR.

    Aha! A feasting fatling man of favour
    Snores on the mead
    Lets on him feed
    To make him light makes usselves heavier.

ACTRESS. I fear the fire, good Wedlock,
    And that mightily.

HAM. Come sir, show valour,
    And that speedily.
    This man is richly got
    We've not a lot
    Why should this be?
    Remember the tale of Dives
    And Lazarus the poorest man
    Who sat by Abram
    While the richer went his way
    To flame infernal.
    Come, draw your sword,
    And that without a word,
    For his soul eternal.

ACTRESS. By our lady then do I
   Better his soul to save
   By making his purse light
   Else he should as a rich man meet his grave,
   And endless night.

HAM (*to* ACTOR). Come, sir, your purse.

ACTOR. Ah! Footpads! Help! Hark! Ho!

ACTRESS. Your purse, sir.

ACTOR. No.

HAM. Why then to Abram's bosom you must go.

   They stab and rob him.

   So come, good master, from this place we hie
   Else we're arrested.

   HAM *and* ACTRESS *withdraw, changing to a* TAX-
   COLLECTOR *and a* PRIEST *respectively, as* ACTOR *sits up
   to explain:*

ACTOR. I am not dead, but deathly lie,
   Save I'm assisted.

   Lies down.

ACTRESS. A Priest am I, a goodly man of God
   On virtue paramount in every one
   Faith in my riches, hope of more
   And love of all I own.

ACTOR. Help, help! Is none by?
   (*To audience:*) I weakly moan.

ACTRESS. I cannot hear — for I am seeming deaf,
   A woe that comes quite suddenly today,
   And charity begins at home, tis saith —
   And home's that way.

ACTOR. Help! Help! My death is nigh.
   I thinly croak.

ACTRESS. And hearing not what this sad merchant spoke,
   I pass on by.

ACTOR. O! O! Will no one help me from my death!
   (*To audience:*) I'm very near to my last living breath.

HAM. A levious tax-collector me
   Full up of tithes,
   Of tenths, fifteenths, and heriots and fines
   St Peter's Church would fill.

ACTOR. Help! Help! I'm very ill,
  And thus cry out for succour still.

HAM. I hear a shout:
  Why sir, what ails you, out!

ACTOR. Help! Help! I'm robbed and like to die!
  And near bereft of breath to cry.

HAM. And he is robbed, then taxes none he'll pay —
  What profits me I stay?
  So I pass by.

ACTOR. O! O! Will none hear me, by our mother?
  I'm reaching near the ending of my tether.

ACTRESS (*as a Jew*). I am a wandering, wondering Ebrew man,
  Scratching a living as I can,
  Poor and the victim of much cuss,
  For my forbears in murthering of Gentle Jesus
  In old time.

ACTOR. Help help!

ACTRESS. Speak up!

ACTOR. Help help again!

ACTRESS. By all the saints it is a Christian man!
  Fallen and wounded.
  I should make great cheer
  But suffering can I nor look on so near,
  Save that I mend it.
  Now come, sir, let's see to your hurting.

ACTOR. By Mary, 'tis a Jew of Jerusalem
  Who'll poison all as soon as look at 'em
  Pray, sir, I beg you, show me mercy!

ACTRESS. Good sir, I owe you no cursing
  Come, let me mend you, bind your wounds,
  Comfort with oil and wine,
  Be it ever so costly
  Priceless is it to feed he that starves,
  To sate the thirsty.

ACTOR. Why sir, you'd salve a Christian man?
  (*To audience*:) Methinks 'tis succour strange
  Being he's Ebrew and so wealthy.

ACTRESS. For God, sir, we are all as one.
  Art now well mended?

ACTOR (*leaping up*). Ay, ay, and thus your charity's upended
  Making me healthy. (*Draws his sword.*)

ACTRESS. Why, sir, what haps, why do you champ and frown?

ACTOR. Why, for the murthering of your black race.

ACTRESS. Some dark intention read I in your face.

ACTOR. Ay, that being robbed, to rob you back in turn.

He knocks ACTRESS *down and robs her.*

ACTRESS. O Woe! That kindness so rewarded be!

ACTOR. O Joy! That profit I of this man's gentlery.

HAM. So ken the weight of this our parable
Our time's a pain and grievance terrible,
For rich man or thrall,
The reaper grim waits for every man,
For Bishop, King or wretched villein
He cares not at all;
And ken that charity's grown cold
And friendship freezes,
Save in outward show
And he you help may grant you his dis-eases
Ere you go
Whether to Winchester it is you hie
To fall for thieving men
Or on the road to Jericho
From fair Jerusalem.

*They bow. Silence. Turn to go. A drum-beat. During this
sequence, the* ACTORS *lines are punctuated by percussion, ,
drums, rattles, bangs from unseen* TOWNSPEOPLE. *Also,
lights fade up and down on the* ACTORS.

HAM. Your pardon, sirs?

Rattle.

You wish for more, sirs?

Bang bang.

You wish for no more, sirs?
Either way, live-a-day.

Turns back. Rattle.

What will you, sirs, more or no more?

ACTRESS. What's their matter, Ham?

HAM. I don't know, do I?

ACTOR. They're looking black.

HAM. Shut up and keep smiling.

Bang.

O we do all varieties, good sirs. Entertainments, interludes, divertissements, morals and mysteries of every place. We can dance you a Cornish jig, or set you a fair french foursome — threesome — or sing a Brussels ballad, or a Dutch ditty, or an Oxford ode . . .

Bang.

A Brussels ballad, yes. And conjuring, do that as well . . . And juggling too.

To ACTOR:

Give them a juggle quick.

ACTOR *searches in baskets.*
Bang.

Oh wandering people, sirs. Here one hour and gone the next. With any luck.

Drum.

Yes, as the Jew in the play, sir, very like the Jew.

Rattle.

ACTOR. I thought that Jew was a mistake.

HAM. Shut up and juggle.

ACTOR. I can't find the sticks.

HAM. Oh, I know not, where were we last? At Windsor, peradventure, playing afore the king and all his valiant knights? Highly valiant, they were.

Rattle.

Aye, Flanders, sirs.

A sudden, violent rattle and bang. ACTRESS, *who has been trying to sidle out, rushes back to the others, the group reforms rapidly.*

HAM. You what? A witch? My Meg a harridan?

ACTRESS. A what?

HAM. A harridan. Why sirs — ha-ha — my Meg a harridan? She can't even fly, sirs, can you?

Two slow drum beats.

Go on, try and fly, then, show the people.

Slight pause.

ACTRESS (*nervously flapping her arms about*). Try, try, try to fly.

HAM. See? Meg fly? Half the time, she can hardly walk.

Three drums. HAM has an idea, turns wooden sword upside down, so it looks like a cross. ACTRESS nervously tries to look happy.

And look, she don't flinch at the cross, now, sirs? Flinch like there's no tomorrow, at the holy cross, the harpies do.

Four drums.

Ah, and there's another test. The marks. Old Nick's ice-cold kiss. Our Meg's got skin like alabaster, haven't you?

ACTRESS. Ay, like alabaster. Very like that.

HAM. Show 'em your leg then.

ACTRESS. Show 'em my leg?

HAM. You'll be showing a lot more if you don't.

ACTRESS crossly hitches up her skirt. She has black marks on her thighs. ACTOR realises, as does HAM. They both point their wooden swords, uselessly, into the darkness. Five slow drum beats.

Well, yes, sirs. On the surface, yes, it does look like the pestilence, I grant you that, but on the other hand —

Blackout as tremendous drumming, rattling and banging. Lights fade up on DICCON looking at the ACTORS, lying dead. All we see of HAM is his legs sticking out from under a blanket.

DICCON. God-a-mercy. God-a-mercy.

Enter WILLIAM carrying tools.

WILLIAM. What's to do here, Diccon?

DICCON. Jesters, troubadours. Killed, ever one.

WILLIAM. Weren't their jests good?

DICCON. No, that's not the cause, William.

Pause.

Eh, what you bearing, in the name of Christ?

WILLIAM. My tools to the church.

DICCON. Are you the only man in the green world knows not? There'll be no church-building now.

WILLIAM. Why, Diccon?

DICCON (*gesturing towards the* BODIES). Plague.

Pause.

WILLIAM. Them here? They're dead of plague?

DICCON. Aye. Aye, or killed for bearing it.

WILLIAM *goes towards a body.*

Don't touch! D'you know nothing at all?

WILLIAM *stands back.*

Saw two pigs today. Sniffling and rooting round some beggar's corpse, all black with oozing. Not ten minutes gone, they both fell to the ground. Dead like a snapped stick.

WILLIAM. Well, let's be running, Diccon.

DICCON. Where to? How'er fast you go, plague's faster. All there's to do is hide and hope.

WILLIAM. And pray.

DICCON. Pray? Why?

WILLIAM. The priests'd tell us, pray.

Pause.

DICCON. The priest from the church. You know? I saw him die. The first to go. (*Pause. Harshly:*) And praying. I once prayed. In Italy. (*Pause. Shrugs:*) And all, they say the judging's come. So why should we be caring? Didn't sweet Jesu say he'd come again to save the wretched poor? Let's go.

Exit DICCON. WILLIAM *follows. One of* HAM*'s legs move. Then the other. He sits up, still covered with the blanket. Takes it off. Looks round, sees the bodies. He stands, goes to them, lifts up their arms, confirms they're dead. In the midst of them, under an upturned basket, he finds a big, black, dead rat. He lifts it up by the tail.*

HAM. You too?

No response.

You too.

Blackout, rattling of drums, and lights on an old BISHOP *in the pulpit.*

BISHOP. Childer,
    A voice in Rama has been heard,
    Much weeping sounds throughout the mortal globe,
    Where joy abounded, dismal sorrow reigns
    The world is rid with plague.

And let me speak with voice on clear brass
That none of ye so deaf as cannot hear
This is a visitation on your pride,
God's patience has run out.

Slight pause.

Not all concur.

Slight pause.

Some say it is but Kings and courtiers are struck down
And that the poor and humble folk are spared
To live a thousand years of earthly bliss
Before the Wrathful Day.
Returning to that Golden Age,
It pleased our God Omnipotent to look upon.

Slight pause.

But they forget.
Ay, what?
Old Adam and his sin.
That laid on men, by men, the yoke of servitude,
Creating order, station and degree
In consequence of that old Eden evil, and
It's just and needful remedy
That selfish pride should not like chaos run amok,
And break down nature's ditch.

Pause.

Some others speak of Job, and say
That like that goodly man
At last all shall be unto ye restored
Yea fourty-fold
And that the pestilence is but a test
From Satan, that the world
For but a passing season must endure.

Slight pause.

O foolishness. O fond simplicity.

Slight pause.

For Job bore such a weight of righteousness,
Such heaviness of virtue, that were made light as air
One thousandth part of it, not one of you could lift.

Pause.

No, childer, think instead of hell.
And hear my solemn fantasy:
That and imagine ye a mount of sand,

As large as all the universe,
And each an hundred thousand year,
One grain is taken of it,
At last, the mountain will be flat.

Slight pause.

But in that time hell's torments will be less
By not a jot.
And ending will no nearer be than when the first grain took.
O, and the damned were told it were,
Hell's ovens all would shake at their rejoicing.

Pause. Huge.

So tremble. Tremble at this visiting!
Pray, weep, moan, curse youselves!
Talk not of a new age or the end of time,
But Old Nick waiting with his furnace stoked!
The reaping's come, the sharpest scythe is whet,
The grapes are ripe, and cast into the press.
And none is spared!

Blackout.

Scene Five

A WOMAN *singing, wordlessly. Her song goes on throughout
the scene.*
Lammas Eve. Light fades up on JOHN, *a grey friar, kneeling on a
round mat, surrounded by open books, praying. A* READER *with
the Bible.*

SINGER. And John the grey friar at the dead of night,
    When graves are left and howling are the damned,
    Kneels in his coldest of cold cells contrite,
    Dreams of an age before the sin of man:
    When was no need for law or punishment,
    The earth itself bore fruit, not sown or ploughed,
    And great with groaning good each tree was bent,
    And wine and nectar in each river flowed;
    Before foul greed was born into the world,
    To set a price on love and joy and mirth;
    And avarice our golden one-ness spoiled,
    And made division of the very earth.
    But reading of this age before man's sin,
    The grey friar asks: Could it not come again?

READER. And I saw in the right hand of him that sat on the
    throne a book written within and on the backside, sealed with
    seven seals. And I saw when the lamb opened one of the seals,

and I heard, as it were the noise of thunder, one of the four beasts saying, come and see.

A white-clad MONK, *with a long white train, carrying a crown, enters. He puts the crown on his head, takes the train from off his neck, and ties it to* JOHN's *left hand, as:*

And I saw, and behold a white horse: and he that sat on him had a bow; and a crown was given unto him: and he went forth conquering, and to conquer.

JOHN. Father forgive them, for they know not what they do.

READER. And when he had opened the second seal, I heard the second beast say, come and see.

A red-clad MONK *enters with a sword. He strikes* JOHN, *takes off his red train, and ties it to* JOHN's *right hand, as:*

And there went out another horse, that was red, and power was given to him that sat thereon to take peace from the earth, and that they should kill one another: and there was given unto him a great sword.

JOHN. Woman, behold thy son: son, behold thy mother.

READER. And when he had opened the third seal, I heard the third beast say, come and see.

A black-clad MONK *enters with a glass of wine in one hand and a small loaf of bread in the other.* JOHN *reaches out towards them. The* MONK *pours the wine on the floor and crushes the loaf in his hand, so the crumbs fall. Then he ties the black train round* JOHN's *waist as:*

And I beheld, and lo a black horse; and he that sat on him had a pair of balances in his hand. And I heard a voice in the midst of the four beasts say, A measure of wheat for a penny, and three measures of barley for a penny; and see thou hurt not the oil and the wine.

JOHN. I am thirsty.

READER. And when he had opened the fourth seal, I heard the voice of the fourth beast say, come and see.

A pale-clad MONK *enters holding a baby's skeleton, and ties his train round* JOHN's *neck, as:*

And I looked, and behold a pale horse; and his name that sat on him was Death, and Hell followed with him. And power was given unto them over the fourth part of the earth, to kill with sword, and with hunger and with death, and with the beasts of the earth.

JOHN. O God, O God, why hast thou forsaken me?

Taking JOHN *as the centre of a compass, the* WHITE MONK
*goes east, stretching the train out so it runs from his hand to
the side.*

READER. And when he had opened the fifth seal, I saw under
the altar the souls of them that were slain for the word of
God, for the testimony which they held:

The RED MONK *goes west.*

And they cried with a loud voice, saying, How long, O Lord,
Holy and True, doest thou not judge and avenge our blood on
them that dwell on the earth?

The BLACK MONK *goes north.*

And white robes were given unto every one of them; and it
was said unto them, that they should not rest yet for a little
season, until their fellow-servants also and their brethren,
that should be killed as they were, should be fulfilled.

The PALE MONK *goes south.*

JOHN. Verily I say unto you, today shalt thou be with me in
paradise.

The MONKS *ripple the trains.*

READER. And I beheld when he had opened the sixth seal, and,
lo, there was a great earthquake; and the sun became black as
sackcloth of hair, and the moon became as blood: And the
heavens departed as a scroll when it is rolled together; and
every mountain and island were moved out of their places:

Three skeletons, in the costumes of the KNIGHT, *the* BISHOP
and the LORD *descend a little from the flies and hang above*
JOHN.

And thus I saw the horses in the vision, and by these three was
the third part of men killed, by the fire, and by the smoke,
and by the brimstone: And the kings of the earth, and the
great men, and the rich men, and the chief captains, and the
mighty men, and every bondman, and every freeman, hid
themselves in the dens and in the rocks of the mountains.

JOHN. It

READER. And said to the mountains and rocks, fall on us, and
hide us from the face of him that sitteth on the throne, and
from the wrath of the Lamb.

JOHN. Is

READER. For the great day of his wrath is come; and who shall
be able to stand?

JOHN. Finished —

The MONKS *drop the trains and exit. The skeletons rise again. A gold light falls on* JOHN.

READER (*quieter*). And when he had opened the seventh seal, there was a silence in heaven about the space of half an hour.

JOHN. Father —

READER. And I looked, and, lo, a lamb stood on the Mount Sion, and with him a hundred fourty and four thousand, which were redeemed from the earth.

JOHN. Father —

READER. And I, John, saw the holy city, new Jerusalem, coming down from God out of heaven, prepared as a bride adorned for her husband.

JOHN. Father —

READER. And I heard a great voice out of heaven saying, Behold, the tabernacle of God is with men, and he will dwell with them, and they shall be his people, and God himself shall be with them, and be their God.

JOHN. Father —

READER. And God shall wipe away all tears from their eyes; and there shall be no more death, neither sorrow, nor crying, neither shall there be any more pain: for the former things are passed away.

JOHN. Father —

READER. And he that sat upon the throne said, 'Behold, I make all things new.

The singing builds up. And JOHN *stands, still holding the baby skeleton.*

JOHN. Father. Into thy hands I commend my spirit.

Blackout, the music continues.

Scene Six

Music cuts out and lights. June 1948. DR HENDERSON *stands in front of the altar, looking at the cross. He's in his mid-30s.* HILDA, *who's about the same age, wearing slacks and a sweater, enters with a stack of chairs. She starts to distribute them, then notices* HENDERSON, *goes up to him, sees he's looking at the cross.*

HILDA. Beams. From the roof.

HENDERSON. What? Oh, I see.

Pause.

Woodworm?

HILDA (*smiles*). No, a bomb, in '44. Missed the works, got three slum streets and the vestry. Still a ruddy great hole in the ceiling.

Pause.

John left it as it was, and put that up. Kind of memento mori.

HENDERSON. Yes.

Slight pause.

John who?

HILDA (*surprised he didn't know*). Hammond. The vicar.

HENDERSON. Oh.

Pause. HILDA *smiles, then goes and distributes chairs. A few moments.*

Excuse me, are you from the theatre company?

HILDA. Yes?

HENDERSON. I'm Dr. Henderson. I'm supposed to be giving some sort of talk.

Slight pause. Then HILDA *realises.*

HILDA. Oh, yes, I'm sorry. Of course. Edmund told me.

HENDERSON (*patiently*). Edmund?

HILDA. Sorry. Edmund Wolfe. The author of the play. I'm Hilda.

They shake hands.

HENDERSON. How do you do?

Pause. HENDERSON *looks at his watch.*

HILDA. I'm afraid people are always late in this business.

HENDERSON (*smiles, then:*) Can I give you a hand?

HILDA. Oh, thanks.

They distribute the chairs. Pause.

HILDA   }   How long have you —
HENDERSON } (*simultaneously*).   Could you tell me a —

HILDA. Sorry, go on.

HENDERSON. Oh, I was just going to ask, about the play, really.
I wasn't told very much.

HILDA. Well, it's all to do with the anniversary, I think. That's
where Edmund and John got the idea.

HENDERSON. The anniversary?

HILDA. The Black Death came to England six hundred years
ago.

HENDERSON. A commemoration.

HILDA. That's right. To the month, actually. Depending on your
historian. July, 1348, the plague came to England.

HENDERSON. The play's on in July?

HILDA. Opens on the fifth, God help us. Look, I'm so sorry
people aren't —

HENDERSON. The fifth?

HILDA. Yes. Why?

HENDERSON. No, just an odd coincidence, that's all.

HILDA (*smiles*). I see.

Pause.

In what respect?

HENDERSON. Well —

Snap blackout.

Act Two

Scene One

Lights on exactly the same position as the end of Act One. Enter HAMMOND, *briskly. He wears a clerical collar, and is in his late 30s.*

HAMMOND. Dr Henderson?

HENDERSON. That's right.

HAMMOND. John Hammond, how do you do.

HENDERSON (*shaking hands*). Hello.

HAMMOND (*to* HILDA). Where is everyone?

HILDA. Late, is where everyone is.

HAMMOND (*to* HENDERSON). Oh, I'm sorry.

HENDERSON. It really doesn't —

Enter NEVILLE, *late 30s, and* NORMAN, *early 30s.*

NORMAN. Good evening, all.

HAMMOND. Speak of two devils.

HILDA. Hello, you two, come and meet the doctor.

NORMAN. What me, in my state of health?

NEVILLE. It's being so cheerful keeps her going. Hello, doctor. I'm Neville.

As HENDERSON *shakes hands:*

HILDA. You'll have to forgive them, doctor. They've both got a touch of the harpics.

NORMAN. What?

HILDA. Clean round the bend.

NORMAN *and* NEVILLE *nudge each other in appreciation of the joke as enter* HARRY, *aged 30, good looking, smoking a pipe and wearing bicycle clips. During the following* NEVILLE *sits, starts going through his script.*

HARRY. Hello, all. (*He sits and takes his clips off.*) Guvnor not in yet?

HAMMOND. Er, Harry . . .

HARRY. Yes, padre?

HAMMOND. House of worship, Harry.

A moment before HARRY *realises.*

HARRY. Oh, I'm sorry. (*He puts his pipe out.*)

HILDA. Doctor, this is Squadron Leader Harry Morgan.

HARRY (*stands*). Pleased to meet you, sir.

HENDERSON (*shakes hands*). Hello.

HILDA. Harry's our tame D.F.C.

HARRY. Oh, Hilda, for Christ's sake —

NEVILLE (*looks up from his script*). Um — house of worship, Harry.

Slight hiatus.

HAMMOND (*to cover*). Who are we missing, Hilda?

HILDA. Well —

Enter AGGIE, who's 24, and FRANK, late 20s.

AGGIE. Sorry. Bus. Are we the last?

HILDA: No, there's still George and Edmund.

AGGIE. Oh, well . . . (*She sits, takes out her script.*)

NORMAN (*conspiratorially, to AGGIE*). New hair-do, Aggie?

AGGIE. That's right, Norman. How clever of you to notice.

HAMMOND. Frank, come and meet Dr. Henderson.

FRANK (*towards HENDERSON*). Oh, yes, of course —

Enter WOLFE, stridently. He is in his mid-50s and a hurry.

WOLFE. Good evening, everyone. I am covered with shame, I bow, I scrape, I am, with Tennyson, wild with all regret. Dr Henderson.

HENDERSON. That's right.

WOLFE. We will waste no more of your valuable time. Everyone be seated please. More — light. (*He strides off into the vestry.*)

HILDA (*to HENDERSON*). Edmund.

HENDERSON. Ah.

The COMPANY *get seated. More lights come on. Re-enter* WOLFE.

WOLFE. Right. That's better. Doctor, have you met everyone?

HENDERSON. Well, more or less . . .

WOLFE. That's splendid. Well. The good doctor has very
generously agreed to give us some medical background on
bubonic plague. Most of you die of it, so you may as well
know of what you are dying. Now, do you want to —

HENDERSON. I thought, I'd just run through the basic facts and
then, answer any questions . . .

WOLFE. Just what I was about to suggest. Splendid.

> WOLFE *sits, leaving* HENDERSON *the only one standing. He
> decides to sit. He refers to notes.*

HENDERSON. Well. Simply, what is now called the Black Death
is a form of bubonic plague, as you said. And it is caused by
the bacillus *pesteurella pestis,* which is passed on from infected
rats to men by way of fleas. In simple bubonic plague, I'll
describe the complications in a minute, the flea is called
xenopsylla cheopsis, and the rat is a big black chap called
rattus rattus.

> GEORGE *has entered. He is mid-to-late 20s, untidy and lost-
> looking. All turn to him.*

NEVILLE. Evening, George.

GEORGE. I was — reading, in the library, and um, my watch,
seemed to stop, I'm —

HILDA. Come and sit down, George.

GEORGE. Right. (*He sits. Slight pause. To* WOLFE:) Sorry.

WOLFE (*smiles*). It's all right, George.

> (*To* HENDERSON:) Do carry on, please.

HENDERSON. Well, as I say, basically, disease of rats passed on
to man by fleas. Now. There are three types of plague. Simple
bubonic is characterised by swollen lymphatic glands, called
buboes, in the armpit and groin, and subcutaneous
haemorrhages that blotch the skin. Very painful, after about
five days, buboes burst, victim dies. Number two is
septicaemic plague, when the bacilli get into the blood. The
flea in this case is the *pulex irritans,* which doesn't need rats
and lives on men. Very quick, kills before the buboes form.
Number three, most virulent, is pneumonic plague. Effectively,
when the bubonic victim catches pneumonia, his lungs are
infected, he coughs blood, spraying the bacilli into the air,
thus spreading the disease directly, man to man. It's when this
form becomes prevalent that the pestilence ceases to be merely
epidemic and becomes pandemic.

> *Slight pause.*

Is that all clear?

COMPANY (*variously*). Oh yes, absolutely, utterly clear, yes, no problem.

HENDERSON. Well, good. That's the nitty gritty, anyway. So, any questions . . .?

Pause.

WOLFE. Anyone?

Pause.

NEVILLE. Pandemic, doctor.

HENDERSON. Yes?

NEVILLE. What does pandemic mean, doctor.

HENDERSON. It means general, prevalent over a whole country or even continent, as opposed to epidemic which is much more localised.

NEVILLE. General. Prevalent. Fine.

Pause.

WOLFE. Anyone else?

AGGIE. Did they know, about the rats causing it?

HENDERSON. No, they didn't. And it's important to remember we're not talking about sewer rats, George Orwell territory. *Rattus rattus* is a sleek, rather handsome, friendly sort of chap.

AGGIE. So what did they think caused it?

HENDERSON. Well, you name it. The most popular theory was that it was carried in the air, a kind of vapour. There was an Arab physician, (*He checks a note.*) Ibn Khatimah, if that's how he's pronounced, who argued that at the centre of this cloud you couldn't breathe, or burn a light. And then . . . Galen of Permagus, who was the classical authority, he thought it came from marshes and ponds, and there were various other theories . . . One had it that it was in the eyes, quite literally, that looks could kill.

FRANK. Did they treat it, the doctors?

HENDERSON. Well, yes, in a rather ineffectual way. There were lots of potions and folk remedies, closer to magic than medicine, most of them — not that that's exclusively medieval, of course . . . Oh, there's one prescription I thought might give you an idea . . . (*He reads.*) Take one ounce of best gold, plus eleven ounces of quicksilver, dissolve over a slow heat, let quicksilver escape, add 47 ounces of water or borage, keep airtight for three days over a fire, and drink. And then there were the usual bleedings, and leeches, and cauterization, and so on. Not the best time in history to be ill.

Pause.

Also, there was a certain fatalism, which is more of a religious question, but it didn't help the doctors . . . And, topically enough, medicine was self-restricted, too. Doctors weren't inclined to treat patients who might not live to pay them.

Pause.

GEORGE (*suddenly, intensely*). What do you think of Malthus, doctor?

HENDERSON. What?

GEORGE. The theory that it had to happen, that plague and famine and war are necessary, from time to time, when there's overpopulation, that they're necessary forces, to, control, what do you think of that, as a theory?

HENDERSON. I think it's abominable.

GEORGE. Good, good; that's all I wanted to ask.

Pause.

HAMMOND. Why do you think it was so extensive?

HENDERSON. Well, the reasons I've said, really . . .

HAMMOND. No, I was thinking of things like, greater freedom of movement?

HENDERSON. Well, yes, that's not medical of course, but yes.

HAMMOND. A larger volume of trade . . .

HENDERSON. Yes, that's the same —

HAMMOND. People concentrated in towns and cities . . .

HENDERSON. Yes, yes, certainly.

HAMMOND. Progress, in fact.

Pause.

HENDERSON. I'm not quite sure —

WOLFE And, of course, the worst thing to do, wasn't it, was to try and help, because if you did, if you befriended a sufferer, you were liable to catch it, whereas, if you shut your doors, and watched them die, in the street, alone, then you and a thousand others might be saved. I suppose that's true, isn't it.

Pause.

HENDERSON. Well —

Pause.

AGGIE. Can we cure the plague?

HENDERSON. Yes. Warfarin kills rats, DDT kills fleas, and antibiotics cure the thing itself.

Pause.

HARRY (*to* WOLFE, *suddenly*). What did you mean by that?

WOLFE. Mean by what, Harry?

HARRY. About the worst thing to do.

Pause.

WOLFE. Well. I think the point that both John and I were making, in different ways, and George too, in an oblique fashion, is that civilisation, which claims to eradicate our friendly, equine buddies, plague, hunger, war, has in fact perhaps tended to encourage them, that easier communications, reliance of cities on imported food, armaments technology, have not eliminated but made more deadly those forces of destruction . . . (*To* HENDERSON:) Mm?

HENDERSON. Is that a question?

WOLFE. The punctuation is optional. But, um, you said yourself the medical profession hardly comes through the plague with all flags flying.

HENDERSON. No, no, and I'd agree with your implication, too: that even now, doctors are often ignorant, and won't admit it, arrogant, without cause, and avaricious: then, as now, not only friends in need, but friends in need of money; I'd admit all that, quite freely.

WOLFE. Physicians, heal thyselves?

HENDERSON. Well, yes, indeed . . . Could I ask, while we're on the subject, Mr Wolfe, was it intentional that your play should open on the date the National Health Act comes into force?

Pause.

WOLFE. Shall we say, it was a happy coincidence.

COMPANY *look surprised.*

Any more questions?

Pause.

Right. We won't keep you any longer. Our heartfelt gratitude. Company, ten minutes, then act two.

HILDA. Can I have a hand with the chairs?

WOLFE. And can Hilda have a hand with the chairs.

All stand. WOLFE goes slightly apart, with HENDERSON. HILDA and one or OTHERS start shifting the chairs. During the following, all but WOLFE and HENDERSON go.

WOLFE. I take it, from what you said, that you espouse the minority view in your profession?

HENDERSON. Well, yes. . . . But it's not so much a minority. It's always the biggest wallets make the most noise. Easy if you're an underworked consultant in Mayfair, spend your time lobbying the Ministry of Health. Harder if you're a South Wales GP with twice the number of patients to cope with.

WOLFE. You think they'll go in?

HENDERSON. Sure to. Only niggling 'cos it's Labour.

WOLFE. No misgivings? Nationalising hospitals?

HENDERSON. I think, really, most people would prefer to see the hospitals financed by the state, rather than by whist drives and flag days, don't you?

WOLFE. I meant, professional independence.

HENDERSON. You know, there's odd double standards, about essential services. The chairman of the BMA tells Bevan: you need the doctors, we have the doctors — and he trots out a list of concessions as long as your arm. But when it's you need the dockers, we have the dockers, then Attlee slaps on Emergency Powers and sends the troops in.

WOLFE. What a vision. The paras landing on the roof of Barts.

HENDERSON. I take it you've little faith in the prospects of the NHS.

WOLFE. Well, not in itself . . . But it's just administration, isn't it. The issue's not the coupon's surely. It's what the food's like, mm?

HENDERSON. Well, not exactly . . . I think you'll find they're more related than that . . . (*He glances at his watch.*) But I must go.

WOLFE. Of course. It's been most useful.

HENDERSON. Good. I look forward to seeing it.

WOLFE. Well, you can read it if you like.

HENDERSON. Thanks. I would.

WOLFE gives him a script.

WOLFE. Subject to alteration without notice, as they say. Well, goodbye for now.

HENDERSON. Goodbye.

Exit HENDERSON. Pause. WOLFE rubs his neck.
Enter HAMMOND.

WOLFE. Bright chap. For a doctor.

HAMMOND. Mm.

Pause.

Well, what's the verdict?

WOLFE. Delicately put. But not a chance.

HAMMOND. I see.

Pause.

Any idea how long?

WOLFE shakes his head.

Hamburg.

WOLFE. Indirectly, yes. It's academic, anyway.

Pause.

I get this, funny stiffness, in the neck. And sleepy. That's why I was late. Just, fell asleep.

Pause.

HAMMOND. I had some news today. A letter, from my old associate.

WOLFE. It's true?

HAMMOND. It's true, yes.

Pause. HAMMOND sits on the altar steps.

Do you remember when the news came through, the siege of Leningrad was raised. I was in Farnborough, mucking about with little strips of foil, to blind their radar. And then, the news, of all that sacrifice, but real, not like the bomber crews, real sacrifice, courage, heroism, real, in that it was to build a better . . . Felt there was nothing, then, could not be done.

WOLFE. Before you found out what was, being done.

HAMMOND. Exactly.

Enter HARRY. WOLFE *looks at his watch.*

WOLFE. Ah. Act Two. Where's Hilda?

HAMMOND. Vestry.

WOLFE (*going to vestry*). Good, I want to try the masks today . . .

HARRY. Mr Wolfe, I wonder if I could have a word . . .

WOLFE. Not now, Harry. Afterwards. All right?

Exit WOLFE. HAMMOND *stands.*
Blackout.

Scene Two

Immediately, in the darkness, and continuing:

CHOIR. Kyrie eleison
      Christe eleison
      Kyrie, kyrie eleison

During the Kyrie, after a few moments, a procession, in dim, torch-light, from one end of the nave to the other: An ABBOT, *borne by* ACOLYTES. *It's so dark, we can't see the* ABBOT's *face. The smell of incense.*
Curtains at the end open, revealing a NOBLEMAN, *a* NOBLE-WOMAN *and their* ATTENDANTS. *Chairs and cushions. The whole atmosphere of a decadent parody of a mass, though clearly in a house, not a church. The whole scene formal, choreographed.*
The ABBOT *reaches the end, stands, is given a cup of wine, holds it up, as if for consecration.*
The Kyrie reaching its climax.
The ABBOT *turns. His face is a skull mask. He blesses the company.*
The Kyrie climaxes. Silence.
The ABBOT *suddenly rips off his hood and the skull mask. It's* HAM. *He grins at us.*

HAM. Old Player Ham
     Does as he çan
     Sports in the Holy, All-Hallows season
     As Abbot of Unreason

He drinks as spot on the SINGER, *who sings a couplet. During this, in a formal movement,* HAM *is sat down, his drink refilled, and the* COMPANY *sit around him, on cushions, as if paying court.*

SINGER. Sceptre and crown
   Tumble must down
   And in the dust be equal made
   With the poor crooked scythe and spade

*The scene freezes and lights cross-cut to the other end,
discovering the* LADY.

LADY. We tried to escape. We ran like the wind. But the wind
   was faster. We had to leave our carriage, walk along the
   plough-tracks to the house. A week, or two, of quietness.
   Now, my husband's growing pale.

Enter CLERK.

CLERK. Good morning, Madam. How's my uncle?

LADY. Tired.

CLERK. He mustn't sleep.
   Slumber of day, as sudden excitation,
   Are both a dangerous excess.
   He must employ his thoughts.
   I'll see to him.

Exit CLERK.

LADY. Employ his thoughts? On what. No business. Trade has
   died. The fields lie fallow, sheep and oxen running free, with
   no one tending them.

Cross-cut lights to HAM. *At each cross-cut to* HAM *the area
of light on him decreases.*

NOBLEWOMAN. Will you sing for us, Lord Abbot?

HAM. Indeed, my lady. All Abbots are good for, some say,
   singing. (*He sings:*)

   To God in heaven we complain —
   Kyrie eleison —
   That the priests cannot be slain —

COMPANY (*joining in*). Kyrie eleison

HAM. Now we see that God is just:

COMPANY. Kyrie eleison

HAM. For he's slain them all for us:

COMPANY. Kyrie eleison

And, again, spot on SINGER *for a couplet, as* HAM's *glass is
refilled, he is disrobed of some of his vestments, the*
COMPANY *changes its tableau.*

SINGER. And golden lads and girls all must,
    Like chimney sweepers, come to dust

Freeze scene and cross-cut to LADY. *Enter* CLERK.

CLERK. Lady, your husband —

LADY. Sick.

CLERK. There's nothing certain yet.

LADY. He's sick?

Pause.

How could he catch it here, seeing no one?

CLERK. There's little can protect us from the air.
    I'll try to bleed it out.

LADY. And that will help?

CLERK. Madam, each organ has its own emunctory,
    Through which the poison, entered through the pores,
    May drawn out be,
    From where the sickness may be lodged,
    The heart, the liver or the brain.
    The heart's emunctory is underarm,
    The liver's is the legs between,
    And of the brain, the throat.
    The blood is drawn, the sickness should abate.

He turns to go.

LADY. If he dies master, you'll inherit his estates.

CLERK. If you have no issue, madam, yes.

LADY. How could I have an issue.

Pause.

Can bleeding do him any good?

CLERK. It is the most our present science has.

Exit CLERK.

LADY (*to herself*). I said, can it do good?

Lights cross-cut to HAM, *who is becoming quite merry.*

NOBLEMAN. My Lord Abbot, a question.

HAM. Yes, my son.

NOBLEMAN. Plague rages through the land.

HAM. Indeed it does, my son.

NOBLEMAN. How can we counter it, my lord?

HAM. Three views, my son, three attitudes. Some say, flee, up all, and run away.

NOBLEMAN. Well, then?

HAM. Too many others are of that opinion, sir, the roads are all clogged up with folk, going all ways, belching and blowing and spitting all on each other, in short, a right health hazard, so I say, take care of fleeing, sir.

NOBLEMAN. And so, the second?

HAM. Well, there are those who argue for preventive remedy, for stillness, care of all activity, slow moving, hang the house around with burning woods, ash, juniper and vine; and aromatics, mastic, wood of aloes, amber and sweet musk.

NOBLEMAN. Well, then?

HAM. Too many others tend to that position, sir, all aromatics are in shortage, and you can't get musk for love nor money, so I say, take care of careful, odorous sobriety.

NOBLEMAN. The third?

HAM. Well, there's those inclining to abandonment, my son, to lush and black excess.

NOBLEMAN. Well, then?

HAM. A lot of that persuasion, too, not in itself a disadvantage, but there are hazards in this policy.

NOBLEMAN. What hazards?

HAM. Notably, hellfire, damnation and the racks of flame eternal, sir.

NOBLEMAN. Then what is your conclusion?

HAM. That, all in all, it is an ill time to be sick in, sir. But taking of the three, I'd go, on balance, for abandonment. For either road's as like to end up in the grave.

NOBLEMAN. That's well said.

HAM. Oh, I try to please, and if I don't, I'm pleased to try again.

NOBLEMAN. Then you are a philosopher.

HAM. If I'm not, God save me sir . . . And if I am, then God must save philosophy.

And as the COMPANY, *again, reform the tableau,* HAM *losing all but his surplice, a spot on the* SINGER.

SINGER. And Jack the Miller grinds small, small, small,
And the King's son of Heaven shall pay for it all . . .

Freeze scene and cross-cut to LADY. *Enter* CLERK, *coatless, bloody and furious.*

CLERK. My bleeding's done.

LADY. He's well.

CLERK. No, no.
>So neither may I be;
>And so the nearer you may stand to me,
>The nearer are to sickness.

LADY. But he's still alive?

CLERK. Oh, yes, what little comfort may he had
>I've stolen from him.
>But, for an hour or so, he'll live.

LADY. I want to see him.

CLERK. No.

LADY. I want to see him, if he's going to die.

CLERK. There's other remedies —

LADY. Yes, yes, in half an hour, but now, please go.

>*Exit* CLERK.

>So saw my husband. Told him of his death. But in death, life. And in the grave is victory. I tell my husband — sir, I am with child. No man else knows. Your lady is with child.

Lights cross-cut to HAM. HAM, *now drunk, is not immediately aware of what the* NOBLEWOMAN *and her* ATTENDANT, *are up to as they move in closer to him.*

NOBLEWOMAN. Lord Abbot, you said that if we live a life of pleasure, we'll be damned.

HAM (*pouring himself a glass of wine*). True, madam.

NOBLEWOMAN. But if we live a pious, sober life, we're saved?

HAM (*drinking*). Not true, madam.

NOBLEWOMAN. And why not?

HAM. Well, lady, we are taught that with no priests to tell us and instruct us, all men are beasts and sinners, as in Adam's time. And all the priests are fled or dead.

NOBLEWOMAN. Then aren't we better, being virtuous without them?

HAM. No, no, for if we don't sin, without their counsel, then we spit on scripture, and we must be damned. And further, as this is, they say, God's punishment on universal vice, then to be good, and thus deny his judgement, seems like blasphemy. So either road is broad, and straight, and leads direct to hell. (*He drinks.*)

NOBLEWOMAN (*pouring him more wine*). So then, Lord Abbot, you must give dispensation to excess.

HAM (*a bit doubtful*). Well, yes, my lady.

NOBLEWOMAN. You said so, my lord.

HAM. O, yes, indeed, as a matter of theology . . .

NOBLEWOMAN. But practically, my lord, a dispensation to all forms of sin?

HAM (*nervous*). O, yes, so, all available, all sins, venial and mortal, deadly and original —

NOBLEWOMAN. Name them.

HAM. Name which?

NOBLEWOMAN. The deadly sins available.

HAM. O, why, there's seven of them . . . gluttony — and wrath — and pride — and envy — sloth — and avarice.

NOBLEWOMAN. That's only six, my lord.

HAM. Why then there's gluttony, wrath, pride — and envy, sloth, avarice — and wrath.

NOBLEWOMAN. You said wrath twice, my lord.

HAM (*swallowing*). Why then there's pride, gluttony, wrath, sloth, and envy, avarice and, lech —

NOBLEWOMAN *suddenly kisses* HAM, *who breaks free.*

HAM. Madam, I'm your servant —

NOBLEWOMAN. Then, master, aren't I your mistress? Mm?

HAM *is assaulted, then bold, spot on* SINGER, COMPANY *reform tableau,* HAM *left in his Act One clothes.*

SINGER. And lovely girls who get a green gown,
Lie with many, die alone.

Freeze and cross-cut to LADY. *Enter* CLERK.

CLERK. You stayed too long. He's dead.

LADY. Then you have work to do.

CLERK. What work?

LADY. For the estate that's fallen to you, master.

Pause. CLERK *exits.*

The Lady thus keeps secret she's with child,
The Clerk inherits all her husband's gold.
The Lady doth discharge her due and right,
That she may flee and find her gentle knight.

Exit LADY *as cross-cut lights to* HAM. *Now no more than a spot on his face.*

HAM. What about this plague, then, eh? (*He chuckles.*) Eh? What about this plague? (*He chuckles.*) Then eh? (*Pause.*)Eh? (*He notices the silence.*) Eh?

He takes a torch, goes to one of the COMPANY, *who's dead, their face a grisly death-mask.*

HAM. Ah.

He goes on round. All are dead, death-masked. Then to the NOBLEWOMAN, *sitting upright, staring.*

Mistress?

A black stain appears on the NOBLEWOMAN's *dress, at the neck. It spreads down her body.* HAM *watches. Then he has an idea. He goes round the* COMPANY, *taking hats, clothes, accessories, props from them. He sets them up in front of him, as if for some kind of performance. Perhaps he moves a body into a better position as audience. Then, when ready, he raps the floor for silence, has a little cough, and begins. Through the play, he uses the props he's collected to differentiate the characters. The play starts at an even pace, then speeds up.*

Open the door and let us in
We hope your favour we shall win
We'll do our best to please you all
Each one of us, from short to tall
If you believe not what I say
Enter the King of Egypt — clear the way!

(KING.)
I am the King of Egypt as plainly does appear
(SABRA.)
I am his daughter Sabra, a chastely maiden fair
(GEORGE.)
I am Prince George who did the scaly dragon slaughter
(KING.)
And married was unto the King of Egypt's daughter
(TURK.)
And I am the Black Prince Paradise, the Turkish Knight

Come of fair Araby for you to fight.

He pauses for breath. Changes costume, realises he's still the
TURK, *changes back.*

I come to kill St George my foe
When he's done in back home I'll go.
Be he a Christian, or he wear a crown
Mahummet shall him quickly strike well down.
(SABRA.)
O George pray do not fight lest he you kill!
(GEORGE.)
No I mun stop this black-faced infidel!
(SABRA.)
O George I pray again, you mun be slain!
(GEORGE.)
Not so to do would be a greater blain!
(SABRA.)
O very well.
(GEORGE.)
Then hark at you —
(TURK.)
And you —
(GEORGE.)
And you again —
(TURK.)
Thrust I you through
A ten time ten —
(GEORGE.)
Then nigh am I to die,
(TURK.)
Tis true!
(SABRA.)
O George look what it is you do!

He stops for another breather.

(KING.)
Prince George has fallen
(SABRA.)
O my lover's slain
(GEORGE.)
I'm dead!
(KING.)
So who can we call on
(SABRA.)
Who would cure the pain
(GEORGE.)
That's in my head?

(KING.)
Is there a doctor to be found,
All ready, nearby at hand
To cure this deep and deathly blow
And make the champion stand?

HAM *looks round desperately for a prop, finds a cap, puts it on.*

(DOCTOR.)
I am a doctor
(KING.)
Doctor?
(DOCTOR.)
Ay.
(KING.)
From whence and why?
(DOCTOR.)
For whither of the world around
For why to cure him on the ground.
(KING.)
What can you cure?
(DOCTOR.)
O any diseases
Freezes and sneezes whatever ye pleases
The stitch, itch, the ague, scratch, the palsy and gout,
The murrain within and the murrain without,
The vapids, the vapours, the blight of the lame,
And for half a pence more, the dead raise up again.
(KING.)
And what is your fee?
(DOCTOR.)
A seven pound is all my fee,
The money lay you down,
But as 'tis such a rogue as he
I'll do for half a crown.
So drink this jug —
(GEORGE.)
Slurp slurp glug glug —
(DOCTOR.)
And stand to claim your crown!

HAM *stands as* GEORGE *and takes another breather.
As* SABRA.

My son! My son is elevated!
(KING.)
Look! Lo! My love is levitated!

HAM *corrects himself.*

(KING.)
My son! my son is elevated!
(SABRA.)
Look! Lo! My love is levitated!
(TURK.)
Then must I fight Prince George once more
(DOCTOR.)
Where is my fee?
(GEORGE.)
Then let's to war
(DOCTOR.)
Thus am I cheated?
(TURK.)
Then I you clout –
(GEORGE.)
I flout –
(TURK)
I lout you true –
(GEORGE.)
So in and out
I thrust you through.
(TURK.)
Again? Then fain I'm slain
No doubt!
(GEORGE.)
So pray your last with fear devout!
(TURK.)
So thus I die
(DOCTOR.)
Where is my fee?
(GEORGE.)
You scurvy rogue, begone!
(SABRA.)
With joy I cry
(GEORGE.)
Please marry me
(KING.)
So thus our tale is done.

Very breathlessly, to finish:

Godbless you sir afore your roaring fire,
Godbless your mistress in her fine attire,
None in your cheery house would we to chide,
And ye but bless us on this Christmastide.

Pause. Helpfully, to AUDIENCE:

It's a play for Christmas, see.

*He falls on to his bottom. He pours a glass of wine.
He starts to chuckle as lights fade to blackout.*

Scene Three

KNIGHT (*calling in the darkness*). Diccon! Diccon!

Lights on the nave area. On the ground three bodies. HAM sits where he was, but all his props and the rest of the scene has gone. He stares. WILLIAM and DICCON stand, looking across the area at the KNIGHT, who's just entered.

KNIGHT. Diccon. (*He goes to DICCON, nearly tripping over a body.*) Three days I've searched you, sir!

DICCON. Well, now you've found me.

KNIGHT. I'm called to war, in France. You coming?

Pause.

DICCON. No, sir.

KNIGHT. No?

DICCON. Save I get double wages, sir.

KNIGHT. What?

DICCON. You heard, sir.

KNIGHT. Diccon!

DICCON. Double, sir.

KNIGHT. I'll find another rascal then.

DICCON. Do that.

KNIGHT. I shall.

DICCON. If you can find one, sir.

Pause.

KNIGHT. A half again.

DICCON. No, sir.

KNIGHT. That's all I can —

DICCON. Then have you a good journey, sir. (*To WILLIAM:*) Come on, William. Each one should have a purse on him, left for his burial, and he don't, we leave him.

They each go to a body, find a purse, and start stripping them of what looks valuable. KNIGHT looking on in horror.

KNIGHT. What are you doing?

DICCON (*stops work*). Someone's got to, sir. Time for all to soil their souls, and they want to keep 'em.

Slight pause.

Where's your lady, sir?

KNIGHT. Lady? What, lady.

Exit. DICCON *shrugs, back to work.*

WILLIAM (*holding up an arm to show a shirt-sleeve*). What about this, eh?

DICCON (*feels it*). No. Shoddy. No market for it, see.

VOICE (*off*). Morning, Diccon!

DICCON. Morning, Master Bull!

BULL, *a sexton, and another* SEXTON, *pull in a cart.*

BULL. All done, are they?

DICCON. Nearly.

BULL. Good, good. Come on, you, get loading.

The SEXTON *goes and pulls a body, towards the cart. Making rather heavy weather. During this,* WILLIAM *taking another body to the cart.* BULL *to* DICCON, *they share money and booty.*

BULL. Cold enough to freeze your plums off, eh, Diccon?

DICCON. Aye, I'd thought, too cold even for plague, now.

BULL. O no, fear not, the plague's a hardy beast. Not like some of us, who flake out at the first whiff of privation. (*To* SEXTON:) Eh, boy?

SEXTON *scowls.* WILLIAM *gives him a hand to get his body on the cart. Then* DICCON *goes and helps with the other body.* BULL *counting. During all this:*

DICCON. Eh, did you hear, Master Bull, so short on burial ground in France, the Pope has consecrated all the River Rhone. So folks just drop 'em in.

BULL. Eh, I hope there's no talk of that here . . .

DICCON. Most saintly fish in all the world, they swim in liquid paradise . . .

Enter, as if pushed, the SINGER, *as a* PRIEST, *followed by* BUNG, *a third sexton.*

BULL. Ah, Master Bung.

BUNG. Found one.

WILLIAM (*to* DICCON). What's a priest for?

DICCON. They pay for Christian burial, that's what they're going to get.

BUNG. He says he'll do ten requiescats for a penny, and full requiem for two and hapence.

BULL (*to* SINGER). Let's hear you, then.

SINGER. Libera me domine, de morte aeterna in die illa —

BULL. Enough, you'll do.

DICCON (*to* WILLIAM). Some of 'em just dress up as clergy, for the stipend, see.

BULL. Come, Master Bung.

He and BUNG *to another body, about to pick it up when they notice the* LADY *has entered.* ALL *stop work, look up.*

LADY. Sirs, I'm — sirs, I am looking for a knight.

Pause.

A green-dressed knight, that's back from France and Italy. Italy.

Slight pause.

And you've seen him, sirs —

BULL (*laughs*). No knights here, lady.

BUNG (*laughs*). Save endless night, mebbe.

BULL *doesn't get it so* BUNG *jabs him in the ribs.*

Endless — night.

BULL. O, aye . . .

They laugh merrily, as they pick up the body.

LADY (*to* WILLIAM). You've not seen him, sir, a green-dressed —

WILLIAM. Aye, we seen him.

Pause.

LADY. Where?

DICCON. He's gone. Run away. To escape the plague.

BUNG *and* BULL *loading the body on to the cart*

LADY. Thank you for telling me.

She turns to go.

WILLIAM. Lady, have you any with you?

LADY. No, sir.

WILLIAM. You can't be alone now, lady.

DICCON. William —

WILLIAM. We'll be your service.

BULL (*seeing* HAM). Now, what's this one, eh?

He and BUNG *to* HAM, *look at him, as:*

DICCON. William, we've enough to keep usselves —

WILLIAM. Or I'll be . . .

Slight pause.

LADY. Thank you, I —

BUNG. He dead?

BULL. I don't know. Ask him.

BUNG. Are you dead, sir?

LADY. I've nothing I can pay you.

DICCON. O, by our mother, William —

WILLIAM. That's no matter, lady.

> LADY *smiles at* WILLIAM, *who picks up his share of the booty, preparing to go, as:*

BUNG (*concluding*). Dead.

BULL. No purse.

BUNG. O, charity.

> *They make to pick* HAM *up.* HAM *suddenly lashes out at them, knocking* BULL *over.*

BULL. Wrong, Master Bung.

HAM (*shouts*). WHAT ABOUT THIS PLAGUE THEN EH?

> ALL *still, looking at him. He wipes his armpit and groin, in great pain.*

> Nothing you can do. Once there. The little, hardness. Hurting. O, pretend, an hour or so, not there. But — is. And grows and grows. Till, pop. Just hope, it's soon. (*A spasm of pain.*) You'd best keep away. All virtues deadly now, but charity is deadliest. O yes, charity's a killer, kindness kills and friendliness is fatal, yes — (*Shouts.*) ABOUT THIS PLAGUE THEN EH?

> *Pause.* HAM *is still.*

BULL (*getting up*). Mind gone. We'll pick him up tomorrow. Now, we go.

He pushes the SINGER, *who starts chanting, very badly.*
BULL, BUNG, SEXTON, SINGER *and the cart exit.*

SINGER. Libera me domine, de morte aeterna in die illa
tremenda: quando coeli movendi, sunt et terra —

They're gone. LADY, *suddenly, to* HAM, *kneels, looks at
him.*

WILLIAM. No, leave him lady —

DICCON. Leave her, William, leave her and let's go —

LADY. There's nothing wrong with him.

Pause.

WILLIAM. What you mean?

LADY. Look. No tokens. Not a mark. He hasn't got the plague.

WILLIAM. Then why —

LADY. He thought he had. He's wrong.
It's in his mind.

WILLIAM *turns to* DICCON, *smiling.* DICCON *is staring at*
HAM.

WILLIAM. Diccon. Diccon?

DICCON (*surprised, himself, by the certainty of his sudden
decision*). I'm going.

WILLIAM (*smiling*). O, Diccon . . .

DICCON (*collecting his booty*). Going.

WILLIAM. Eh, Diccon, no, we'll be . . .

DICCON (*very hard*). Going. Of men dead in their mind.
Thinking they've plague when they've none.

Pause.

In Italy. One day. Venezia, we were. Whole mob of folk.
Crusaders, starving, in the name of God. So prayed, to him.
And he said, said, walk on. Walk on, my childer, to Jerusalem.

Slight pause.

There's naught but sea there, William. Walked into the sea.
A ten, a hundred, and a thousand, walked into the sea and
drowned. No reason, William. God's telling. God, Almighty
God.

WILLIAM. Eh, I thought you'd no time for God, Diccon.

DICCON. What else? Just fear.

Slight pause.

I ran then. Up the road, to France. Afore was my mind, went.
Afore I walked into the sea. I ran then, seeing dead minds,
and I'm running now.

He runs out. WILLIAM *doesn't know whether to follow.* HAM
comes to.

LADY. Good morning, master. You've been sleeping.

HAM. Sleep? Not dead?

LADY. No, no.

HAM. I'm not in hell? You're not the whore of Babylon?

LADY. No, no.

HAM. Well, then. Well — then. Eh?

Fade to Blackout.

Scene Four

ADVENT. *The stage is a church. A second* PRIEST *kneels at
the altar.*
WILLIAM, HAM, LADY *among the congregation. Psalm 38, the
third penitential, is sung, verses 1-10. From far away, early in the
psalm, we hear drumming. Nearer.* JOHN, *in a red robe, enters at
the back of the church, drumming. He slowly walks towards the
altar, drumming.* PRIEST *turns. At verse 10 of the psalm,* JOHN
throws his drum down. The psalm fades. Pause.

PRIEST. What do you want?

JOHN. Nothing. I have found what I want. I am here.

PRIEST. What do you mean?

JOHN. I want what I can find only here, in Christ's house. For
he came to preach the gospel to the poor, and I have come for
the poor, that you, as his servant, shall feed the hungry.

PRIEST *doesn't know what to say.*

For you, as I, have taken on the yoke of poverty, as did
the Apostles, who had all in common, and possessed no thing
of their own. We are hungry, then. Feed us.

PRIEST. There is nothing here.

JOHN. But, sir, there is. You are too modest.

*Takes the plate of the Host and the chalice from the altar
and lifts them up.*

Here! Here on God's table there is bread and wine.

PRIEST. That's —

JOHN *eats the Host and drinks the wine. Then he lays them in the centre of the aisle.*

JOHN. Now, eat — come — eat.

PRIEST. This is blasphemy —

JOHN. Come. Eat. You are hungry. There is no dread. I have eaten, I have drunk, and I am not struck down.

Silence.

Perhaps you are thirsty, not for wine, but for understanding of the visitation that has come. For you have heard your priests mumble of retribution, and yet you've seen the good struck down. And they have told you to come here, to church, for understanding, yet the plague goes on.

To the lectern.

But it's all written, in this old book.
Hear and understand.

He opens the Bible.

That there is spoken of a time when civil discord, wars and droughts, famines and tyrants shall oppress the world. That time is now. That there is spoken of a beast, the son of all perdition, who will rise in the appearance of a saint, and do the devil's work, enslave the earth. His name is Antichrist. That time is now. And the beast is carried on a great whore, who had laid with all the kings of the earth, deliciously, and sits on the waters of the world, which is the people of the world, and spreads her filth throughout the clear waters. This whore is Babylon. That time is now. That there is spoken of a time when Babylon shall suffer with all famines, and all curses, and all plagues, and it shall fall. And all the merchants of the world shall weep, O weep terribly, for no one buys their gold or silver, or their linen, or their ivory, or sheep, or souls of men. And the poor shall in their place live a thousand years of bliss. That time is now. (*To* WILLIAM:) Who is the Antichrist? Who is the whore?

WILLIAM. Aren't they to be born in the East?

JOHN. No. No. No. They are already here. He sits, the Antichrist. The whore lies already under him. (*Gently, explaining:*) The Antichrist is the priest of Rome, and Babylon's his church. The fat priest is he that wears the robes of innocence to hide his putrid nudity. His church it is that fornicates with all the kings and princes.

The PRIEST *rushes to* JOHN, *pulls him round.*

PRIEST. Who are you?

JOHN. I am the Baptist of the King that once was killed and
sleeps, waiting to rise with all the righteous ones. It's there —
it's in the book. You only have to read.

PRIEST. If you are what you say you are, if you are greater than
the church, show us a miracle.

*JOHN smiles. He takes from his belt a pouch. In it is powder,
which he pours in the shape of a circle around him. He takes a
candle, lights the powder, which flares round him.*

HAM. That's a miracle. Look, priest, that's a miracle.

JOHN. No. It's a trick. You could make that powder. I'll show
you a miracle.

He goes to the LADY, *takes her hand and leads her to the
centre.*

He asked me where I came from. But he's a wormy old man.
You ask me, in his place.

LADY. Where have you come from?

JOHN. Nowhere.

LADY. What are you?

JOHN. I am not.

LADY. Where do you lead?

JOHN. To untrammelled freedom.

LADY. What do you call that?

JOHN. When a man does only what he wants to do.
What do you want to do?

LADY. I want to find my love.

JOHN. Then you want paradise. And where is that? In Eden.
In old Adam's time. Before the stream of man was forded
from the sea of God. But it can join again, and mingle in the
clearest waters. We can make us innocent. Kiss me.

She kisses JOHN.

Guilty? Feel guilty?

LADY. No.

JOHN. Then there's a miracle. Look, you're clothed with the sun.
You are incorruptible. Look, there's a miracle.

The PRIEST *rushes out of the church.* JOHN *speaks quickly.*

JOHN. And now I can tell you the meaning. For the hordes are
not destroyed by God, but men. It's there. The hundred and
fourty and four thousand of the just who are to chain the
Antichrist. And where are they? Not in the East. But here.
Amongst the poor. Those who make the wheaten bread but
never chew it. Those who are robbed of labour, to maintain
the pomp of riches. For, know this, the plague is in their
purses. It is the rust of gold that burns their flesh like fire.
And let them puff themselves up as much as they will, these
tares, still they will go beneath the flail. For God's a reaper
and a leveller too. And they should howl. But you — no,
you won't howl. For as Isaiah says, you will drink at the
breast of consolation, as one whose mother comforts him,
so you shall be comforted in Jerusalem.

HAM. Where is it then?

JOHN. Again. It's here. When all is held in common, like the sky
and sea, as in old Adam's time, and each man has enough.

The BISHOP *has entered in full habit, carrying his crook,
at the back of the church. The* PRIEST *skulks behind him.*
JOHN *sees him.*

BISHOP. Leave my house.

JOHN. It is not your house. It is the house of God. It is our
house, for we are God.

BISHOP. That's the most dreadful blasphemy.

JOHN. No, it's the best theology. For God is in each stone,
and every limb, as sure as in the Eucharist bread. All is divine.

BISHOP. Have you no thought of sin?

JOHN. How could I. For if we sin, then God sins. It is his work.
Nothing is sin except we think it so.

BISHOP. If God is all, then God is nothing.

JOHN. Yes, of course. We are God, so we have no need of him.

BISHOP (*to* WILLIAM). Sieze that man! I order you.

Pause.

WILLIAM. No sir, God save me.

BISHOP. He will not.

Pause.

Will none seize this man? Are you all blinded by the devil's
light?

Pause.

Then I must do God's work alone.

He raises his crook to strike JOHN. WILLIAM *suddenly stands, and knocks the* BISHOP *over.* WILLIAM, JOHN *and* LADY *are before the altar.* PRIEST *rushes to help the* BISHOP, *who pushes him away. The* BISHOP *stands, raises his crook again, and charges to* WILLIAM *etc., brings the crook crashing down on the altar. Lies on the steps.*

JOHN. So who will not follow me now? To the houses of the rich, to the fine mansions, to the marble halls. For see, I make all things new.

Pause. Blackout.

Act Three

Scene One

In the darkness:

JOHN. So who will not follow me now? To the houses of the rich, to the fine mansions, to the marble halls. For, see, I make all things new.

Lights. Same tableau as the end of Act Two but the ACTORS in their 1948 costumes, and ACTORS not in the scene standing watching. WOLFE stands.

WOLFE. Well done everybody. Just a couple of notes.

Tableau breaks. PEOPLE get chairs, or sit on steps, or stand. Amond the standees, HARRY.

Any lines, Hilda?

HILDA (*with the book*). Well, Neville got a bit snarled up in the middle of Saint George . . .

NEVILLE. Yes, I know. Sorry.

HILDA. And Aggie transposed a couple of speeches in scene one . . .

AGGIE. Did I?

HILDA. Mm. And George cut the church fornicating with all the kings and princes.

GEORGE. Where's that?

HILDA. Just after the fat priest hiding his putrid nudity.

GEORGE. Oh, yes . . .

WOLFE. Generally, I felt that was very good. Norman, bit slow towards the end of two, and Hilda, still a bit more lust?

HILDA, a look at NEVILLE.

The only other major thing is, um, Harry, I feel your performance generally, we all go through a dip, perhaps lacking in conviction . . . It needs a quality of, hard satire, which we had, but I think we're losing it. All right?

Slight pause.

HARRY. If you don't feel my performance is up to it, Mr Wolfe, I'm sure you can find an understudy.

Pause. WOLFE thrown. All surprised.

WOLFE. No, of course, I didn't mean that, Harry —

HARRY. I think perhaps I find it hard to come to terms with the material.

Pause.

WOLFE. What do you mean?

HARRY. The moral of your play, I'm not sure I'm in sympathy.

WOLFE. Harry, we go up in two weeks —

HARRY. Being used as a puppet, too, I think I find difficult to take.

WOLFE. What is this all about?

HARRY. Particularly by you.

Pause, he takes a letter from his pocket.

WOLFE. Harry, perhaps we could discuss this aft —

HARRY. Mr Wolfe, I have a friend who served in the Ministry of Information. According to him, the Ministry asked you to participate in the propaganda effort on the 21st of June 1940. On the 24th of June, you boarded the Queen Mary at Southampton, bound for the United States, from which you did not return until the 27th of December 1944.

Pause.

WOLFE. Yes.

HARRY *surprised, not quite the effect he expected.*

You think that was wrong?

HARRY. Wrong? I think with your talents, it was treachery.

WOLFE. You're so right.

Pause.

HILDA. Edmund, should we perhaps break, until —

WOLFE. But, what to do? One man, faced with that enormity. You're right, but what to do?

Pause.

HARRY. Mr Wolfe, I have studied your play. Like everyone involved, I've been somewhat mystified by it. Now I think I begin to see. You have used the plague as a symbol, of the war in which I fought, in which 360,000 Englishmen died, and which you watched from the safety of America.

Pause.

WOLFE. I knew Germany. And I knew the Nazis. And that Sunday, when the news came through, 'consequently we're at war with Germany,' I believed it was a noble thing, a war against those thugs, that thug, that gangster. (*Hard:*) An illusion which was rapidly dispelled.

HARRY. 360,000 people died for what you call —

WOLFE. Because it grew quite clear that we weren't fighting Nazis, we were fighting Germans. Once again. Fighting for influence, for markets, economic stamping-grounds, glossed with imagery of Empire, as we'd done in 1916, as I'd done, a sewer-rat, knee-deep in Europe's slops — you know the image, *All Quiet on the Western Front*, the film, the soldier who'd survived it all, just reaches from his cover for a flower . . . Bang. A waste. And all of those deaths, waste. And now the same old war again. And, yes, I said I'd watch the game this time, not play, just watch the score, five million, ten, fifteen, then twenty, thirty million, realised. The Great War's waste was nothing on this waste. This war would make all useless sacrifices of the past seem puny. This was waste upon a cosmic scale. The only hope was that the world would learn, and change. Resolve to end the rule of monsters — poverty and warfare and disease — create the New Jerusalem.

Pause.

What do we see now. Poverty, again, as in the thirties, now they call it wage restraint, austerity, but still — And war. A million bearing arms. And Greece. And Palestine. Berlin. Disease. We — now — what man has cured he makes . . .

Pause. WOLFE *seems in pain.*

But you can't see. You bind your eyes up with the union jack, whatever, you can't see. Jerusalem's not coming. Not on the agenda. Because there cannot be another lesson like this lesson, and if men won't learn from this they'll never learn. And then it ceases to be merely waste, refuse on the roadside, ugly but not pre-emptive of a better world. It blocks the road. Denies the new world. Becomes tragedy. That's what my play's about.

Pause.

AGGIE (*stands*). It was a butterfly.

WOLFE. What was a butterfly?

AGGIE. *All Quiet on the Western Front.* It was a butterfly, not a flower, he reached out for.

Pause.

I'm — going now, I think. Do some work on the lines. You coming, Frank?

FRANK. Yuh, sure.

    FRANK *and* AGGIE *exit. Pause.*

HARRY. In 1941, Mr Wolfe, I was one of a bomber crew of five. By 1943 —

WOLFE (*furious*). We can't create the new world when so many people think like you, believing that the way to build it is to fly a Lancaster to Dresden, find a line of refugees, and push the button.

HARRY. I find this most offensive, I'm afraid.

WOLFE. My heart is bleeding.

HARRY. And I therefore must —

WOLFE (*suddenly vague*). Oh, go away . . .

HARRY. Tender —

WOLFE. Please . . . go away . . .

    He walks, stumbling, away from the OTHERS, *and sits. Pause.*

GEORGE. I agree with what he said.

HARRY. You would.

HAMMOND (*stands*). All right. Hilda, what's the call tomorrow.

HILDA. Um, seven, for Act Three.

HAMMOND. Right.

    Pause.

NEVILLE (*stands*). Well, TTFN, all. Norm, d'you want to catch the pub?

NORMAN. Why, is it infectious?

NEVILLE. Come on, Norm.

    Exit NORMAN *and* NEVILLE. *Pause.* HILDA *to* WOLFE, *with a hard look at* HARRY *as she passes him.*

HILDA. Mr Wolfe, I'm sorry, but I do need to discuss the light plot for act three — (*Pause.*) Mr Wolfe. (*Pause.*) Mr Wolfe?

    WOLFE *falls over.*

    Oh gosh.

HAMMOND (*quickly, as he goes to* WOLFE). Hilda, have you got your car?

HILDA. Yes, what's —

HAMMOND. Can you take Edmund, now, to the hospital. Tell them it's a tubercular condition. I'll ring them, anyway.

HILDA. Yes, of course.

HAMMOND. George, give us a hand —

GEORGE, HAMMOND *joined by* HARRY, *lift up* WOLFE *and carry him out,* HILDA *follows. A few moments, then enter* HAMMOND, *going towards the vestry, followed by* HARRY.

HARRY. Padre.

HAMMOND. Yes?

HARRY. What is it.

HAMMOND. Tubercular meningitis. Increase of fluid in the skull, can't secrete, eventually it presses on the brain. It's a manifestation of TB.

HARRY. TB.

HAMMOND. Yuh, he picked it up in Hamburg. TB proper that is. He was working there, in 1945, among refugee children, in the slums. Or what the RAF had left of the slums. And he went to a sanitorium in England, and they thought they'd cured him, and they hadn't, and it re-emerged as tubercular meningitis, as I said and that is what it is.

HARRY. I'd no idea, of course . . .

HAMMOND. No, of course you hadn't.

HARRY. Is it curable?

Pause.

He will, it's curable?

Pause.

HAMMOND. I've got to phone the hospital now, Harry.

Exit HAMMOND *to vestry. Blackout.*

Scene Two

Mid-December. In the darkness, a hymn:

HYMN. Whoe'er to save his soul is fain
    Must pay and render back again
    His safety so shall he consult
    Help us, good lord, to this result.

Ply well the scourge for Jesus' sake
And God through Christ your sins shall take.
Woe! Usurer, though thy wealth abound
For every ounce thou makest, a pound
Shall sink thee to the hell profound.
Ye murderers and ye robbers all
The wrath of God on you shall fall.
Mercy ye ne'er to others show,
None shall ye find, but endless woe.
Had it not been for our contrition.
All Christendom had met perdition.

Light on a MASTER *of the Flagellants. He stands in a circle of light, in the same position as* JOHN *at the end of Act One. He wears a shirt and cap, both with red cross before and behind, and a long skirt. He carries a heavy scourge, with four leather thongs and metal spikes.*

MASTER. Welcome.
Welcome, you sinners to our brotherhood of Christ.
You've seen our marching, heard our solemn dirges,
And now are come.

Slight pause.

Then see. We stand. As in a circle. Silent. Bowed.
We stand in robes of innocence.
We strip our filthy bodies bare.

He rips off his shirt and throws it to the ground. His torso, chest and back are torn and bleeding.

Then down usselves we throw.
Down, to the ground, signing the world, and God,
By gesture, of our sins and infamy.

He walks to the edge of the light.

You brother hold three fingers to the air
Your face is set with shame.
You are a perjurer,
That is your crime.
You lie.

He beats the floor five times.

Howl, howl, howl, howl, howl.

Slight pause.

Now rise. Rise by the honour of pure martyrdom,
And henceforth guard 'gainst sin.

Moves.

You brother hide your face
And rub it in the slime
You signify adultery's your crime.
You fornicate.

He beats the floor five times.

Howl, howl, howl, howl, howl.

Slight pause.

Now rise. Rise by the honour of pure martyrdom,
And henceforth guard 'gainst sin.

Suddenly shouts.

All rise! All rise and hear the cause!

He takes a letter from his pocket.

For this I hold, this letter is the cause!
See, it shines with mystic light.
But know you what it is?

Pause.

This letter — bow and tremble, foulnesses —
This letter is from great Jerusalem
St Peter's church of Sion, there it came:
From — God.

Pause.

What does it say?

Pause.

It says that God Almighty and Omnipotent
Rages so furiously against the sin of men,
That plague and earthquake spent,
To curb their pride and wilfulness,
He had resolved each living thing to kill
And end the world in slaughter.

Pause.

But his hand was stayed.
For why?
Because his Holy Mother, and the saints
Begged him to stay his hand.

Pause.

For three and thirty years.
The span of Jesus' life on earth.
That's all.
Then shall the trumpet sound.

Pause.

Save but one thing.
That good enough is found in all the world
To make it worth to save;
That Brethren of the Cross shall three and thirty days
For three and thirty years
Three times a day
Make solemn imitation of his suffering
And they that bleed, they only shall be saved.

Pause. Loudly.

For only through unceasing suffering:
A bloody, mindless, vicious suffering
May we approach the font
Of Resurrection.

The SINGER *appears.*

SINGER. A soul! a soul! a soul-cake
Please good missus a soul-cake
An apple, a pear, a plum or a cherry,
Any good thing to make us all merry,
One for Peter, two for Paul,
Three for him who loved us all

God bless the master of this house,
And the mistress also
And all the little children,
That round the table grow

A soul! a soul! a soul-cake, *etc.*

The lanes are very dirty
And my shoes are very thin,
I have a little pocket
To put a penny in

If you haven't got a penny,
A ha'penny will do:
If you haven't got a ha'penny
Then God Bless You.

Scene Three

Mid-December. Drums. Enter LORD, KNIGHT *and* SOLDIERS.
A CHILD *stands at the side, with a begging bowl, motionless.*
DICCON *stands near, cold, desolate.*

LORD. Through coldest of cold snows, without slumber
    The army marches:

In the deepest of deep mid-December
The plague still rages.

KNIGHT. From France the few fighting men are called
The soldiers come,
From honourable war abroad
To strife at home.

DICCON. The faithless bowman ran, in mortal fear
To save his mind,
Tries to escape, but plague is everywhere —
The army finds.

KNIGHT. There's a man I know.

LORD. We need him then.

KNIGHT. Diccon! Diccon!

DICCON. Sir Knight. You're not in France?

KNIGHT. Turned back at Dover. There's a truce. We're for
the town, where there's a rising.

DICCON. Aye.

KNIGHT. You with us?

DICCON. Now, sir, I've not much choice.

KNIGHT. Good. (*Turns away.*)

DICCON. Your lady sir. I saw her, in the town.

KNIGHT. She's not with her lord?

DICCON. No, sir.

KNIGHT. Where is she?

  Pause.

  Where is she?

DICCON. I don't know, sir.

KNIGHT. Where?

  Pause.

DICCON. I left her with my people, sir.

KNIGHT. Then I must find her. If she's with them, I must find
her, Diccon.

DICCON. This a time for courting, sir?

  KNIGHT *doesn't reply.* LORD *steps forward.*

LORD. The Lord strides forth, into the biting wind
Looking before, he dare not look behind.

Exit LORD *and* SOLDIERS.

DICCON. The bowman joins the soldiers in their fight
Freedom to starve is but an empty right.

DICCON *follows* LORD.

KNIGHT. The Knight joins not his bowman in the war.
Deserting, flees to find his belle amor.

He turns to go. The CHILD *steps forward, speaks impassively,
not looking at the* KNIGHT.

CHILD. Sir. Sir.

KNIGHT. What is it?

CHILD. Alms, sir, for God's love.

KNIGHT. Alms?

CHILD. For Christmastide, good sir.

KNIGHT *looks at the* CHILD *a moment, then shakes his head
and runs out, a different way to the* ARMY.

CHILD (*without looking after him, or changing tone*). A merry
Christmas, sir.

Blackout.

Scene Four

Christmas. A carol throughout the scene. lights and enter the
BISHOP, *with* MONKS, *to meet the* LORD.

BISHOP. Well? What's happening? Have your soldiers stopped
them tearing down my churches and beating my priests?

LORD. Not all of them, not yet, my lord —

BISHOP. Then see to it. You are a soldier, see to it.

LORD. We'll stop them, never fear. Their leader, he rides on these
simple people like a sledge. But now, the pestilence is
spreading through their ranks. He cannot save them, so they'll
leave him. Then, he'll be taken.

BISHOP. And see that he's well burnt. I want no relics. Too much
light, it's blinded them. The time now, bind their eyes up
with the holy shroud. (*To the* MONKS:) Come, now.

LORD. There's a new heresy, my lord.

BISHOP *turns back.*

Chastisers. Drawing common folk, again.

BISHOP. Chastising who?

LORD. Themselves. With great delight and pleasure, seemingly.

BISHOP. Then it will be extremely hard to punish them. Come, sir.

LORD. No less, my soldiers will disperse them.

BISHOP. No! no, not in any way.

LORD. They're causing passion in the town, my lord. They say they're imitating Christ himself.

BISHOP. Better they parody his suffering, than that they imitate his Godhead and his glory, sir.

Pause.

So leave — them — be.

He exits with the MONKS. *The* LORD, *angry, exits the other way. Fade up carol and Blackout.*

Scene Five

Candlemas. Lights come up quickly. Enter JOHN, *backing away from a* SOLDIER. *He is pale and has been sick down his robe. He turns, confronts another entering* SOLDIER. *He turns to face* DICCON, *entering in soldier's clothes. He's surrounded. He gives up, kneels, shuts his eyes.*

JOHN. Holy Mary, pray for me.

DICCON *signals to the* SOLDIERS *not to attack. He goes to* JOHN *and takes his arm.*

DICCON. Leave him be. Come, Sir Prophet-on-the-Poor.

JOHN *looks up to* DICCON.

I must take you away to prison, sir.

JOHN. Where are my people.

DICCON. Save beating their masters, sir, they've taken to beating theyselves.

JOHN. They have no cause.

DICCON. No, sir. Save there's a general madness in the air. Your purse, sir.

JOHN *looks questioningly.*

You'll have no use of it.

JOHN *gives him his purse.* DICCON *helps him up.*

You heard that soldiers coming?

JOHN. Yes.

DICCON. You should have run sooner, then.

JOHN. How could I leave my people?

DICCON. They've left you.

JOHN *suddenly falls into* DICCON's *arms, retching.*

JOHN (*smiles*). The pestilence will rob the fire.

DICCON. Your soul may cheat it, sir. Your body won't. They'll burn it, anyroad.

He signals to the SOLDIERS, *who come and support* JOHN.

JOHN. Set me free, soldier.

DICCON. You're a good man, surely, sir, but you're a poor man's prophet. And I work for him who'll pay.

SOLDIERS *take* JOHN *out.* DICCON *opens the purse, finds the powder. Doesn't understand. Turns in the direction* JOHN *has gone, strides after, as if to ask him something. Blackout.*

Scene Six

Passion Sunday. In the curtained recess, the LADY *lies in bed, about to have her baby. In an open area, a table, set with food.*

SINGER (*SONG, then*).
    A lady once, upon a mortal season
    A player met, and saved him of unreason
    Then met she with a prophet of the poor
    And he was taken, and prophesies no more
    Now, come the holy day of Christ's torment
    Lies breeding, bleeding, all her passion spent.

HAM. Well, masters. Here am I again, old Ham. Of player to midwife go I. Of St George and all his company to old Joseph, the angel's cuckold in the manger. (*Softer:*) She's dying. It's a race to get it out of her afore she goes.

LADY. Did you hear what happened to him, Master? The good Baptist in the church?

HAM. No, ma'am, but I imagine — no.

LADY (*spasm*). Ham, I think it's coming.

HAM. Right. Old Joseph to his task.

(He quotes, out front:)
Your angel-tale I've heard Mary
But I must own it false
And you didn't get that bairn of me
It musta bin somebody else.

*He turns back to her, lights cross-cut to the table.
Enter the CLERK and his WIFE. They are expensively, but
soberly dressed. They sit and eat.*

CLERK. I am to build the church, madam.

WIFE. Why?

CLERK. The mason died. I am, on the commission of the Bishop,
to complete the work.

WIFE. Why you? You're no mason.

CLERK. No, but I've money, madam, to employ a mason.

They eat.

The style will be less gaudy. Straighter. For the spirit of the
times.

*Cross-cut lights to LADY and HAM. HAM stands, holding a
baby.*

HAM. Well, ma'am. The little bastard's out. And he's a pretty
one. O, yes. Your eye, ma'am, as a brown berry in his face.

LADY. He is a bastard, Ham.

HAM. O, and he has the look of it, a wicked eye.

LADY. No, I mean — he is a bastard.

HAM *(turns)*. O, ma'am, I'm sorry, but I thought —

LADY. I know what you thought, Ham. But he's a love-child,
bastard, true enough.

Pause.

HAM. Your knight, ma'am?

LADY. Yes. Before the feast of Trinity.

Lights cross-cut to CLERK and WIFE.

WIFE. Is the arising over?

CLERK. O, yes.

WIFE. And the chastisers gone?

CLERK. O, yes. *(Smiles.)* They scared the priests and nobles
well enough.

WIFE. That's good?

CLERK. That's good. They'd ruled too long.

They eat. Lights cross-cut to HAM *and* LADY. HAM *has put the baby in a crib. He sits on the bed, holding the* LADY's *band.*

LADY. Master, will you give me the last unction?

HAM. Eh?

LADY. Last unction, Ham, before I die.

HAM. That's a priest's office.

LADY. There are no priests. So will you, Ham?

HAM. O, ma'am, but I don't know the sacraments. Last unction, in particular. I mean, a penance, or a matrimony I could have a crack at. But last unction, no. Why, I've never had cause to hear it.

LADY. Then make it up. You're a player.

HAM. O, I can make a jig or a joke, ma'am, or a humorous citation, fine on them, but not a sacrament. You need wisdom for sacraments, and holiness, and Latin, and I've never been that well up on any of 'em.

LADY. Try.

Pause.

HAM. I'll tell you a tale I heard. 'Bout God. How's that?

LADY. Anoint me as you tell it, Ham.

HAM *takes oil, sits on the bed again.*

HAM. Well. There's this abbey, see. And this old monk, he's been out, doing his stuff, distributing largesse, performing the odd office, here and there, as he finds the need for it, and he comes back to the abbey, all tired and thirsty, hoping for a glass, a vesper and then off into the arms of Morpheus. Well, he pops into the church, you see, to check the candles, count the offertory, and in the corner, sitting down, all wretched and alone, is God. And the old monk throws hisself down on the ground — just as you might expect — and says, O God, Almighty God, what are you doing here. And he says — God says, well, I'll tell you, monk. It's like this. For the last four thousand years I've sat on my great throne and watched what all you lot have done to one another, and to me, and now, to be quite frank, my dear old monk, I'm tired.

Pause. He anoints her face.

And the monk says back — well, God, I understand you're tired, we all get a bit tired, from time to time, so why not give us your weapons, so that we can, as you might say, carry on. I mean, you got the powers of relief of suffering, redemption, miracles, and magic, grace. So why not lend 'em us. Just for a while. Just till you're feeling better.

Pause.

And God made no reply. And the want of his reply filled up the church, and the abbey, and the town, and the country, and the sea, and the world, and the universe. And the monk, the old monk, went suddenly — and quickly — and extremely — and quietly — lunatic.

Pause.

Like me.

Pause. He anoints her face with oil again.

I'm sure you'll go to heaven, lady.

Pause. HAM lifts the LADY's hand. It's lifeless. He hears voices. He stands, picks up the baby, and exits. Enter the KNIGHT, who carries a candle, and WILLIAM, to the LADY. They stand, and look at her. Cross-cut lights to CLERK and WIFE. They're finishing their meal.

WIFE. And it will come again, the plague?

CLERK. It may. Next time, we'll know the cause.

WIFE. We will?

CLERK. We must, my lady.

They stand and hold. Cross-cut lights to KNIGHT and LADY. WILLIAM has gone. The KNIGHT kneels, before his candle.

KNIGHT. Mother accept my solemn pledge and promise
No couch my body rests, in hall or palace
My eye nor shuts, until the Holy Land
Be Christian again
And Blessed Virgin grant my undertaking
A candle I'll keep burning without ceasing
Till comes that glory-dawn with you I stand
In fair Jerusalem
Whereas I break this vow
Show me no ruth
Forever is my pleading now
I pledge my truth

He stands, takes the candle, turns, and sees himself, a man dressed exactly as he is, holding a candle, who follows his gestures exactly, in a mirror image. It is the KNIGHT'S DEATH. *Establish the mirror-image, then the* KNIGHT *speaks.*

KNIGHT. Who is it?

DEATH. It is yourself.

KNIGHT. I shall die, of plague?

DEATH. No, you escape the plague, and die in war.

KNIGHT. The Holy Land?

DEATH. No, Normandy. Outside a little town. A battle's won. Back in your tent, you're thirsty. See a brook, go there, in your shirt, without your shield, or armory, or differencing. You drink. One of your soldiers, thinking you are the enemy, cuts off your head.

KNIGHT. There's nothing I can do?

DEATH. No, nothing.

They shrug. His DEATH *puts the candle in front of him, pulling the* KNIGHT's *with it, who can't resist.*

DEATH. So, goodbye.

They blow their candles out.

Scene Seven

Easter Saturday. At once, a carol, in the darkness. It builds up, through the following speech, and into the scene. During the scene, other carols sung.
The speech, by a VOICE, *begins in darkness, then lights fade up. The skeletons of the first act slowly descend, the* LORD's *nearly to the floor. The* CLERK *and his* WIFE *go to the skeletons. She takes the* CLERK's *coat, then takes the coat from the* LORD *skeleton, and dresses the* CLERK. *During this,* WILLIAM *comes in, carrying a flagstone. Throughout the scene, he will carry flagstones from one side of the stage to the other.*

VOICE. Lately, a great part of the people, and especially of labourers and servants, has died during the pestilence, and some, perceiving the pressing need of the lords, refuse to serve unless they receive excessive wages. We have had treaty and deliberation upon this matter with the experienced persons assisting us, by whose counsel we have ordered: that every man or woman in our realm, being able in body and below the age of 60 years, if he shall be required to serve in any suitable service, shall receive only such wages, hire or salary, as were accustomed to be offered in the place where he is to serve, in the twentieth year of our reign, or in the average five or six years previously.

The CLERK *goes to* WILLIAM, *gives him coins from his purse;* WILLIAM *nods acknowledgement;* CLERK *and* WIFE *exit; as the voice goes on:*

Given under our privy seal at Westminster, the year of Our Lord one thousand-three hundred and forty-nine, the twenty-first year of our reign in England, and the ninth year of our reign in France.

WILLIAM *still working. Enter* DICCON.

DICCON. Hail to you, Master William.

WILLIAM. Diccon! What's with you?

DICCON. What's that singing? On a Saturday?

WILLIAM. The Easter songs. Practising, for tomorrow.

DICCON. And how do you find your labour, Master William?

WILLIAM. It's good enough. There's a gang of us — no guild or apprentices or journeymen — so all's as one, and paid the same.

Pause.

What you doing?

DICCON. Still a soldier.

WILLIAM. But there's no war.

DICCON. O, now there's peace. Land needing tilling, churches building. But it won't go on. And when it comes again, well, old Diccon's going to make his mark on it.

WILLIAM. How's that?

DICCON *looks round, then shows* JOHN's *purse of powder to* WILLIAM.

DICCON. Cannon's powder. Looks calm and dandy. But set light to it, blow this church to the ground. And I know how it's made. And I'm making it, and I'm going to sell it.

WILLIAM. It's a miracle.

DICCON. No, it's a trick. But a trick as'll make me gold.

WILLIAM. Well done ye, Diccon.

DICCON. No virtue, being free and poor, now is there, eh?

Enter HAM. *He carries the baby. He sits, cooing it.*

Who's that?

WILLIAM. You know. Master Ham. The mad one. Here, most days.

DICCON. Oh, ay. (*To* HAM:) Good morning, Master Ham!

HAM *nods at him.*

And how's your fine son? (*He looks at the baby. Then to* WILLIAM:) There's no bairn there. A roll of rags, no more.

WILLIAM. I know. But he don't.

DICCON. I'm going.

WILLIAM. God be with you, Master Diccon.

DICCON. Ay, master, and with you.

Exit DICCON. WILLIAM *goes back to work. A few moments.*

WILLIAM. Well, let's see your teeth on a fine spring morning, Master Ham!

HAM *smiles, not looking up.*

That's better. There's been a great deliverance. Worth smiling for.

Pause.

And if the new world's still a poor and bleak one, well — our time'll come, eh? Even and we may not see it. As this great place.

Pause.

We don't know what the world is, no better. But there's no more plague.

Pause.

HAM. Mebbe it's waiting.

WILLIAM *looks at him, carries on working.* HAMMOND, *still as the* CLERK, *but without the* LORD's *coat, mounts the pulpit. The singing ends.* HAM *and* WILLIAM *hold.*

HAMMOND. Estimates of the numbers killed in the Black Death are difficult to assess accurately. But it is generally accepted that the plague killed one third of the population of Europe. It returned in 1361, 1390, 1405 and 1665. There are now no known pandemic diseases which cannot be cured.

Pause. WILLIAM *and* HAM *as if to stand, as if that's it.*

I'd like to read you a description of two places of suffering.

Neither WILLIAM *or* HAM *knew this was coming. They are thrown, but remain in their places.*

'In both cities, the scale of the disaster brought city life and industry virtually to a standstill. Even the clearance of debris and the cremation of the dead trapped in it do not seem to have been begun for more than a month, and members of the Mission still stumbled upon undiscovered skeletons. The impression which both cities made is of having sunk, in an instant, to the most primitive existence.

Witnesses say that people directly under the explosion in the open had their exposed skin burnt so severely that it was charred brown or black; these people died within minutes, or at most hours. Burns on exposed skin were very severe up to about 1,500 yards from the centre of the damage, mild burns extended to distances of two and a half miles and more.

The most important radioactive action appears to have been that from penetrating radiation. Even those severely irradiated probably did not show the characteristic symptoms, nausea, vomiting and fever, for 24 hours, and rarely died in less than a week. Disasters as vast as these are difficult to fix in numbers. Most of the city records were destroyed and in the chaos which followed little note was taken of the fate of individuals when the population was in mass-flight. The Mission had to content itself with estimating that the number of people killed in Hiroshima lay between seventy and eighty thousand.'

That was a report of the British Mission to Hiroshima and Nagasaki, published in July 1946, two years ago.

Pause. WILLIAM *and* HAM *again move, and are stilled by* HAMMOND *speaking.*

I have to tell you that two months ago, on May 12th, the Minister of War admitted, in answer to a question, almost unreported, that Britain is developing atomic weapons. Of its own. Of course, they will take some time to build. But I have to tell you something else. And this is secret. Britain will have these monstrous weapons, on her soil, prepared to strike, in eleven days time.

Last month, the Secretary for Foreign Affairs, Mr Bevin, acceded in a confidential correspondence to the United States' request that Britain provide bases for these weapons. The bombers, and their bombs, will arrive on 16th July. How I obtained this information is irrelevant. That it is secret is monstrous. That it is true is horrifying. I am sure I am breaking the law by telling you this. But I could not stay silent, knowing that these engines of destruction, more dreadful even than the plague, because they are man-made, are coming here, to stand upon our soil, and mock at us.

He nods to the ACTORS *and exits. The* ACTORS *stand, not knowing quite what to do. They put their arms out to the wings. Some* OTHER ACTORS, *those not in the beginning of the next scene — and not* WOLFE — *enter, raggedly, and prepare to bow to the* AUDIENCE. *Snap Blackout.*

Scene Eight

At once, in the darkness, some one whistling 'Happy Days are Here Again'. Lights. AGGIE *stands, looking at the skeletons. She's just come in, carries her bag.* GEORGE *sits on the altar steps, reading the script. Enter the whistler. It's* NORMAN.

NORMAN. Evening all.

GEORGE. Hello, Norman.

NORMAN. Any news?

AGGIE. No, I wondered if you had. You were sounding so cheerful.

NORMAN. No. Just keeping happy, know what I mean?

AGGIE. Not really.

   Pause.

NORMAN. Have you?

AGGIE. What?

NORMAN. Heard any news?

AGGIE. Well . . . apparently the doctor's still rushing about . . . Not saying anything, of course. John says it's no hope, bar a miracle.

NORMAN. It's been ten days.

AGGIE (*shrugs*). It's been ten days.

   Enter HARRY.

HARRY. Any news?

AGGIE. No, there isn't.

   HARRY *sits, takes his clips off. Pause.*

GEORGE (*stands, intensely*). I've been reading it a lot, since. And it seems to me, he must have known. It must be, of all the things he wrote, the one he wanted, most to do. That's how it seems to me.

AGGIE. Well, it's going to get done, isn't it?

NORMAN. Is it?

AGGIE. John'll bring someone in, I suppose.

GEORGE *sits, reads again.*

NORMAN. Well, he's taking his bloody time over it.

Enter HILDA, carrying the LORD's coat. She puts it on the skeleton.

HILDA. Norm, Harry, give us a hand, get these up.

NORMAN. Course.

NORMAN, HARRY *and* HILDA *pull up the skeletons.*

HILDA. Thanks.

Pause.

HARRY. When are we supposed to start?

HILDA. Well I said six thir—

Enter HENDERSON, carrying the script. They all turn to him. Pause.

AGGIE. Is he dead?

Pause.

HENDERSON. Well, actually no.

HILDA. But is he going to —

HENDERSON. No.

Pause. The ACTORS can't believe it.

You see, the problem is, with science moving so fast, some doctors, particularly, in the rural areas, don't always know about developments . . .

Slight pause.

Streptomycin. It's an antibiotic. Like penicillin. Very recent. Cures almost immediately. I didn't want to say, until I was sure it was going to work. But now — he'll be up, in a day or two.

Slight pause.

(*Smiling.*) Had quite a row with him, actually. When he came round, wouldn't believe it.

Pause.

GEORGE (*stands*). Well, that's because it undermines what he's saying, doesn't it. 'Maybe it's waiting.' It's there. In the play. And, it was, for him. And now it isn't.

HILDA. George.

GEORGE. Well, I'm right, aren't I?

Pause.

(*To* HENDERSON:) Aren't I?

HENDERSON. Well, I don't think it's finding streptomycin, undermines the play. If that's what you mean.

GEORGE. Go on.

HENDERSON (*uncertain, looks round. Then shrugs, continues*). Well, I'd say it would be, if we cured diptheria. Which we know *how* to do. The drugs. But we don't know how to administer the cure. It's work like that, it seems to me. Boring, unspectacular. Not great leaps forward. Sanitation. Cleaner water. Drains. That kind of thing.

Pause.

You see, what I feel is, we've always talked about eradicating war, disease and poverty, and when we've failed, we've said, to, I don't know, to keep us sane, that they'll always be with us, but — in fact, it's not till now, we've had the tools to do it.

Slight pause.

And, of course, those tools will be misused, but then again . . .

Slight pause.

We've got the tools to change that too. Well, I think.

Slight pause.

Actually.

He half-smiles. WOLFE, *heavily muffled up, has entered behind* HENDERSON. *The* OTHERS *notice him.* HENDERSON *turns.*

You should be in hospital.

WOLFE. I discharged myself.

HENDERSON. You shouldn't have. (*To* HILDA:) See he goes back, in an hour or so, all right?

HILDA *nods.*
Exit HENDERSON. *Pause. Then* HARRY *forward, shakes*

WOLFE's *hand. The tension breaks. The* OTHERS, *except*
GEORGE, *forward too, to shake his hand.*

WOLFE. Well, ladies, gentlemen. We must rehearse. We have a
play to do.

At once, lights off WOLFE *and the* OTHERS, *and,*
simultaneously, a spot finds the SINGER.

SINGER. The moon shines bright,
And the stars give a light,
A little before 'tis day:
And bids us awake and pray.

Awake, awake, good people all:
Awake and you shall hear,
Our Lord our God died on the cross
For them he loved so dear.

O fair O fair Jerusalem,
When shall I come to thee?
When all my grief is at an end,
Thy joy then we may see.

Destiny

To Ron and Di

DESTINY was first presented by the Royal Shakespeare Company at the Other Place, Stratford-upon-Avon, on 22 September 1976. The production transferred to the Aldwych Theatre, London on 12 May 1977, with the following cast:

TURNER	Ian McDiarmid
GURJEET SINGH KHERA	Marc Zuber
COLONEL CHANDLER	David Lyon
MAJOR ROLFE	Michael Pennington
PETER CROSBY	Paul Shelley
PLATT	Clyde Pollitt
MRS CHANDLER	Judith Harte
FRANK KERSHAW	Dennis Clinton
BOB CLIFTON	Paul Moriarty
SANDY CLIFTON	Frances Viner
PAUL	Greg Hicks
TONY	Leonard Preston
MONTY GOODMAN	Paul Shelley
DAVID MAXWELL	John Nettles
RICHARD CLEAVER	Bob Peck
DRUMONT	David Lyon
PRAKASH PATEL	Dev Sagoo
ATTWOOD	David Lyon
MRS HOWARD	Judith Harte
LIZ	Cherie Lunghi
INSPECTOR	Hubert Rees
EMMA CROSBY	Judy Monahan
DIANA WILCOX	Denyse Alexander
CAROL	Cherie Lunghi
PARTYGOERS/MEMBERS	Denyse Alexander
OF THE PATRIOTIC	Michael Cashman
LEAGUE/POLICE	Jack Galloway
	Alfred Molina
	Judy Monahan
	Martin Read
	Hubert Rees

Directed by Ron Daniels
Designed by Di Seymour
Lighting by Leo Leibovici

The constituency of Taddley, where most of the play is set, is a fictional town to the west of Birmingham.

The Nation Forward Party, the Taddley Patriotic League, the Association of Diecasters and Foundrymen, the Baron Castings Co. Ltd, the United Vehicle Corporation and the Metropolitan Investment Trust are fictional organisations.

None of the characters seen in the play has ever existed.

ACT ONE

'The Conservative Party by long tradition and settled belief is the Party of the Empire. We are proud of its past. We see it as the surest hope in our day. We proclaim our abiding faith in its destiny.'

Conservative Party Manifesto
General Election, 1950

'The Right is acutely aware that the kind of Britain it wishes to preserve very largely depends on Britain remaining a great power. . . Everything about the British class system begins to look foolish and tacky when related to a second-class power on the decline.'

Peregrine Worsthorne,
Conservative commentator,
April 1959

Act One

Scene One

Darkness. We hear a sonorous VOICE:

VOICE. Long years ago, we made a tryst with destiny, and now the time comes when we shall redeem our pledge, not wholly or in full measure, but very substantially. A moment comes, which comes but rarely in history, when we step out from the old to the new, when an age ends, and when the soul of a nation, long oppressed, finds utterance. At the stroke of the midnight hour, when the world sleeps, India will awake to life and freedom.

Slight pause.

Jawaharlal Pandit Nehru, 14th August, 1947.

Lights snap up, and with them, sounds of celebration in the distance. We are in the box room of a British Army barracks, near Jullundur in the Punjab. On the back wall hangs a huge, dark painting of the putting down of the Indian Mutiny. It dominates the set. A door to one side, two chairs, several packing cases, a stuffed tiger, a trunk, all covered with dust sheets. A British Army Sergeant, in tropical uniform, stands by the door. He has just switched the light on. His name is TURNER; *he is from the West Midlands, about 20, and harrassed.*

TURNER. Oh, bloody hell. (*Exit. Shouts, off.*) Khera! Khera! (*Pause.*) For Christ's sake, Khera, where the bloody hell you hiding?

Sound of running feet. The voice of a young Indian:

KHERA. Sir?

TURNER. Where the hell you been? (*Pause.*) Aw, come on. Look what I found.

TURNER *comes back into the room with* GURJEET SINGH KHERA, *an 18-year-old Sikh servant, who wears a turban, and has a steel bangle on his wrist and a knife at his belt. When talking to* KHERA, TURNER *speaks loudly and slowly.*

TURNER. Right. See this stuff? It's going. Out. You, me, get this stuff out, right? (KHERA *nods and does nothing.*) Well, come on, let's get weaving. Get these sheets off, see what we got. (KHERA *and* TURNER *begin pulling sheets off furniture and packing cases.* KHERA *is just dropping the sheets.* TURNER *notices.*) Hey, you. Don't just drop 'em anywhere. Fold 'em up. (KHERA *does nothing.* TURNER *waves his folded sheet as an example.*) Fold, yuh? Savvy? (KHERA *nods wisely.*) Well, get a move on, then. (KHERA, *still nodding, starts folding a sheet, very slowly and precisely.*) Jesus Christ.

TURNER *returns to his work. Sounds of celebration, a little louder.*

Your people having a good time then, eh?

Pause.

I said, your people having a good time?

KHERA (*stopping work*). Oh, yes. Having a wizard time. (*As if explaining to a child:*) Independence.

TURNER. Oh, I wondered what it was.

Pause.

All right, get on. (TURNER *pulls the dustsheet off the tiger.*) Now what's this here?

KHERA (*helpfully*). Tiger. Stuffed.

TURNER. You know, I just about worked that out for myself.

KHERA. They shoot them, then they stuff them.

TURNER *looks to heaven, then back to folding. Enter a* COLONEL, *43 years old, upper class.* TURNER *snaps to attention, salutes.*

TURNER. Sir!

COLONEL. It's all right, Sergeant.

TURNER *looks to* KHERA, *who has not responded.* KHERA *becomes aware of his negligence, slowly and lackadaisically comes to attention. Pause. Then:*

Oh, Lord, is this some more?

TURNER. Yes, sir.

COLONEL (*to the tiger*). Ah. What have we here?

KHERA. It's tiger, sir.

TURNER *looking daggers.*

Stuffed.

COLONEL (*smiling*). Yes.

TURNER (*to cover*). I found this trunk, sir, I don't know
what. . . .

COLONEL. Do we know whose it is?

TURNER. No, sir. Reckon it's been here a long time. Don't
think anyone's been in here for years.

COLONEL. Well, let's take a shufti. Is it open?

TURNER. I'll try it, sir. (TURNER *opens the trunk.* COLONEL
kneels and looks inside.)

TURNER (*to* KHERA). You can be getting this stuff down to
the lorries.

KHERA *is taking the stuff out as:*

COLONEL. Well, well. (*He takes out a red hunting coat.*) Can't
jettison the fancy dress, can we?

TURNER. I'm sorry about him, sir, he's —

COLONEL. No matter, Sergeant. After all, it's their day. No
doubt all his chums are whooping it up in Jullundur.

TURNER. Yes, sir.

COLONEL. Now, what else . . . ah. (*He takes out a bayonet,
desheathes it.*) I'll bet this hasn't seen service for a year or two.
(*He looks at the sheath.*) It's certainly not us . . . Indian Army,
I'd say . . . (*He shrugs and sheathes the bayonet, puts it back
in the trunk. Finds a bottle of whisky.*) Good Lord, it's
scotch. That's a turn up for the books. I wonder how long
that's been there?

TURNER. Don't know, sir.

COLONEL. Well, it doesn't go off, does it? Where's the boy?

TURNER (*to the door, shouts*). Khera!

KHERA (*off, from a distance*). Sir?

TURNER. Let's have you! Sharpish!

Enter KHERA, *who deliberately speaks to the* COLONEL
rather than to TURNER.

KHERA. So sorry, sir, I am taking —

COLONEL. Look, will you nip down to the mess and fetch
three whisky tumblers. Got that? Say I sent you.

KHERA. Right away, sir. Three tumblers, right sharpish. (*Exit.*)

TURNER. Three, sir?

COLONEL (*stands*). Yes. Why not? (*He shuts the trunk.*) I'm afraid I think we'd better take it all.

TURNER. Yes, sir.

COLONEL. God alone knows where we'll put it.

Slight pause.

TURNER. There been any trouble today, sir?

COLONEL. Not as far as I know. All having a good time. The real shindig here'll be when they decide the boundary. Hence the rush.

TURNER. If you ask me, sir . . . (*He thinks better of it.*)

COLONEL. No, go on.

TURNER. They didn't have all this trouble in the old days, sir. I was in Calcutta last year, the riots, and I can't see they're much more than savages, sir, whatever they say.

COLONEL. Well, ours is not to reason why.

Pause. Enter KHERA *with three tumblers on a tray. He puts them on the trunk.*

Ah, splendid. Do you fancy a tipple, um —

TURNER. Khera, sir.

COLONEL. Khera? (KHERA *doesn't understand.* COLONEL, *waving the bottle:*) Drink?

KHERA. Oh, please, yes.

COLONEL. Splendid. (*He pours the whisky, handing glasses to* KHERA *and* TURNER.) Know what you're going to do when we've all gone home, Khera?

KHERA. Oh, I don't know, sir.

COLONEL. Perhaps you'll come to England one day. See the natives on their own ground, mm?

KHERA. Yes, sir, I would like to come to England very much.

COLONEL. Well, here's to . . . yes, why not. To the King. With whom we need not, I think, couple the name of Mr Attlee.

TURNER. Winston, sir?

COLONEL. Yes, splendid. The King, and Mr Churchill.

They are raising their glasses as MAJOR ROLFE *bursts into the room. He is nearly 30, brusque, and at the moment, in a filthy temper.*

ROLFE. Oh, there you are, Sergeant, I've been looking all over — *(He sees the* COLONEL.) Oh, I'm sorry, Colonel.

COLONEL. That's all right, Major. The Sergeant and I just found ourselves caught up in the general atmosphere of jubilation. Do join us.

COLONEL *nods to* KHERA, *who gives his whisky to* ROLFE. *As* ROLFE *takes it:*

ROLFE. Some bloody wog's whipped the battery from the Landrover.

COLONEL. Oh, not again.

ROLFE. Broad daylight. Anything that isn't nailed down. They've stripped the cellar.

COLONEL. We'll have to do something about the battery.

ROLFE. If we want to get out of here, yes. Your health, Colonel. *(He takes a swig. Slight pause.)*

COLONEL. Your health. *(He and* TURNER *drink.)*

ROLFE *(to* KHERA). Well, don't just stand there gawping. I assume all this stuff's got to be moved?

TURNER. Yes, sir.

ROLFE *(to* KHERA). Well, get moving it.

KHERA *(with a mock salute)*. Yes, sir! *(He picks up a packing-case and goes.)*

COLONEL *(refilling glasses)*. Quite a bright little chap, that one. Half devil, quite possibly, but hardly half child.

ROLFE. I'm sorry, Colonel?

COLONEL. Kipling. Don't you know it?
'Take up the White Man's burden —
Send forth the best ye breed —
Go, bind your sons to exile
To serve your captives' need;
To wait in heavy harness
On fluttered folk and wild —
Your new-caught, sullen peoples,
Half-devil and half-child.'
We used to have to learn it by heart at preparatory school.

ROLFE. I didn't go to a preparatory school, Colonel.

COLONEL. I know you didn't, Major.

ROLFE. Nonetheless, it sounds an eminently appropriate
description.

Pause.

TURNER. Is it true, sir, they'll all be able to come to England
now, to live?

COLONEL. I believe Mr Attlee is preparing legislation, now
India is in the Commonwealth.

ROLFE. Do you approve of that, Colonel?

COLONEL (*quite sharply*). Of course. It's an obligation. We are
the mother country, after all.

ROLFE. I have some reservations.

COLONEL. And you're welcome to them.

Pause. The COLONEL *drains his drink.*

I suppose I'd better go and sort out this battery business. See
all this stuff gets loaded, Sergeant.

TURNER. Sir.

COLONEL (*meets* KHERA *coming in*). Carry on the good work,
Khera.

KHERA *smiles. Exit* COLONEL.

ROLFE. Well, Mr Khera, apparently you've just become a
British citizen. (*He pours himself another drink.*)

KHERA. Sir?

ROLFE. Get on with it.

KHERA. Do you want tiger, sir?

ROLFE. Of course we want the bloody tiger. We shot it.

*KHERA takes the tiger out. ROLFE takes out his cigarette
case, offers it to TURNER.*

Smoke, Sergeant?

TURNER (*not sure of the protocol*). Er . . .

ROLFE. Oh, for Christ's sake, if Mountbatten can hand over the
Raj to a bunch of half-crazed dervishes, you can smoke on
duty.

TURNER (*takes a cigarette*). Thank you, sir. (*He lights his and*

ROLFE's *cigarette*.) Do you think Mr Churchill will do anything about it, sir? When the Conservatives get back in?

ROLFE. When were you last in England, Sergeant?

TURNER. 1945, sir. Just after VE Day.

ROLFE. A lot has changed.

Slight pause.

TURNER. You going straight back, sir?

ROLFE. No, not straight away. I want to go soutn, to Tiruppur. Old garrison. Just once, again, before I go.

Enter KHERA.

Well, best get on.

TURNER. Right, sir. Khera, I want the rest of this stuff down in ten minutes.

Pause.

ROLFE. You say 'yes, sir', don't you?

KHERA. Yes, sir.

ROLFE. Let's get this bloody show on the road. (*Exit* ROLFE *and* TURNER.)

KHERA *goes to the trunk, is about to take the tray off it. Then a second thought, he pours himself a whisky. Then he notices the painting of the Indian Mutiny. He looks at it. He touches the canvas. Then he turns out front, raises the tumbler in a mock toast.*

KHERA. Civis — Brittanicus — Sum.

Blackout and music: Handel's Music for the Royal Fireworks — covers the change.

Scene Two

Dim light on a portrait of the COLONEL, *in uniform, in India. Music fades.*
A spot fades up on the COLONEL, *at the side of the stage. He is very old.*

COLONEL. In '48. Came on home.
        Colonel Chandler. Monochrome.
        Another England,
        Rough and raw,
        Not gentle, sentimental as before.

Became a politician, not to master but to serve:
To keep a careful finger on the grassroots Tory nerve;
Like any born to riches, not to plunder but to give:
Always a little liberal, a great Conservative.
But as his seat grows marginal, his power's less secure,
His responsive elder statements sound increasingly
    unsure;
Colonel Chandler, past his prime:
Dignified. Worthy. Out of time.
Colonel Chandler, oyster-eyed,
One fine summer morning, died.

Exit. Lights up, the portrait, we now see, is on the back wall of a drawing room. A door. A table, with coffee set out, and a telephone. Enter PETER CROSBY, who is in his late 20s. Like all the men in this scene, he wears a sober suit and a black tie. He goes to the telephone, picks it up, dials.

CROSBY. Extension 237, please. Hallo, Maggie? Look, I'm at — (*Checks on the phone.*) Taddley 3721. T-A-D-D-L-E-Y. Well, it's somewhere near West Bromwich. Anyway, I'll be here 20 minutes, gone an hour, back till about 5.30. (*Smiles.*) No, it really is a funeral. My uncle.

Enter PLATT, middle-aged, West Midlands accent, unsure of his surroundings. About to speak to CROSBY when he sees he's phoning, so looks at the portrait.

Hardly. He was very old. Now, look, Maggie, can you get me running yields on all the Inter-Americans first thing. That's right. And get Bill to check me futures on the Chicago softs, sometime before lunch. No, that's all. (*Smiles.*) And you, sweetheart. (*He puts the phone down, notices PLATT.*)

PLATT. Business goes on, eh, Peter?

CROSBY. I'm afraid the market is no respecter of grief. Coffee?

PLATT. Thanks very much. (CROSBY *pours the coffee.*) We were all right sorry to see him go.

CROSBY. Yuh. I'd think, actually, you constituency people knew him rather better than I did.

PLATT. Could be.

CROSBY. Milk and sugar?

PLATT. Just — milk.

CROSBY (*giving* PLATT *his coffee*). I imagine it was a much safer seat, in the old days.

PLATT. Oh, ar. Rural, indeed. Now, of course, with the new estates, it's very dodgy.

CROSBY. Did he ever think of retiring?

PLATT. Talking for ten years. But they don't, do they?

CROSBY. Old Tories never die, they just get redistributed.

PLATT *smiles.* CROSBY *looks at his watch.*

Off, soon.

PLATT. Um, Peter, it's probably not the right time to bring it up, but the by-election writ's on the cards any day, and I gather Smith Square were thinking of, keeping it family . . . Perhaps we could have a chat.

CROSBY. Yes, indeed. Why don't we, I'm in no hurry to get back up, have a drink or something afterwards?

PLATT. Fine. We'll go up to the Club. Get your face known.

Slight pause.

Be others in the running, of course. Can't take nepotism to excess.

CROSBY. No, of course. Anything I should push, or steer clear of?

PLATT. Well, I'd keep quiet about Chicago softs, for a start. Concentrate on hards from Longbridge. (CROSBY *smiles.*) Otherwise, bear in mind we're in Enoch country and you'll be all right.

CROSBY. Enoch country?

PLATT. The ground fairly thick with our commonwealth cousins. .

CROSBY. Well, yes, o˙ that one, I should make it clear —

PLATT. I shouldn't.

CROSBY. Shouldn't what?

PLATT. Make it clear, cos all they'll say is, you don't have to live with 'em.

CROSBY. Well, yes, but —

KERSHAW *opens the door, lets* MRS CHANDLER *enter and follows her in. They are both in their mid-fifties.*

MRS CHANDLER. Hallo, Peter.

CROSBY (*kisses her*). Aunty.

MRS CHANDLER. I'm so glad you could come.

KERSHAW. Coffee, Sarah?

MRS CHANDLER. Yes, I'd love some, please. (KERSHAW *pours some coffee.*) Oh Peter, I'm sorry, do you know Frank Kershaw?

CROSBY. Yes, of course I know Frank.

MRS CHANDLER. Central Office very sweetly sent him up to represent the party.

KERSHAW. That's not quite true, Peter. Dozens of them wanted to come, but your aunt insisted that she wanted it kept as small as possible. (*He gives* MRS CHANDLER *her coffee.*)

MRS CHANDLER. Thank you, Frank.

Pause.

Do you know if they've arrived?

PLATT *coughs.*

CROSBY. Oh, I'm sorry. Frank, this is Jim Platt, foreman, isn't it?

PLATT. Works Manager.

CROSBY. Sorry, works manager at Baron Castings, local foundry. And more importantly, constituency chairman. Jim, this is Frank Kershaw, whose many commercial concerns are too numerous to mention.

PLATT. Oh, yes, we all know Mr Kershaw.

KERSHAW. I didn't know my fame had spread so far.

MRS CHANDLER. There, you see, Frank —

PLATT. Cos, actually, we're one of his numerous concerns.

Pause.

CROSBY. Small world.

KERSHAW. What did you say your —

PLATT. Baron Castings.

KERSHAW. Oh, yes, of course.

Slight pause.

You're doing rather well, aren't you?

PLATT. Well, that's not quite correct, Mr Kershaw. It'd be a bit more accurate to say we're doing rather badly.

Pause.

CROSBY. No-one's doing well, after all.

Slight pause.

KERSHAW. See the trade figs, Peter?

CROSBY. I did. Of course, a lot of it's still oil . . .

KERSHAW. That doesn't mean we don't have to pay it.

CROSBY. Roll on the North Sea, say I.

KERSHAW. As soon as Mr Wedgwood Benn rolls off it . . .

PLATT (*breaks in, as a joke*). Oh for the days of Empire, eh, Peter? Send in the gunboats, sort the Saudies out that way.

CROSBY (*smiles*). The sun will never set, eh, Jim? Last for a thousand years?

MRS CHANDLER. There was something to be said for it.

CROSBY, *taken aback by her tone, looks to* KERSHAW, *who nods at the portrait.*

CROSBY. Oh, I'm sorry, I didn't mean —

MRS CHANDLER. It's all right, Peter. Of course, I know it's changed. The nation, and, indeed, the Party. Once we stood for patriotism, Empire. Now it's all sharp young men with coloured shirts and cockney accents, reading the Economist. We stand or fall, how capable we are. Perhaps, however, not inspiring — quite . . .

Pause.

KERSHAW. I think I heard the car —

MRS CHANDLER. You should hear Peter, Frank. He's really very witty. Especially when they talk about the Dunkirk Spirit. Says we must be the only nation in the world that's inspired by battles it lost.

CROSBY. I'm sorry.

MRS CHANDLER. Are you going to stand?

CROSBY. Stand?

MRS CHANDLER. For the candidacy.

CROSBY (*carefully*). I had thought of it. But it's entirely up to you.

MRS CHANDLER. I'd be delighted.

A knock. KERSHAW *goes and speaks to someone outside.*

CROSBY. Really?

MRS CHANDLER. Really.

KERSHAW. They're ready, Sarah.

MRS CHANDLER. Off we go, then.

Exit KERSHAW *and* MRS CHANDLER.

PLATT. Look, Peter, if you'd rather not bother today, after the funeral, and that . . .

CROSBY. No, it's fine.

PLATT. Another day, if you prefer . . .

CROSBY. No, it's fine.

PLATT *goes.* CROSBY *looks at the portrait.*

You old bastard. You're laughing at me.

Blackout.

Scene Three

In the darkness, the voice of a young Brummie, PAUL.

PAUL. Bob! Hey, Bob!

Lights. The bar of the Labour Club. A table, on it three pints and an ashtray. Stools. CLIFTON *and* SANDY *are playing darts. He's in his early 30s, dressed in an oldish corduroy suit and tie. She's perhaps a little younger, from the North, neatly dressed in denim.*

CLIFTON (*throws a dart, then*). Paul!

PAUL *appears. Mid-20s, wearing jeans, denim jacket, open-necked shirt, carries a rolled-up piece of paper.*

PAUL. Bob, I think we done it.

CLIFTON (*marking up his score*). How d'you work that out?

PAUL. Well, get a load of this.

SANDY *throws as* PAUL *makes a space on the table and spreads out his piece of paper. We see it's a map, with sections coloured in. He weighs down the chart with the ashtray and a glass.* SANDY *marks up and comes over.*

CLIFTON. That pint's yours. Hey, have you met Sandy?

PAUL. No. How d'you do?

SANDY. Hallo.

CLIFTON (*going to the board and throwing*). Paul's in charge of getting me the nomination, darling. He thinks I'm a bit fuzzy on Clause Four, but he's backing me because of the opposition. He's what the Express calls an unrepresentative, militant minority. He started reading Tribune at the age of two, he hates Roy Jenkins just a little more than Adolf Hitler, and Reg Prentice gets apoplexy at his very name. (*Coming back to the table.*) But what he doesn't know about the Labour Party Rulebook isn't there. That's right?

PAUL. That's right.

CLIFTON. Now.

SANDY *to throw, as.*

PAUL. Right. Calculations as follows. 40 union delegates eligible. And on my estimate, them as turns up breaks circa 50/50. And odds and sods like women, YS and the Co-op, all for you. OK?

CLIFTON. Fine.

SANDY (*returning*). Yours, Bob.

CLIFTON. 'Scuse I.

CLIFTON *to throw*, SANDY *looks at the chart.*

SANDY. That looks very impressive.

PAUL. It's just a matter, know the rules.

SANDY. And then, exploit them?

PAUL. Use.

CLIFTON (*returning*). OK.

He sits, indicating a suspension of the game. SANDY *sits.*

PAUL (*pointing at the chart*). Right. So the key's the wards. That's over half the delegates. Now, right-wing wards, the ones you lost already, marked in pink. That's Greenside and Fenley Heath. The reds you got, no bother: Grimley and Broughton Park. The floaters, Stourford and West Thawston, see?

CLIFTON. I see.

SANDY. D'you think, the other feller, what's his name —

PAUL. John Smalley? Not a chance.

SANDY. Not even — as an ex-MP?

PAUL. Especially, as an ex-MP. (*He takes a xerox sheet from his pocket. To* CLIFTON.) Now, as it happens, neither of the floaters got their full quota of ward delegates for the General Management Committee. In Thawston, nothing like. And they can nominate from now until they fix election day. And so — the strategy — recruit new members like there's no tomorrow, pack the GMC with folk'll vote for you, it's in the bag. OK?

CLIFTON. Won't Smalley too?

PAUL. He'll try. But here's the point. Cos obviously, them two, we're talking of our pals from overseas. And, as it happens, on that, Mr Smalley's got his drawers in something of a tangle.

He waves the xerox. SANDY *comes over to them.*

Hansard, Parliamentary Report. Second reading, Kenya Asians Bill, Feb 1968. The Hon. John Smalley, then MP for Sheffield East. I quote. (*He reads.*) "Whatever one's sympathies — and I have many — with these unfortunate people, one must accept that the indigenous population will not for ever stay silent, faced with what appears to be the thin end of a very thick black wedge."

CLIFTON. He said that?

PAUL. There in black and . . . well, you know.

CLIFTON. That's great.

PAUL. We do it as a leaflet. Bung it round. We got him by the plums, Bob. Like a jerbil in a bucket.

CLIFTON *goes to throw.*

SANDY. So what about the Tory?

PAUL. Eh?

SANDY. You got Bob candidated, or whatever. What about the Tory?

PAUL. Well . . . (*Confidentially, to both.*) The Tory. Two in it, so I hear, like us. On one hand, Chandler's nephew, chap called Peter Crosby. You know, bright, high-flier, all slim suits and unit trusts. The other, something altogether different.

CLIFTON. Well?

PAUL. One Major Rolfe. Wild man, with eagle eye. Who thinks
the Carlton Club is in the pay of Moscow, and would put
himself just slightly to the Right of Ghenghis Khan.

CLIFTON. He's possible?

PAUL. Who knows? With that lot. Does it matter, anyroad? (*He
picks up his pint.*) Whatever, come the day, it's hallo Robert
Clifton, honourable member.

CLIFTON *raises his glass.* SANDY *follows suit.*

I give you, comrades — the Collapse of Capital.

PAUL *and* CLIFTON *clink and drink.* SANDY *sips her beer.
Blackout.*

Scene Four

Lights. Empty set. ROLFE, *now in his mid-50s, stands centre.
He wears a black overcoat, with medals, and a poppy.*

ROLFE. In '47. Came on home.
Major Rolfe. A face of stone.
Another England, seedy, drab,
Locked in the dreams of glories she once had.
The Major looks at England and bemoans her tragic
    fate,
Condemns the mindless comforts of a flaccid,
    spongers' state,
Despairs of trendy idiocies repeated as a rote,
While the knot of old school tiredness is still tight
    round England's throat.
Sees leaders fat with falsehood as they lick up every
    lie,
The people's blood grown sickly with their driving
    will to die.
Major Rolfe, sees the light,
Calls for a counter from the Right:
Major Rolfe, starboard seer,
Loses, for they will not hear.

Enter KERSHAW, *dressed similarly to* ROLFE.

KERSHAW. Lewis.

ROLFE. Frank.

KERSHAW. How are you?

ROLFE. Fine. And you?

KERSHAW. I'm fine.

Pause.

How's the boy?

ROLFE. Alan? He's fine too. Just got promotion. Captain.

KERSHAW. Splendid.

ROLFE. Sails for Belfast on the midnight tide.

KERSHAW. That's fine?

ROLFE. Arrives in time to see the dawn rising over Ballymurphy.

KERSHAW. Breathtaking.

ROLFE. Indeed.

Pause.

KERSHAW. And business?

ROLFE. Brisk. And yours?

KERSHAW *shrugs, smiling.*

I didn't get the candidacy, Frank.

KERSHAW. What?

ROLFE. Do you remember? I was going for the Tory nomination, Taddley.

KERSHAW. Oh, yes —

ROLFE. Didn't have a chance, of course.

KERSHAW. Oh, surely, I thought by now you're due for —

ROLFE. Up against the perfect opposition.

Slight pause.

KERSHAW (*smiling*). Well, go on.

ROLFE. Oh, Frank, he looked just right. Knew all the right words, too — concerned, humane, constructive, moderate . . . With just the right note of apology in his voice when he had to admit to being a Conservative as well . . .

KERSHAW (*slightly embarrassed*). Bitter.

ROLFE. Perhaps. His hatred of privilege, you see, doesn't stop him showing off his stripy tie.

KERSHAW. In fact, I know him, Peter Crosby. Nephew of a friend of mine.

ROLFE. So then you'll understand.

Pause.

What's it matter, anyway? The state the Party's in.

KERSHAW. What state is that?

ROLFE. Self-loathing. Gutless. Genuflecting to the fashionable myths.

KERSHAW (*with some irony*). What myths might they be, Lewis?

ROLFE. Oh, the full employment myth, the ever-rising wages myth, the higher public spending myth, the whole social-democratic demonology of workers good and bosses bad, all those myths . . .

KERSHAW. Now, surely, Lewis. All that's changed. I read my Daily Teleg-

ROLFE (*interrupts*). Oh, yes, we'll say, the Party's changed, at last we've understood, we have the Right Approach, and yes, of course, at Party conference, our new and True-Blue leaders, to a person, bang the drum and flap the flag . . . It's just, you see, we learn from history, in practice, come the crunch, the flag they wave omits the red and blue.

Pause.

KERSHAW. What's the alternative?

ROLFE. That is the question.

Slight pause.

KERSHAW. OK, Lewis. I've got the message. Brimstone and hellfire. So, how must we be saved?

ROLFE. There's a group of us have lunch from time to time.

KERSHAW. That's nice.

ROLFE. To talk about what happens after.

KERSHAW. What happens after lunch?

ROLFE. What happens when the river breaks its banks.

KERSHAW, *perhaps deliberately, not understanding.*

The cold Class War hots up.

KERSHAW. Oh, Lewis, surely not.

ROLFE. Not what?

KERSHAW. Not Suffolk military geriatrics, drilling private armies on their croquet lawns.

ROLFE. Of course not. There's no need for private armies.

KERSHAW. Well, exactly —

ROLFE. When, already, we've a public one.

Slight pause.

One of our little group is Alan's Brigadier.

Pause.

KERSHAW. You're seriously suggesting — army into Government?

ROLFE *shrugs.*

In England?

ROLFE. All right. What happens? Wage control collapses, unemployed take over factories, council tenants massively refuse to pay their rents, in name or not, another General Strike, the pound falls through the floor, the English pound, the English river's burst its English banks . . . So what d'you do? You either let the deluge, deluge, or you build a dam against it. Mm?

Slight pause.

We've got to think about it, Frank —

KERSHAW. Wasn't it R.A. Butler said — politics, the Art of What Is Possible.

ROLFE. No. It wasn't.

KERSHAW. Oh, I'm sure it —

ROLFE. Butler borrowed it. From Bismarck.

Pause.

KERSHAW. Why talk to me?

ROLFE. I'm testing water.

KERSHAW. Only mine?

ROLFE. No, any Managing Director of a major British company whose shares were two pounds fifty eighteen months ago and at the close on Friday just topped sixty-four.

Pause. KERSHAW brusque.

KERSHAW. No, Lewis.

ROLFE. No? Why not.

KERSHAW. Can't see it in those terms.

ROLFE. Won't see it.

KERSHAW. Still have some faith in people's reason.

ROLFE. Reason? Your shop stewards, reasonable men?

KERSHAW. In people's loyalty.

ROLFE. To what?

KERSHAW. The national interest.

ROLFE. Whose? Whose loyalty? The miners? Students? Irish? Blacks?

KERSHAW. Lewis, there's no need —

ROLFE. And whose interest, hm? You talk of our national interest, and they listen? Come on, Frank. They know which side they're on. And so should we.

KERSHAW. The dogmas of class war . . .

ROLFE. Yes, yes. And why?

KERSHAW. Tell me.

ROLFE. Because if we turn craven, we collaborate, we are betraying people who, if they're not on our side, are left in no-man's land, ripe for defection. The NCO's. The lower-middle-class.

KERSHAW. Yes, well?

ROLFE. Who, on all counts, have been betrayed. Their property no longer secure. Their social status, now, irrelevant. And in the place of what's important to them, national destiny and hope, we've given them . . . You see, Frank, it's not true that we've lost an Empire, haven't found a role. We have a role. As Europe's whipping boy. The one who's far worse off than you are. Kind of — awful warning system of the West. And to play that role, we must become more shoddy, threadbare, second-rate. Not even charming, quite unloveable. And for those — the people that I come from, that despair is a betrayal.

Enter DENNIS TURNER, *stands upstage. He is nearly 50, dressed soberly, wears a poppy, carries a wreath.* KERSHAW *and* ROLFE, *sensing the ceremony is about to start, move to stand upright, together.* ROLFE *quietly, to* KERSHAW.

And if they go, we've lost. And go they will, unless they feel defended. So for them we must arm the national interest. Fortify it. Build the dam, for them.

Pause. A VOICE.

VOICE. Let us commemorate and commend to the loving

memory of our Heavenly Father, the shepherd of souls, the giver of life everlasting, those who have died in war for our country and its cause.

'They shall grow not old, as we that are left grow old. Age shall not weary them, nor the years condemn. At the going down of the sun, and in the morning, we will remember them.'

RESPONSE (TURNER, ROLFE *and* KERSHAW). We will remember them.

A very long silence. TURNER *lays the wreath. The Last Post is played on a bugle. As it finishes.*

VOICE. The Legion of the Living salutes the Legion of the Dead.

RESPONSE. We will not break faith with ye.

KERSHAW *speaks quietly to* ROLFE.

KERSHAW. Maybe.

Blackout. KERSHAW *and* ROLFE *go.*

Scene Five

Immediately, a spot hits TURNER.

TURNER. In '47. Came on home.
    Sergeant Turner, to a Midlands town.
    Another England, brash and bold,
    A new world, brave and bright and cold.
    The Sergeant looks at England, and it's changed
       before his eyes;
    Old virtues, thrift and prudence, are increasingly
       despised;
    Old values are devalued as the currency inflates,
    Old certainties are scoffed at by the new
       sophisticates:
    And big capital and labour wield an ever-bigger clout,
    And it's him that's in the middle and it's him that's
       losing out —
    Sergeant Turner, NCO:
    Where's he going? Doesn't know.

Full lights. TURNER's *Antique shop. 1970 Election Conservative Party posters on the wall: Vote Conservative for a Better Tomorrow. Enter* TONY, *blonde, late teens, and* PAUL, *a few years younger than when we last saw him. They carry an antique table.*

TONY. Turner's Antiques. Employee: Tony Perrins. Like the work. And learn a trade. Investment for the future.

PAUL. Turner's Antiques. Employee: Paul McShane. Dislike the work. But, out of school, job market bleak, just take what you can get.

They set the table and go out.

TURNER. Selling old things. Beautiful things. Heavy with craft.

Enter PAUL and TONY with two antique chairs.

TONY. Years ago. June, 1970. Election results. Labour lost. Pollsters confounded. Gaffer's pleased.

PAUL. Years ago. June, 1970. Election results. Tories won. Lame ducks and rising unemployment. Selsdon Men. A Black Day.

They set the chairs either side of the table. TONY takes TURNER's overcoat from him; goes out and re-enters, as:

TURNER. An end to six years of socialist misrule. At last, the little man will get his chance against the big battalions.

Enter MONTY, about 30, Jewish, cockney accent, long hair, brushed denim suit, open-necked shirt. He carries a union jack carrier-bag and smokes a thin cigar. To TONY:

MONTY. 'Morning, flower. See the boss?

TONY. Someone to see you, Mr Turner.

TURNER looks to MONTY. Some distaste.

MONTY. Good morning, Mr Turner. Montague Goodman. New neighbour. Thought it time we had a chat.

Slight pause.

Just call me Monty.

TURNER. Neighbour.

MONTY. That's correct. We are developing next door.

TONY. Look of surprise, the gaffer's face.

PAUL. Horror, more like.

Exit TONY and PAUL.

TURNER (*sits*). Developing next door to what?

MONTY (*sits*). A shop.

TURNER. I hadn't heard.

MONTY. So hence our chat.

TURNER. What kind of shop? It might affect my trade.

MONTY. It will, old love. Antiques.

Pause.

TURNER. What d'you mean, antiques?

MONTY. Selling old things. Beautiful things. Heavy with nostalgia.

TURNER (*stands*). Who are you?

MONTY. Didn't I present my card? (*He stands, gives* TURNER *his card. Out front.*) I told him to ignore the company. It being what you might call defunct.

TURNER. You what?

MONTY (*out front*). Quite elegant, the system, as it happens. Buy a name, in our case several, firms that've stopped trading but still have listed Boards and all that stuff . . . And in that name you go to an estate agent, in our case several, and buy a series of adjacent properties, separately of course, complete the deals, wind up the firm.

TURNER (*sits*). I don't get what you mean.

MONTY (*out front*). So told him. Idea was to conceal a whole row being bought by one developer. And, naturally, that developer's identity. But nothing he could do, and liked his face, so told him. (*Sits, to* TURNER:) That you, Dennis Turner, are now a tenant of the Metropolitan Investment Trust.

TURNER. You what?

MONTY. They've sold the building, love.

TURNER. Who has?

MONTY. Your landlord.

TURNER. But —

MONTY (*out front*). Though, truth be told, he put up quite a fight. (*He stands and walks about.*) In fact, eventually, we had to ring the council, do a bit of bartering. Luckily, we found they were but bursting to erect a SupaParkarama down the road, needing to demolish a pair of properties at that time in our gift. So we said, look, old chums, you don't want all the fuss of buying us out, why not slap a CPO on number 27, grounds of rot, and we can call it quits. Well then, of course, we told his landlord, purchase order on its way, you

couldn't see his signature for dust. Wouldn't even have
matched our offer, see.

TURNER. What's happening to my shop?

MONTY (*out front*). I told him, plan was for a precinct, geared
towards the younger end. Boutiques, hair stylists, soda
fountains, drive-in legal aid facilities, antique emporia, self-
service massage parlours, all that kind of thing. (*To* TURNER:)
And this particular retailing zone is pencilled in as a zen
macrobiotic luncheon take-away, old love.

TURNER. You're joking. I've got a 12 year lease.

*MONTY sits, picks up his union jack bag, plonks it on the
table, takes out a document, as he speaks.*

MONTY. Now there you are correct. Unfortunately the law, in
that majestic way it has, does give a little leeway. Quote: the
rent is subject to a periodical review. Sunbeam, you have
just been periodically reviewed. Direction: up.

TURNER. You can't do that.

MONTY. Now there you're incorrect.

TURNER. I'll pay it. I'll refuse to go.

MONTY. Oh, petal, please.

TURNER. Why shouldn't I?

MONTY (*out front*). I hate this bit. (*He stands, facing away
from* TURNER.) Tulip, I don't know if you've noticed, but
among the merry navvies labouring next door are several of
our Caribbean cousins. Simple, cheery folk, all charmers to
a man, but tending to the slapdash. Natural exuberance, you
see. The kind of natural exuberance that pushes bits of
scaffolding through windows, picking off the Georgian
porcelain.

Pause. He neatly stubs his cigar out on the table top.

TURNER. You bastard.

MONTY (*back to the table, putting the document back in his
bag*). No, not bastard. Selsdon man.

TURNER. But why destroy my livelihood.

MONTY (*harsh, quick, nearly angry*). Because, my love,
destroying you will make someone somewhere some money.
All it is. Cupidity. What you got, but just not enough. Cos

we, we make our money out of money. We covet on a global
scale. We got cupidity beyond your wildest dreams of
avarice. And you, the little man, the honest trader, know your
basic handicap? You're suffering a gross deficiency of greed.
(*Briskly, as he goes:*) You've got three weeks, old love.

MONTY *goes. Pause. Enter* TONY *and* PAUL, *either side.*

TONY. We came in. Saw the gaffer. Shattered.

TURNER. Lunch, you two.

PAUL. It wasn't half past twelve.

TONY. We told him so.

TURNER. I said, it's lunch.

PAUL. We went.

PAUL *goes. Pause.* TURNER *waves* TONY *out.* TONY *goes.*
TURNER *stands, looks at the table and the stubbed-out
cigar.*

TURNER. So where do I go now.

Blackout.

Scene Six

*Lights on an upstairs pub room. The date is 20 April, 1968.
Tables, chairs. On a table an old Grundig tape-recorder. An
easel, with a picture on it, covered in a red cloth.* MAXWELL,
*a thin, neat man in his early twenties, is finishing the distribution
of the chairs.*
Then enter CLEAVER, *mid-fifties, distinguished, and* DRUMONT,
*a middle-aged French Canadian, who carries a glass of scotch, and
has a raincoat over his arm.*

CLEAVER. Thanks very much, David.

MAXWELL *nods and goes.*

Well?

DRUMONT (*tossing his coat over a chair*). Looking good,
Richard.

CLEAVER. We think so.

DRUMONT. Whole world over. Detroit to Grosvenor Square.
Particularly here. The sell-out blatant. Deeper rot. Unthinkable
ideas beginning to be thought. What an opportunity.

CLEAVER. Indeed.

DRUMONT. I would be so confident, Richard, but for one factor.

CLEAVER. Which is?

DRUMONT. You. The revolutionary movement. The essential vanguard. Where are you, Richard?

CLEAVER. Edward, you know . . .

DRUMONT. No, Richard, no. I'll tell you where you're at. You're stuck in 1930. You're still fighting old battles, tearing yourselves apart with petty sectarian squabbles that you should have settled years ago.

CLEAVER. Edward, the reason why — (*A knock. Impatiently:*) Yes?

Enter MAXWELL.

MAXWELL. I think everyone's here now. They're in the bar, and they're wondering . . .

CLEAVER (*looks at his watch*). Oh, yes, of course, tell them to come up. (MAXWELL *goes. To* DRUMONT:) The will is there. It's money.

DRUMONT. When the movement in Britain demonstrates that it is seriously committed to unity, then money follows. Simple.

CLEAVER. We're having talks —

DRUMONT. On unity?

CLEAVER. That's right.

DRUMONT. Then see that they're concluded.

CLEAVER. Yes. Of course.

DRUMONT. Richard. It's nineteen hundred and sixty-eight. Student riots. Workers striking. Chaos and decay. In ten years time, where could you be? I tell you. Out of the cellars, Richard. Out of the basements and into the sun.

A knock.

CLEAVER. Come in.

The door opens and a number of PARTYGOERS *enter. In the main, young. Most have drinks. Some greet* CLEAVER. MAXWELL *is with them.* DRUMONT *picks up his coat to go.* CLEAVER *to him.*

CLEAVER. You going?

DRUMONT. I want an empty ritual, I go to church. So — au revoir.

CLEAVER. Goodbye.

DRUMONT goes. MAXWELL to CLEAVER.

MAXWELL. Who was that?

CLEAVER. Edward Drumont. Canadian. The man with all the money.

MAXWELL. And?

Slight pause. CLEAVER shrugs.

CLEAVER. Let's get the formalities over with.

MAXWELL and CLEAVER move to the centre. MAXWELL bangs a glass for silence. During his speech, the PARTYGOERS group round, some sitting.

MAXWELL. Comrades. If I could have your attention. Comrades. It's my pleasure to ask Dick Cleaver, on behalf of the movement, on this very special day, the 20th of April 1968, to propose the toast of fealty.

Applause. During CLEAVER's speech, MAXWELL takes a tray of candles from below a table, and lights them.

CLEAVER. Thank you. Comrades, I'm not going to make a long speech . . .

SOMEONE. That'll be the day!

Laughter. CLEAVER smiles.

CLEAVER. Though I do believe that a good speech should be like a woman's skirt: short enough to arouse interest, but long enough to cover the subject. (*Laughter.*) Anyway, all I really want to say is how good it is to see a group of people like this, particularly the young ones, in this day and age . . . (*Laughter.*) You probably know, you probably saw in Grosvenor Square last month, a lot of today's students are attracted to communism as an alternative to the evils of the capitalist system. And they're right. It is an alternative. Under capitalism, man is exploited by man. Under communism, it's precisely the other way round. (*Laughter.*) But we know that, don't we. Anyway.

SOMEONE. That's cos you told it last year!

CLEAVER (*smiling, good humoured still*). And there's more where that came from! No, just the one, I promise. There's these two Jewish businessmen on a train. And they're discussing ethics. And one says — I tell you a story that illustrates perfectly the problem of ethics already. Here am I in this shop I run with my partner Hymie. And this man comes in for his suit. And I give it him and I say that is £10 and he gives me the money. But when he has gone I find he has given me by mistake £20 already. So here as I say I have the ultimate ethical problem. Do I, or do I not, tell my partner.

Laughter. Suddenly, serious.

But I don't have to tell anyone here about that kind of ethic. Or the degeneracy of youth today. Or how our beloved country is being deliberately destroyed. I needn't tell you that. You've got your noses. You can smell the stink.

Slight pause. Jovial again.

Well, that's my lot. So, without further ado, can I ask you to raise your glasses and join with me in toasting the memory of the man whose birthday we have come together to celebrate. David —

The PARTYGOERS *take candles from the tray.* SOMEONE *switches off the light, leaving the scene candle-lit.* MAXWELL *takes the curtaining off the picture. It is Adolf Hitler.*

The Fuehrer.

ALL (*raising their glasses*). The Fuehrer.

MAXWELL *switches on the tape recorder. A German recording of the SS marching song, the Horst Wessell Lied. The* PARTYGOERS *take off their jackets. Some are wearing armbands, showing the sunwheel symbol; others put on armbands, badges, flashes. By small additions to basically black, brown and blue costumes, their ordinary clothes become uniforms. As each* PARTYGOER *finishes changing, they salute the portrait, and go and stand by the tape recorder, joining in the song, with English words.* CLEAVER *is the last to salute the picture of the Fuehrer.*

SONG. We march and fight, to death or on to victory,
Our might is right, no traitor shall prevail
Our hearts are steeled against the fiery gates of hell
No shot or shell can still our mighty song.

> Our sword is truth, our shield is faith and honour,
> In age or youth, our hearts and minds we pledge,
> Though we may die to save our people and our land
> This course will stand, our millions marching on.

A knocking starts at the door. The song peters out.

> We close our ranks, in loyalty and courage,
> To God our thanks, for comrades tried and true . . .

MAXWELL (*switching off tape recorder*). Who is it?

DRUMONT (*off*). Drumont.

CLEAVER. Let him in.

SOMEONE *puts the light back on. The feeling of panic in the group subsides.* MAXWELL *admits* DRUMONT, *who carries a folded newspaper. He stands, says nothing.*

CLEAVER. Yes, Edward?

DRUMONT *hands the folded paper to* CLEAVER.

DRUMONT. Read that.

CLEAVER. What is it?

DRUMONT. Evening paper. Read. From there.

CLEAVER. What is it?

DRUMONT. Read.

CLEAVER (*upset at being ordered about, nonetheless starts to read*). 'A week or two ago I fell into conversation with a constituent, a middle-aged, quite ordinary working man employed in one of our nationalised industries. After a sentence or two about the weather, he suddenly said: "If I had the money to go, I wouldn't stay in this country". I made some deprecatory reply, to the effect that even this government wouldn't last for ever' . . . . (*He looks to* DRUMONT.)

DRUMONT. Well, go on.

CLEAVER. . . . 'but he took no notice, and continued: "I have three children, all of them have been through grammar school, and two of them married now, with family. I shan't be satisfied till I have seen them all settled overseas. In this country in fifteen or twenty years time the black man will have the whip-hand over the white man".' (*He looks up.*) Edward, who is —

DRUMONT (*takes the paper, turns it over, points*). Now, there. Read on.

CLEAVER. 'The cloud no bigger than a man's hand, that can so rapidly overcast the sky, has been visible recently in Wolverhampton and has shown signs of spreading quickly. As I look ahead, I am filled with foreboding. Like the Roman, I seem to see . . . (*Slight pause.*) "The River Tiber foaming with much blood".'

Pause.

All right. Who is it.

DRUMONT. The Right Hon Enoch Powell, Shadow Spokesman on Defence. Saying what no-one but you has ever dared to say. (*Pause. He lets it sink in. Then to* MAXWELL.)

You a tough guy, soldier?

MAXWELL. I like to think so, sir.

DRUMONT. This hurt? (*He hits* MAXWELL *suddenly in the stomach.* MAXWELL *flinches slightly, shakes his head.*) OK, now take off that stuff.

MAXWELL. I'm sorry, sir?

DRUMONT. Shirt, armband. All that fancy dress.

MAXWELL *looks to* CLEAVER, *who shrugs a nod.*
MAXWELL *takes off his shirt and armband. Again, suddenly,* DRUMONT *hits him.*

Hurt any more? The second time?

MAXWELL. No, sir.

DRUMONT. That's good. (*He turns to the rest of the* PARTY-GOERS.) Right. Comrades. For years, you have been battering against a bolted door. (*He waves the paper.*) And now, it's open. You can join, and build, and move. To do so, you must spurn the trappings. Spurn the fripperies. But not the faith. Not, absolutely not, the faith. (*He walks around,* ALL *watching him.*) For as you grow, you will, of course, be faced with heresies. Two heresies. And rather easy to define. Beware the man – the Right Conservative, the disillusioned military man – who'd take the Socialism out of National Socialism. But, also, even more, beware the man – the passionate young man, the Siegfried – who would take the National out of National Socialism. Guard against them both. Keep strong. Keep faith. And keep your long knives sharp. (*He covers the*

Hitler portrait with the curtaining.) And so. Not always. For a time. (*He tosses the newspaper to* MAXWELL *as he goes.*)

Pause.

CLEAVER. Where was he speaking?

MAXWELL (*looks at the paper*). Birmingham.

Pause.

CLEAVER. Rivers of blood.

The scene freezes, and LIGHTS *cross-cut to a spot on* KHERA, *at the side. He's now in his early forties, bareheaded, short-haired, clean shaven. He wears the protective clothing of a foundry worker, and carries his mask and goggles in his hand.*

KHERA. In '58. Came on home.
     Gurjeet Singh Khera. To a Midlands town.
     Another England, another nation,
     Not the England of imagination.
     The labour market forces have an international will,
     So the peasants of the Punjab people factory and mill,
     The sacred kess and kanga, kachka, kara and kirpan
     The Sikh rejects so he can be a proper Englishman;
     Keep faith in human virtue, while attempting to
         condone
     The mother country's horror at her children coming
         home.
     Gurjeet Singh Khera,
     Once a slave,
     Returns to haunt the Empire's grave.

PLATT (*off*). Khera! Khera! For Christ's sake, Khera, where the bloody hell you hiding?

PLATT enters into a little light on the other side of the stage. He's in a dirty white coat, carries a clipboard. Pause.

KHERA. Sir?

Blackout. Play Handel.

ACT TWO

'The rise of the Nazi Movement signifies the nation's protest against a state refusing the right to work . . . protest against economic order thinking only in terms of profit and dividends.'

Gregor Strasser, National
Socialist Reichstag Deputy,
10 May 1932

'It is because we want socialism that we are anti-semitic.'

Joseph Goebbels, 1931

'The term socialism in itself is unfortunate, but it is essential to realise that it does not mean businesses must be socialised . . . This sharing of the workers in possession and control is simply Marxism.'

Adolf Hitler,
22 May 1930

'Only an anti-semite is a true anti-communist.'

Adolf Hitler, 1931

Act Two

Scene One

Lights. PLATT *and* KHERA *in the same positions. Noise of machines. The* CHARACTERS *have to shout,* PLATT *rather more than necessary.*

PLATT. OK. Now what's all this I hear.

> PATEL *enters. Dressed the same as* KHERA, *stands near him. About 25.*

KHERA. About?

PLATT. About your people banning overtime.

KHERA. It's not decided yet. We'll let you know. (*He turns to go.*)

PLATT. No good, mate. In your contracts. 28 a month.

PATEL. It's also in our contract you speed up the track?

PLATT. Nothing against it, bab.

PATEL. And chargers, casters, knock-out men, no increased pay for increased work?

PLATT. You're not on piecework, mate.

PATEL. Unlike the moulders.

PLATT (*angry*). Oh, for Christ's sake —

KHERA (*quietly*), And, obviously, coincidence that all the moulders white.

PLATT. Look, mate. It's not my fault, all Asians on fixed rates. Not my fault, all the moulders white. You ought to see your union.

KHERA. We are our union. (PATEL *and* KHERA *turn to go.*)

PLATT (*shouts after them*). Cos I don't give a toss, you're black, white, brown, or pink with purple stripes. As long as you keep working, don't —

PATEL. Precisely, Mr Platt.

PLATT (*shouts after* KHERA). Well, Mr Khera?

KHERA (*turns back*). As shop steward, I have called a meeting. Let you know.

PLATT, *angry, leaves.* PATEL *shakes his head, half-smiling at* KHERA, *and goes out.*

KHERA (*out front*). The Foundry industry. Long hours. Hot, dangerous conditions. Asians lowest paid, least chances of promotion, first to go.

ATTWOOD, *white foundryman, but ordinary clothes, crosses the stage, giving no acknowledgement of* KHERA, *and goes off.*

(*Sardonically.*) And taking British workers' jobs away.

He goes, as blackout.

Scene Two

Lights. A meeting hall. Table at the back, on a raised platform. Microphone. PEOPLE *at the meeting include* TONY, *longer-haired than in Act One, with a guitar under his seat;* MRS HOWARD, *an elderly gentleperson; and* LIZ, *lower middle-class, late 20s. Various other* PEOPLE. TURNER *is making heavy weather of pinning up a banner:* TADDLEY PATRIOTIC LEAGUE. *On the banner, somewhere, is a union jack.* MAXWELL *enters. He is now nearly 30, slim suit, tastefully fashionable. He taps* TURNER *on the shoulder. All the dialogue until the meeting proper is unprojected, part of hubbub of general conversation. During it,* ATTWOOD *enters, and sits.*

TURNER. Oh, hallo David. Nearly ready for the off.

MAXWELL. Fine. Just rung Cleaver. Think it's go.

TURNER. That's great.

MAXWELL *sits.* TURNER'*s task is complete.* TONY *goes over to him quickly, as if he's been waiting to catch him.*

TONY. Um, Mr Turner —

TURNER (*looks at his watch*). Yes, Tony?

TONY. You won't forget the poem, will you?

TURNER. Poem? Oh, no, of course not.

TONY *grins, sits.* TURNER *to himself, as he goes behind the table.*

Right.

MAXWELL *suddenly stands, and goes over to him.*

MAXWELL. Oh, Dennis.

TURNER. Ar?

MAXWELL. Just one thing, I noticed. On the banner.

TURNER. Ar?

MAXWELL. You've got the flag the wrong way round.

TURNER (*coming round to look at the banner*). Oh, blimey, have I?

MAXWELL (*smiling*). Doesn't matter. Sadly no-one notices. But, p'raps, for next time . . .

TURNER. Sure.

He grins at MAXWELL. MAXWELL smiles back, and sits again. TURNER behind the table again. He speaks through the mike, which feeds back.

Good evening ladies and gentle — Oh God. (*He adjusts the mike. It still feeds back.*) Good evening, ladies — (*Away from the mike, he calls.*) Could we, is there anyone in the box? (*Pause. Grins.*) Technological miracle. (*Pause. This time, the mike's dead.*) Testing, testing. Now we've lost it altogether. Testing, test — (*Amplification in.*) — ing, testing. Ah. One, two, three, four. That's better. Ladies and gentlemen, as I was saying before being so rudely interrupted, good evening to you all. Now I've called this meeting, as most of you know, to discuss two things, both of which are related to each other. One is the forthcoming bye-election, in Taddley, and the other is the possibility of the Patriotic League joining forces with a national organisation. And with this in mind, we have here tonight Mr Maxwell, who's leader, is that right, David?

MAXWELL. General Secretary.

TURNER. Sorry, general secretary of the Nation Forward party, a truly patriotic organisation as I'm sure you'll all agree when you've heard what he's got to say. First of all, though, there is the question of paying for the room, and I wonder if someone —

LIZ. I'll do it, Mr Chairman.

TURNER. Oh, thanks, love.

LIZ goes round collecting.

Always collect before the speaker, eh? Now, first of all, I hope you've all seen the new bulletin. If any of you a'n't, we've got a great new system which might not quite work yet.

Anyway, I've got a spare or two. (*He picks up a bulletin.*) Now, we've gone as far as we dare on some of this. I don't mind what the Race Relations people say, but the printers get a bit jumpy. Anyway, one thing I would like to draw your eye to is on page four, the item about parasitic worms at Thawston Junior, cos I did write to the Medical Officer of Health about it. I think he's getting a bit fed up with me, actually. Perhaps eventually he'll get fed up enough to do something about these immigrant problems in our schools. Anyway, he wrote back in his usual soothing vein, I hope some time he'll realise that the patriotic people of Taddley can't be soothed that easily. One of the things I said was that the thing about these parasitic complaints is that they're passed on by cutlery and using the same toilet. Of course that's when these people sit on the toilet. Usually they do other things as you know. Anyway, he didn't say much about that in his reply. Anyway, there was just that one point I wanted to point out before I handed over to Mr Maxwell to explain to us all about Nation Forward. Thank you.

He sits, polite applause. MAXWELL *goes behind the table,* TURNER *adjusts the mike for him.*

MAXWELL. I think, actually, I'll dispense with the electronic aid. (*Not into the mike.*) In fact, I thought, despite Mr Turner's splendid build-up, that I wouldn't launch off into a great diatribe, I think you all know something about Nation Forward, and I think it'd be a lot more useful if we threw the discussion open now, so that you can ask the questions you want answering, and, most importantly, that I can listen to what *you* have to say.

He sits. Pause.

TURNER. Well, that's stunned 'em all into silence, Mr Maxwell.

MAXWELL *smiles. Pause.*

Come on, I'm sure somebody —

Pause. To fill in.

Well, I think one thing people might want to ask is —

MRS HOWARD *stands and interrupts. During all contributions,* MAXWELL *takes notes.*

MRS HOWARD. Mr Chairman.

TURNER. Ah, Mrs Howard. I thought you'd find voice sooner or later.

MRS HOWARD. Mr Chairman, I have been a member of the Conservative Party for 40 years. That's what I wish to say.

Pause. TURNER *starts to ask her if that's it.*

TURNER. Is that, er —

MRS HOWARD (*interrupts*). It would be complete anathema to me to support or vote for any other party.

Pause. Again:

TURNER. Are you saying —

MRS HOWARD (*interrupts*). However. I am afraid that the Party is not what once it was. It has become craven. Once it represented all the finest values of the middle class. Now, gangrenous.

Pause. Again:

TURNER. Yes, well, I'm —

MRS HOWARD (*interrupts*). Values sneered at. Sniggered over. In the Party. The Young Conservatives, who often seem more socialist than the socialists themselves. They look embarrassed, when you talk about the Empire, or self-help, or discipline. They snigger, talk about the Common Market. Sneer, and talk about a wind of change.

Longer pause.

TURNER. Mrs Howar —

MRS HOWARD (*interrupts*). I'm sure it's infiltrated. From the left. The cryptos. Pale-pinks. Sure of it.

Pause. TURNER *does not interrupt.*

I recall it, you will understand, as once it was. That's all I have to say. (*She sits.*)

MAXWELL. Mrs Howard, could I say that yours is exactly our view.

LIZ (*stands*). Mr Chairman, I'd like to say something. I'm sure what the lady says is true, but it's not just politics. My husband — he can't be here tonight — he lectures at the Poly. And he's become convinced of several things. One is that half these so-called foreign students aren't studying at all. They turn up once, then disappear. And, also, he's quite sure at least 75 per cent of the lecturers, and some of them are immigrant, are communists. And cos of this, he may lose his job. Cos he's a patriotic person, and makes no secret of it, when they cut back, and they're going to, he'll be the first to go. The union won't lift a finger. And another thing. It's folk like us, who work for Britain, who are suffering the most. Like when they talk about home ownership, the Tories in particular. What happens? Mortgages go up so far we can't afford the payments. So we say, OK, we'll sell. But even that's impossible. Our house is in West Thawston, and you know, you say that you're from Thawston and they all start talking pidgin English. So we can't sell. Or buy. So people get desperate. Really desperate. There seems no way, you see. (*She sits. Pause.*)

TURNER. Anyone else?

MRS HOWARD (*stands*). In my opinion —

TURNER. Mrs Howard, if anyone else wants —

MRS HOWARD. Just one point, Mr Chairman. Following on what the young lady said.

TURNER (*shrugs*). The floor is yours.

During this, ATTWOOD *is growing irritated.*

MRS HOWARD. In my opinion, the lady is quite right. It is the silent majority who are suffering. In silence. As they watch their green and pleasant land become more and more like an Asian colony. And the do-gooders. Isn't it time, Mr Chairman, that we thought about the victims for a change? And hasn't the tide of permissiveness, the erosion of old values, gone too far? That's what they're saying. The people on fixed incomes. With inflation. No big unions protecting them. What about the people without a union. What about us?

ATTWOOD *stands and interrupts.* TURNER *whispers his name to* MAXWELL. *After a few moments,* MRS HOWARD *sits.*

ATTWOOD. Look, Mrs, let me tell you something. I reckon I'm patriotic as you are, but I'm in a union, and I've voted Labour all my life, and I'll tell you what's bothering me. I'm in motors, steward in a foundry, and what concerns me, with the business like it is, is that if it's a British firm it's going bankrupt, and if it's American, some great Detroit tycoon picks up his phone and says, more profit if we shift the lot to Dusseldorf. And there's summat else. Cos what jobs there are we're not going to get. I doubt if you know Baron Castings, where I work, but come dinnertime there's that many turbans in the canteen, it looks like a field of bloody lillies. And smells like the Black Hole of Calcutta. And if one of 'em gets the push, they're all up in arms, shrieking about discrimination. It's happening now. And I'll be quite frank about the blacks, I hate 'em. And no-one's doing bugger all about it. That's what bothers me. Not the erosion of your bleeding middle-class values. (*He sits.*) Sooner or later, summat's got to be done. (*Angry, to* MRS HOWARD.) So don't you talk to me.

Tense pause. TONY *stands.*

TONY. Er, Mr Chairman —

TURNER. Tony?

TONY. I think, what the last speaker was saying. You know, I mean, you're middle class, and you lost your business, didn't you, I hope you don't mind me saying, but I mean it was the same, big firm taking over . . . And take me. I'm on the dole, in' I? Like you were saying. It just does seem to me, what class you are . . . same, kind of . . .

He's run out. MAXWELL *stands.* TONY *sits, relieved.*

MAXWELL. If I could perhaps come in there. Well, my friends, I said I thought I'd learn a thing or two from you, and by God was I right. We've heard about subversion in the colleges. From Mrs Howard about the Tory Party. And from Mr — (*Checks a note.*) Attwood on the local industry. But it's my view that the last speaker really grasped the point. That what we have in common is greater by far, than what divides us. I'm sure, for instance, that Mrs Howard does not oppose trade unions as such, but only their perversion for political ends. I am convinced that Mr Attwood does not oppose honest profit, but speculative profiteering. Of course, we disagree on many issues. But more, much more, unites us than divides us. It's an old saying, but you can change your class and your creed. But you can't change the blood in your veins.

The odd 'Hear hear'. MAXWELL *smiles.*

But I'm afraid we've something else in common here. To use a light-hearted phrase, we all feel 'Fings ain't what they used to be'. More seriously, we all of us observe a gradual decay, disintegration, in our fortunes and the fortunes of our nation. And perhaps there is a reason — that we have a common enemy.

Oh, of course, it looks like many, different enemies — to the young lady it's the college reds, to Mr Attwood it's the multi-

nationals, to Mrs Howard it's the banks who recklessly
promote inflation and destroy her savings. And it's called by
many names — names representing things we're taught to see
as opposites — socialism, liberalism, communism, finance
capital. Things that, in fact, aren't opposites at all.

You know, there are those who still laugh when we talk
about conspiracy. Even when we look at those people who are
promoting immigration. Even when we look at those supposed
guardians of free enterprise who talk about detente and sell
their grain to bolster Bolshevism. There are people, still, who
laugh at the idea of a conspiracy. A world-wide conspiracy.

But there's one, small group of men and women who don't
laugh. There is one, small, growing party which knows what
is happening and is determined to reverse it. That is Nation
Forward. And I hope, with all sincerity, that you will wish
to join this party, join with us, and make our country great
again.

Pause. He sits.

TURNER. Well, follow that. I think we'd best move straight to
a vote. Um — that the Taddley Patriotic League henceforth
is amalgamated within and serves as a branch of the Nation
Forward Party. I think that does it. All in favour?

All except ATTWOOD *vote. Pause.* ATTWOOD *votes.*

Nem. con.

MAXWELL. I think I can say on behalf of the whole movement
how delighted I am at this decision.

TURNER. Thank you, Mr Maxwell, I'm sure we —

MAXWELL (*interrupts, smiling*). I *can't* say, on behalf of the
movement, anything specific about the bye-election yet, but
we are hoping to stand, and my personal view is that there
could be no more suitable candidate than your Chairman,
Dennis Turner.

Applause.

TURNER (*pleased but taken aback*). Well, David, I don't know
what to say . . . I think anyway we better call it a night . . .

TONY *puts his hand up.*

If there's nothing else —

TONY. Mr Turner —

TURNER. Oh, I'm sorry. One other item. Tony Perrins, here, with a fine show of initiative, he's written a patriotic song, and I'm sure it'd be a very fitting epilogue to such a good meeting. Come on, bab, let's have you.

TONY, *nervous, stands, picks up his guitar, goes to the platform.*

(*To* MAXWELL.) I think, move into the stails, eh, David? (MAXWELL *and* TURNER *move and sit in the body of the hall.*)

TONY (*sits on the edge of the table, takes his guitar out of its case*). It's — I didn't write the words, it's a poem, I just set it to music — (*He strikes a chord, to check the tuning, and breaks a string.*) String gone. Won't take me a second. (*It does. Some shuffling of feet.*) That's it. Um — The Beginnings. By Rudyard Kipling, 1914. Set to music by Anthony Perrins. (*He has a little cough. Then sings. At first not very well, unsure, but growing increasingly assured, harsher, building to the climax.*)

It was not part of their blood
It came to them very late
With long arrears to make good
When the English began to hate

They were not easily moved
They were icy willing to wait
Till every count should be proved
'Ere the English began to hate

Their voices were even and low
Their eyes were level and straight
There was neither sign nor show
When the English began to hate

It was not preached to the crowd
It was not taught by the state
No man spoke it aloud
When the English began to hate

It was not suddenly bred
It will not swiftly abate
Through the chill years ahead
When time shall count from the date
That the English began to hate.

A grin.

That's it.

Blackout. In the darkness, to cover the change, we hear the message of a car loudspeaker.

MAXWELL'S VOICE. People of Taddley. This is Nation Forward, the party which puts Britain first. Our nation is under threat. The scourge of unemployment still ravages. Working people are made to suffer for the mistakes of corrupt politicians, while property sharks and speculators live off the fat of the land. Most of all, treacherous politicians have conspired to flood our country with the refuse of the slums Africa and Asia. Vote for a change. Vote Nation Forward. Vote Dennis Turner.

The tape fades.

Scene Three

Lights. The Labour Club. CLIFTON and SANDY with drinks. PAUL with KHERA, in a suit, and PATEL, in casual clothes.

PAUL. Gurjeet Khera, Prakash Patel; Bob Clifton, Sandy Clifton.

KHERA. How d'you do.

SANDY. Hallo.

CLIFTON (*brisk, but not aggressive*). Right. So what d'you want?

KHERA. We wondered, Mr Clifton, if you knew about the Baron Castings situation.

CLIFTON. Yuh. In part.

KHERA. And if, well, you could —

PATEL. We want support.

CLIFTON. Go on.

PATEL. We gave you ours. We voted for you, delegates from Thawston, and gave you our support. Now we want yours.

CLIFTON. I see. So could you, for the detail, fill me in? "

PAUL. Well, Bob, as I was saying —

CLIFTON. Not you, Paul.

KHERA (*aiding himself with notes*). Well. The dispute at Barons began as a conflict over retimed jobs, required a higher workload for the same reward. And as only unskilled workers don't receive a bonus, and as most are Asian, this job retiming is itself discriminatory. But also this had highlighted discrimination in promotion, whereby high-paid moulders' jobs have gone exclusively to whites. Because of this, the unskilled workers, after due negotiation, have imposed a ban on overtime.

Pause.

CLIFTON. Yuh. Go on.

KHERA (*not using the notes as he grows in confidence*). There is a union, Association of Diecasters and Foundrymen. In fact, within the foundry, it was we who built the union. Now, for five weeks, we have fought, banned overtime, without assistance. We have passed motions, sent letters, proceeded through the correct channels. Even when dismissal notices were served on us, they did nothing.

CLIFTON. So —

KHERA. We occupied their offices.

SANDY. The union?

KHERA. That's right.

CLIFTON. And then?

PAUL. They've made the ban official.

CLIFTON. Good. So what's the problem?

PATEL. So, the ban on overtime's official. On a piece of paper. Registered at Congress House, wherever. Doesn't mean, for moulders, it's official.

CLIFTON. No, of course.

PATEL. And with a racist party, in the bye-election. Making propaganda. Leafletting. And so on.

CLIFTON. Yes.

Pause.

OK. It's clear discrimination. Ban's official. Legal. So I'll make a statement. Backing your dispute. OK?

KHERA *is about to reply when* PATEL *stops him with a gesture.* CLIFTON *notices.*

Problem?

PATEL. Question.

CLIFTON. Shoot.

PATEL. What's in all this for you?

CLIFTON. Why do you ask?

PATEL. We don't have that much reason to have faith in Labour — any British politicians.

CLIFTON. No, you don't. The answer to your question's nothing. It doesn't gain me anything at all, to swim against the tide. So, why? Don't know. Tell me.

Slight pause.

KHERA. Thank you.

CLIFTON. Not at all.

KHERA, PATEL *and* PAUL *go,* PAUL *giving* CLIFTON *a thumb's up sign.*

CLIFTON (*to* SANDY). Members.

SANDY. I beg your pardon?

CLIFTON. That's what he meant. D'you remember. Paul's recruiting drive in Thawston? In a sense, they got me nominated.

SANDY. Ah. I see.

CLIFTON. Not that it's — I mean, I would have backed them anyway.

SANDY. Oh, sure. Bob?

CLIFTON. Yuh?

SANDY. What are you apologising for?

Slight pause.

CLIFTON. Dunno.

Blackout. In the darkness, another car loudspeaker message.

TURNER'S VOICE. People of Taddley. This is Nation Forward, the party which puts Britain first. Our nation is under threat. The scourge of inflation still ravages. Independent business-men are being squeezed out by punitive taxation while social security scroungers live off the fat of the land. Most of all, treacherous politicians have conspired to flood our country with the refuse of the slums of Africa and Asia. Vote for a change. Vote Nation Forward. Vote Dennis Turner.

Fades.

Scene Four

Nation Forward Campaign HQ. Tables, chairs, typewriters. Too much paper, too little space. LIZ is sitting at a table, addressing envelopes.
Two doors: one, with a spyhole, leads into the street; the other to an inner room.
Bell. LIZ stands, checks through the spyhole, admits TONY and TURNER. They both wear union jack rosettes.

TURNER. Hallo, Liz. Mr Maxwell about?

LIZ. He's in the back. Said you'd want to see this. Evening Post. (*She gives him a newspaper.*)

TURNER (*sits*). Oh, ta.

LIZ. Coffee?

TURNER. That'd be lovely.

LIZ. Tony, could you —

TONY. Sure. (*TONY sits, addresses envelopes. LIZ goes into the inner room. TURNER laughs.*) What is it, Mr Turner?

TURNER. The Labour candidate. Bathering on about this nig dispute at Barons. Gonna get his prick caught in his zip, he don't watch out. (*TONY smiles. Enter MAXWELL from inner room.*)

MAXWELL. Hallo, Dennis. Seen the story?

TURNER. Ar, I have. And the Tory's not much better.

MAXWELL. What? No, I meant our statement on the immigrant voters. Page three, top of.

TURNER (*turns page*). Oh, ar?

LIZ *enters with a tray of coffees.*

LIZ. David?

MAXWELL. Liz, you're a treasure.

TURNER (*taking a cup as he reads*). Ta. (*LIZ gives TONY a cup, sits with her own, addresses envelopes, as:*) This is good stuff, David.

MAXWELL. I think it'll capture the initiative.

TURNER. Got to be right.

MAXWELL. By the way, did you manage to glance through the draft election address?

TURNER (*puts down the paper, finds a typescript in his pocket*). Oh, yuh.

MAXWELL. Any worries?

TURNER. Well, yes, actually. One or two.

MAXWELL (*sits*). Shoot.

TURNER. Now, you'll laugh at this, but I found some of it a bit left-wing.

MAXWELL (*smiles*). In what way?

TURNER. Well, a lot of it's great — all the stuff on the nigs, law and order, you know — red hot. But this business about import controls and nationalising banks, I mean — you know what I mean?

MAXWELL. Not exactly.

TURNER. I'm not sure how it'll go down.

MAXWELL. With Tory voters.

TURNER. Yes.

MAXWELL. But we're not just after Tory voters.

TURNER. Well, no. But there's stuff in here about opposing wage controls —

MAXWELL (*slightly impatient*). Of course we are opposed to wage controls. (*Pleasant again:*) Only insofar as we believe that the crisis is created by ruthless international speculators, and that it should not be paid for by the British working class. You see?

TURNER. Well, still —

MAXWELL (*stands*). That's good.

TURNER. And there's the parasitic worms.

MAXWELL. I beg your pardon?

TURNER. The Medical Officer's report on parasitic worms among immigrant schoolchildren.

MAXWELL. Well, yes, I did think, best to keep it fairly general . . .

TURNER. But it proves what I been saying all along.

MAXWELL. Yes, surely but I do think, we've got some general statistics —

TURNER (*stands*). But this is bloody dynamite —

MAXWELL (*patiently*). Look, Dennis. We're not — we can't be, just a pressure group, on any issue, even one as central as the colour question. We're a party, and as such, face other parties whose ideologies are total, all-encompassing. We too must, therefore, show we have a comprehensive view. We are not, merely, hard-line patriots. We are not, certainly, ersatz Conservatives with a particular distaste for immigration. We are British Nationalists, with a cogent and distinct world-picture of our own. You see?

TURNER. I don't think you know them round here.

Pause. Bell. LIZ *goes to answer the door as:*

MAXWELL. All right. All right. I'll bow to your superior local knowledge. We'll insert a specific reference.

LIZ *checks, admits* CLEAVER. *He is slightly older than when we last saw him.*

CLEAVER. Ah. Splendid. Veritable hive.

MAXWELL *nods hallo.*

TURNER. Afternoon, Richard.

CLEAVER. Soldiering on, Tony? How's it going.

TONY. Fine, thank you, sir.

CLEAVER. Splendid. Keep it up. (*To* TURNER *and* MAXWELL.) Mulling over the address?

MAXWELL. That's right.

CLEAVER (*taking the typescript*). Any problems?

MAXWELL. Dennis was worried about some of the economic stuff. Living standards. Banks.

CLEAVER (*leafing through*). That's right?

MAXWELL. I pointed out the need to pose a definite alternative to the bankrupt policies of the old parties.

CLEAVER (*still leafing*). That's good.

MAXWELL. Particularly, that we should dissociate ourselves completely from backwoods Conservative elitism.

CLEAVER. Of course. You see, Dennis, unlike the Tories, we are not unconditional supporters of the economic status quo. Specifically, we oppose the spivs and parasites of credit or financial capital. At the same time, of course, as seeking to eliminate the Marxist wreckers in the factories. Indeed, our view is that financial capital and communist subversion are, in essence, just two pincers of the same conspiracy to undermine the nation's enterprise.

TURNER. It doesn't say that here.

CLEAVER. So it would seem.

Pause.

Dennis, why don't you and Elizabeth go and map out the visiting.

TURNER. Right.

LIZ and TURNER go into the inner room. CLEAVER still reading, TONY listening as he works.

MAXWELL. Jesus Christ.

CLEAVER. What's the matter?

MAXWELL. Turner's obsession with disease.

CLEAVER. I didn't know he had one.

MAXWELL. He has, for starters, a positive paranoia about parasitic worms.

CLEAVER. Parasitic whats?

MAXWELL. Worms.

CLEAVER. David, I'm not totally happy with this.

MAXWELL. Well, it's got to be at the printers by tonight.

CLEAVER. Oh, it's just a few omissions. Tony, go and see if Mr Turner wants a hand.

TONY. Yes, sir.

Exit TONY into the inner room.

MAXWELL. Well?

CLEAVER. Well. (*He reads:*) 'Nation Forward believes that the cause of our present crisis is not the legitimate wage demands of British workers, but the domination of our economy by a tiny clique of international capitalists — the very people who deliberately import cheap foreign labour and cheap foreign goods to undercut our wages and to throw us on the dole.'

Pause.

MAXWELL. Well?

CLEAVER. Drop the wog-bashing and it could be Tribune, David.

MAXWELL. So what d'you want? Wicked unions holding the country to ransom? Eastbourne über alles? Cos that's what Turner —

CLEAVER (*angry, stabbing at the typescript*). Where, amongst all this jolly stuff on the thieves' den of the Stock Exchange, is the support of free productive industry? Where, amid all this merry rhetoric about the plight of ordinary working-folk, is the need to isolate the Commie wreckers? Where, in the midst of all this happy talk of democratic structures and meaningful participation, is the hint, no more, the hint that all men are not equal and that some were born to lead and others only fit to follow?

MAXWELL. Richard, we can reprint Mein Kampf if it'll make you —

CLEAVER. David, I am liable to lose my temper —

MAXWELL. Richard, I've had Turner down my throat all afternoon. I am trying to run a campaign from a disorderly shoebox staffed by juvenile mental defectives and to be frank I couldn't give a toss about your temper.

Pause.

CLEAVER (*icy calm, ripping up the typescript as he speaks*). Were it not, David, for the boundless charity of those of us who, against all the evidence, saw behind your gauche facade the faintest glimpses of potential, you would still be in your army surplus pants and scout-hat goose-stepping up and down in Epping Forest, or, perhaps, organising Nordic Kulturfests on Clapham Common, or, perhaps, being sent down for laughable offences like attempting to arrest the Premier for treason, or, perhaps — (MAXWELL, *furious, takes a wild swing at* CLEAVER, *who catches his wrist.*) Well done, David. For a moment, then, you ceased to look neanderthal. Almost, a prepossessing specimen. For once.

Bell. CLEAVER *and* MAXWELL *still locked. Bell again.* CLEAVER *releases* MAXWELL, *who sits, furiously, and engages immediately in busy activity as* LIZ *enters, goes to the door and checks through the spyhole.*

LIZ. I don't know who it is.

CLEAVER *looks through the spy-hole.*

CLEAVER. Oh, now this is a surprise. Go and fetch Mr Turner, Elizabeth. He has a visitor.

LIZ *exits.* CLEAVER *admits* CROSBY, *who carries a newspaper.*

Good afternoon, Mr Crosby. My name is Cleaver. And this is David Maxwell.

CROSBY. Dennis Turner in?

CLEAVER. Just coming. Do sit down.

CROSBY *sits.*

I read your statement in the Post today.

CROSBY. Oh, yes?

CLEAVER. Do tell me, is it sexual?

CROSBY. What.

CLEAVER. This kick you get from batting for the other side.

Pause.

Nice for you, though. Uncle kicks his boots off, you step in.

CROSBY *is about to reply, when* TURNER *comes in.*

TURNER. Oh, Mr Crosby. To what do we owe —

CROSBY (*stands, gestures with the paper*). Mr Turner, I've just been studying your plans to sabotage this bye-election.

TURNER. Sabotage?

CROSBY. I've come to ask you to reconsider your plans to harass immigrant voters. Quote: 'We do intend to monitor all immigrants who in our view aren't bona fide voters, during this election, at the Polling Stations.' Well?

TURNER. Oh, after the nig-vote, are we?

CROSBY. I — have most unwillingly come.

TURNER. Look, you know as well as I do, half of them's not entitled, and the other half votes twice.

CROSBY. Will you reconsider?

TURNER. Will I hell.

CROSBY. Then I shall report you to the Returning Officer.

TURNER. You do that.

Pause.

CROSBY (*angry*). There's no need, you know, to make the whole
thing mucky, drag us all . . . No need, but I suppose it's all
part of your national regeneration, using these Gestapo
tactics — Oh, I'm sorry. You'd probably view that as praise.
These — red Bolshie bully-boy tactics then. (*He turns to go.*)

MAXWELL. We'd have the reds any day, Mr Crosby. Blood in
their veins. Our most committed people, working-class ex-reds.

CROSBY. Oh, I'm sure you recruit from various lunatic fringes,
not just the one.

MAXWELL. Better to be extremely right than extremely wrong.

CROSBY (*going to the door*). What a fatuous remark, can't you
do better than that?

CLEAVER. Mr Crosby, I have an uncle —

CROSBY. How nice. Mine's dead. Goodbye, Mr Turner —

CLEAVER. — who lives in Southall. Never been involved in
politics. Probably votes Labour. And this harmless old fellow
is quite genuinely terrified that after he's dead, some time in
the future, an Indian temple may be built over his grave.
Which may seem absurd, and, what's the jargon, paranoic to
you. And it might seem very passé, very old-fashioned, very
unhip to say that that old boy did not fight in two world
wars to die, for whatever reason, an unhappy, lonely, terrified
old man.

Pause. CROSBY *is completely thrown.*

CROSBY. I think . . . I think I . . . I don't think there's any more
can usefully be said.
He goes.

CLEAVER (*briskly, as he goes to the inner room*). You see what
we mean, Dennis? Feeble. Flabby. Like all Tories, a slave to
sentiment.

He's gone. TURNER *looks at* MAXWELL. MAXWELL *a wry
smile as blackout and a spot hits* CROSBY, *one side of the
stage, and* PLATT *on the other.*

CROSBY (*to* PLATT). And it was very strange, when talking to
these people; thought, oh, no, these can't be, with their grisly
xenophobia, they can't, or are they, our creation, Demons.
Alter-ego. Somehow. (PLATT *smiles.*) And I remembered,
being small, the Coronation, and the climbing of Mount
Everest, a kind of homely patriotism, sort of, harmless,

slightly precious self-content. A dainty, water-colour world, you know. (PLATT *looks embarrassed*.) And then, their monstrous chauvinism. Dark, desire, for something . . . Kind' of, something dark and nasty in the soul.

Pause. PLATT *has a little cough.*

Felt out of time.

PLATT. Beg pardon? Out of what?

CROSBY. I'm scared.

Blackout.

Scene Five

During the following, fade up lights. PLATT *is still there.* KERSHAW, *in an overcoat and with an overnight case, comes in to him.*

VOICE. This is Taddley. This is Taddley. The train just arrived at platform two is the 15.57 from Birmingham New St, forming the 16.18 to West Bromwich, Dudley, Bilston and Wolverhampton. Platform two for the 16.18, all stations to Wolverhampton.

PLATT *hands* KERSHAW *a thick file.* KERSHAW *opens it, then looks back to* PLATT.

KERSHAW. Look, words of one, Jim. What they after?

PLATT. Extended bonuses. An end to so-called promotional discrimination.

KERSHAW. Can we concede the latter, ditch the former?

PLATT. No chance. Whites won't wear it.

KERSHAW. Why?

PLATT. No cash in it for them.

KERSHAW. And giving them the lot?

PLATT. You'd still have bother, now.

KERSHAW. I see. We'll have to break it, then.

PLATT. Or allow it to break us.

KERSHAW (*looks at* PLATT). Jim, you do understand, why I'm here.

PLATT. Not really. Very small dispute.

KERSHAW. It was. While they were banning overtime.

PLATT. Now, look, that's not my fault. That's bloody union. They said they'd back the ban. They let the whites work normal, didn't they. No wonder that our sunburned brethren lost their rag. Not my fault, that they're coming out on strike.

KERSHAW. Not my fault, sadly true, that with no manifolds or brake-drums, can't make motor-cars.

Slight pause.

PLATT. Think that's called the hyper-mutuality of capital-intensive high technology.

Slight pause.

According to my lad's Financial Times.

Slight pause.

KERSHAW. So. Can the police do nothing?

PLATT. They say no.

KERSHAW. Why not?

PLATT. They can. But won't.

KERSHAW. But come on, Jim, an unofficial strike —

PLATT. You tell the good Inspector. (KERSHAW *looks at* PLATT.) You can see their point. The cameras, press, and all. It's tough for them, politically.

KERSHAW. Can see my point? Three plants, dead stop. Tough, economically, for us.

PLATT. I see. I think that's called a contradiction.

KERSHAW. Jim, for heaven's sake . . .

Pause.

PLATT. I know a young man. Who's in something of a crisis. He decided, 'bout a week ago, he couldn't cope with being a Conservative. Which wouldn't matter if he wasn't standing for election as a Tory in four days. We all have problems.

KERSHAW. Yes.

Pause.

Remind me, the percentage. Black to white.

PLATT. 'Bout six to one.

KERSHAW. Bad odds.

PLATT. What for?

KERSHAW. The picket line.

Pause.

D'you know if Nation Forward know about the strike?

PLATT. Why ask?

Slight pause.

KERSHAW (*suddenly, briskly, walking out.*) An English river, brimming English banks. (*He has gone.*)

PLATT. I don't get what you mean.

Blackout.

Scene Six

In the darkness, on a cassette tape recorder, TURNER *practising a speech. He's not doing it well. During this recording, lights fade up on Nation Forward's HQ, evening.* CLEAVER *and* MAXWELL *sit.* LIZ *and* TONY — *who has the tape recorder near him — are working on a banner upstage.* TURNER *is standing behind a chair, which he'll use as a lectern.*

TURNER (*on tape*). People of Taddley. You've all heard the smears. The lies. The — what's this?

MAXWELL (*on tape, at a distance*). Denigrations.

TURNER (*on tape, after a breath*). Denigrations. You've heard the — is this 'mewlings'?

MAXWELL (*on tape, at a distance*). Yes!

TURNER (*on tape*). All right. The — mewlings of the vested — of the commentators with a vested — sorry, can I start again?

MAXWELL *gestures to* TONY, *who switches off the tape recorder.* TURNER *smiles, shrugs.*

MAXWELL. OK, let's leave that. Try some questions.

Slight pause. CLEAVER *asks the first question.*

CLEAVER. Mr Turner, would you admit to racial prejudice?

TURNER. We all have a natural and healthy preference for our own kind.

MAXWELL. Colour?

TURNER. That's what I mean. Certainly, giving an Asian a British passport doesn't make him British.

MAXWELL (*prompting*). Cat.

TURNER (*rushing slightly, as if a line learnt by heart*). After all, just because a cat is born in a kipper box, it doesn't make it a kipper.

LIZ *and* TONY *look up, react to the joke.* CLEAVER *looks at* MAXWELL.

And have you heard the one about –

CLEAVER (*interrupts*). Turner, there's pressure from the Pakkies for a separate girls' school, religious grounds. Approve?

TURNER. All for it. As long as it's in Pakistan.

CLEAVER. No!

TURNER. Why not? It's funny.

CLEAVER. Flip. You say it shows the immigrants themselves can't integrate.

TURNER (*shrugs*). Ask me another.

MAXWELL. Repatriation.

CLEAVER *holds up three fingers.*

TURNER. Ordered . . . compassionate . . . humane. (*He stops.* CLEAVER *gestures him on.*) But we are honest enough to say that it cannot be voluntary. And that includes all immigrants who were born here.

CLEAVER. No!

TURNER. What's wrong?

CLEAVER. How on earth can an immigrant be born here? Remote control?

TURNER. Well, you know what –

CLEAVER. That's exactly what the hecklers want.

MAXWELL. And on the same score, Dennis, don't say they breed like rabbits.

TURNER. Why?

MAXWELL. Cos then some joker shouts that Queen Victoria did too.

Pause. CLEAVER *looks at* MAXWELL.

CLEAVER. All right. This strike at Barons.

TURNER. The main priority must be — to resist, present attempts to secure a backstairs deal, between the immigrants and the company, um — above, uh —

MAXWELL. Over the heads —

TURNER. Over the heads of the British workers.

MAXWELL. A deal which once again would prove —

TURNER. Would prove —

MAXWELL. The common interest —

TURNER. Of the multi-nationals and the multi-racial elements in our midst.

MAXWELL. So?

TURNER. So, naturally, in the event of management reneging on the interests of the ordinary white workers, we must show our support.

MAXWELL. No, Dennis, no. In the event of management *selling out* the interests of the *rank and file* white workers we must *demonstrate* our *solidarity.*

TURNER. Oh, ar. That's right. I'm sorry.

CLEAVER *looks at* MAXWELL. MAXWELL, *rather self-satisfied, stands and goes to look at* LIZ's *work over her shoulder.* CLEAVER *leans back in his chair.*

CLEAVER. Mr Turner, I wonder, could you tell us just a little more about this common interest, between the multi-nationals and the blacks?

TURNER. Well, it's them attracts them. Them as advertised in all the papers over there. And when they're here, it's them — the multi-nationals — who encourage them to so-called integrate.

CLEAVER. I see. Now why would they do that?

MAXWELL *(still looking at* LIZ *and* TONY's *work).* Wages.

TURNER. Yuh, to undercut the wages of white workers.

CLEAVER. Only wages?

MAXWELL *(still looking at the work).* Jobs.

TURNER. That's right, to take jobs that would normally be given to the whites.

CLEAVER. No more than that?

MAXWELL *looks at* CLEAVER.

Nothing to do with — make-up? Breeding? And the aim, perhaps, to mongrelize . . .

TURNER. You what?

CLEAVER. To turn our nation to a mongrel race of khaki half-castes . . .

TURNER. Ar, and that as well.

MAXWELL (*walks back to* TURNER *and* CLEAVER, *firmly*). Come on, Turner, you're just Fascists in sheep's clothing. Look at Cleaver's Nazi record!

CLEAVER (*scratching his ear*). Look at Maxwell's.

MAXWELL. You're just tinpot Führers, out to overthrow democracy!

TURNER. That's not —

MAXWELL. Come on! Question! Answer it! (*He sits.*)

TURNER. If you'll just let me. There's a simple answer. We want more democracy. We think that at the moment we're controlled by an undemocratic, cosmopolitan elite of Wall Street — puppeteers — who are behind the plot to undermine the nations, the free nations, and impose a One-World State, which would be under their control. Their methods include — strangulation of the national economies by saddling them with debt . . . and, (*Looks to* CLEAVER.) and mongrelisation, and communist subversion, and — (*He looks at* MAXWELL.) the creation of the multi-national monopolies.

MAXWELL. Well done.

TURNER (*during this speech,* CLEAVER *starts laughing, long and loud*). In its place, we wish to build — a truly democratic . . . nationalist society, in which the views, of everyone, are — as it were . . . What's funny?

CLEAVER (*laughing*). Oh dear me.

TURNER (*quite angry*). What's funny?

CLEAVER. Wall Street? In alliance with the Communists? Oh dear me.

TURNER. Well, they financed the Russian Revolution —

CLEAVER (*laughing even more*). Financed the Russian

Revolution? New York bankers? Oh, that's good, that is.

TURNER. Well, it's been said —

CLEAVER (*still jovial*). I mean, for heaven's sake. Name names.

TURNER. Well, Jacob — Schiff, and Otto . . .

MAXWELL. Warburg.

TURNER. Warburg, they gave cash to pay the Bolsheviks to —

CLEAVER (*laughing even more*). Schiff and Warburg? Oh, that's rich, that is. That's really rich. I mean, now, what on earth had they in common with the Communists? Just tell me. What on earth?

Pause. Still smiling.

Just tell me. What on earth. In common.

Pause.

TURNER. Richard, I don't get —

CLEAVER (*not smiling any more*). Or put another way. What British landlords. British tenants. British workers. British bosses. Have in common.

TURNER (*quietly*). Race.

CLEAVER. Can't hear.

TURNER. Their race.

CLEAVER. And so — the others?

Pause.

Warburg. Marx. Schiff. Rosa Luxemburg. Rothschild. Lev Davidovitch Trotsky. What have they in common.

TURNER. Richard, I'm not an anti-sem— (*He stops himself. Pause.*)

CLEAVER. Dennis. The man who took your shop away. What was his name?

Pause.

TURNER. Goodman. Monty Goodman.

CLEAVER. Yes.

The telephone rings. CLEAVER answers it.

Yes? Oh, yes, indeed. Hold on.

He covers the receiver.

And so the questioner's remark about democracy. What is democracy?

TURNER. What serves. Is in the interests of. The Race.

CLEAVER (*stands, walks towards the exit, carrying the telephone on its long lead*). That's right. (*To* MAXWELL.) Goodnight, David. (*He turns at the exit, gestures with the receiver to* TURNER.) It's for you.

CLEAVER *goes out with the telephone.* TURNER *shrugs at* MAXWELL, *follows.* TONY, *his work done, stands, sits on a chair.* LIZ *looks up at* MAXWELL.

MAXWELL. Well?

LIZ. Well what?

MAXWELL. Can't you see what he's doing?

LIZ. Who?

MAXWELL. Herr Obserstgruppenführer?

LIZ *goes back to her work.*

LIZ. Tell me.

MAXWELL. You know, he has this vision of himself, he really sees himself in cap and flashes, striding through Earls Court or somewhere, flanked by cohorts of the brightest and the blondest . . .

Slight pause.

You see, Liz, what he'll never realize, you can't, now, operate a show on Nordic runes and Wagner, there's some people out there going to need convincing, and we must appear . . .

Slight pause.

I mean, OK, the Triumph of the Will, but not just his . . .

TONY. Don't matter what we say, as long as we get votes, that what you mean?

MAXWELL (*drops into a chair*). Oh, blimey. What's the point.

LIZ, *her work done, stands. She takes out a cigarette.*

LIZ. I like things neat.

She lights her cigarette.

I used to do a lot of sewing. Not just clothes, but things around the house. The curtains, chair covers. I even did a bit of tapestry, picked it up at school. The house was getting really nice. But then, with everything, there didn't seem much point.

There was this tenants' group, a lot of them, in fact, were Patriotic League, you know, the thing that Dennis ran. And what was good about it wasn't that they said the things I thought, but that, with them, I could express myself, without apologising.

Why shouldn't I? Why shouldn't I be proud of what I am? Our country's rotting. Fabric's perished. Ripping at the seams. Cos people won't be proud of what they are. I don't care how it comes about. I want a reason to have children.

TONY. Yuh. That's right.

Enter CLEAVER.

MAXWELL. Well, who was that on the —

LIZ (*interrupts*). Banner's finished, Richard.

CLEAVER. Let me see.

TONY and LIZ lift up the banner. A union jack, behind an appliqué white family. The slogan: 'The Future Belongs To Us'.

Yes, that's very good.

Slight pause.

MAXWELL (*suddenly, almost desperately*). Oh, for Christ's sake, Tony, told you, hundred times, the top left white band's broader, look, you got the thing the bloody wrong way round —

TONY. I'm not the only one.

Pause. CLEAVER, as if noticing MAXWELL for the first time since he came back in.

CLEAVER. Oh, David. You still here?

Pause.

Tony, get Mr Maxwell's coat.

MAXWELL. I haven't got a coat.

CLEAVER. Tony, get Mr Maxwell out of here.

TONY goes to MAXWELL. TURNER has entered, he watches the scene.

MAXWELL. Look, I . . . Tony, look, you —

TONY. Heard what Mr Cleaver said?

MAXWELL. Oh, God Almighty.

He turns and quickly exits. TONY *gestures at the banner.*

CLEAVER. It doesn't matter, Tony. Been a long night. (*He sits.*)

TURNER. What's happening? Why's David gone?

CLEAVER (*patiently*). Dennis. There is, in Nationalist politics, a heresy, it's more or less perennial, which argues that true patriots should be opposed, not just to international finance, but to private enterprise in toto. And what follows? An obsession with 'democracy'. Masses, as against the individual. Distrust of leadership. Marx, decked out in patriotic weeds.

Pause.

We've had a little purge.

Slight pause. Briskly.

Right. Once more. The speech.

Blackout.

Scene Seven

Immediately, a spot on TURNER, *in front of the banner. He is miked. His speech is cool, assured, professional. It echoes round the theatre.*

TURNER. People of Taddley. You've all heard the smears. The lies, the denigrations. You've heard the mewlings of the commentators with a vested interest in the notion that our British nationalism is a passing fashion. Well, let me tell them. And tell you.

That from tonight, from Taddley, from this by-election, we are here to stay. Whatever barriers we may encounter, whatever set-backs we must overcome; however long the journey and however hard the road . . . we are the future.

What can stop us now?

Applause, but also heckling. A chant from the HECKLERS: *'Nation Forward, Nazi Party.' It's drowned by the singing of 'Land of Hope and Glory'. Sounds of violence, chairs being turned over. The* HECKLERS *attempt the Internationale. It's drowned by a much louder chant, as sounds of violence grow: 'The Reds, the Reds, we gotta get rid of the Reds.' The spot on* TURNER *fades, as his face progresses from triumph to alarm. Blackout as the chants and sounds of violence go on growing till, suddenly, they cut out, and two single rifle shots are heard.*

Scene Eight.

Lights. ROLFE *stands. He is in a dark overcoat, over a suit which shows signs of hasty travel. The stage is empty, though we are in fact in the Army HQ, Lisburn, Northern Ireland.* ROLFE *holds a union jack, crumpled, in his hands. He almost cradles it, as he would a baby. He looks up at the audience.*

ROLFE. There is a moment in one's life, more terrible, traumatic, even than the ending of a first love, or the consciousness of failed ambition, or awareness of the fact of growing old. It is the moment when you realise you have more time, regard, respect, for those who are your enemies than those you view as friends. That moment came to me at night, while sitting in an aeroplane, and flying northwards, west, across the Irish Sea, to fetch the body of my son.

He was, they told me, on the Lower Falls. Arms raid, just turned his head, a second. And the little boy, the schoolkid at the tenth floor window, with his sniper's gun, aimed just above the hairline, dead on true. Probably been there for hours. Waiting for that second. Patiently.

And on the plane, I realised, I had more time for him, the 12-year-old boy killer in the Divis Flats, the dark child with his Russian rifle, far more time for him, than they. The Generals. The Ministers. Assured us that the sun would never set. The Generals, could not prevent my son, in his high morning, his sun going down.

Yet you still won't see.

Will you? You generals, you ministers, police-chiefs, you won't see, we are at war. Same war. In Belfast. Bradford. Bristol, Birmingham, the one we lost in Bombay thirty years ago, the one we're going to lose in Britain now. Unless you see in time.

Not thugs or lunatics, nor dupes of Moscow. They are ordinary men and women, sane and normal, thousands of them. And there is no time. They're everywhere. Deep, deep, inside the gut. There is no time.

He is crying.

The sun has set. And we should not remember. We should not look back, but should, instead, think only of the morning.

He looks at the crumpled flag.

His fault. He turned his back.

The tears stop. ROLFE *raises the flag, holding it in a high salute.*

We need an iron dawn.

He stands there, holding up the flag. Lights fade to darkness.

ACT THREE

'The misshapen hulk of the modern democratic state poses a serious
serious threat to the ideals that it was originally intended to serve.
The tentacles of bureaucracy and egalitarian socialism are
strangling private enterprise.'

> Robert Moss,
> in *The Collapse of Democracy*,
> 1975

'Private enterprise cannot be maintained in the age of Democracy;
it is conceivable only if the people have a sound idea of authority
... All the wordly goods which we possess, we owe to the
struggle of the chosen.'

> Adolf Hitler,
> 20 February 1933

Act Three

Scene One

*House-lights down. A baby is crying. A doorbell rings, twice.
Lights. CLIFTON's living room. A sofa, chair, coffee-table, on
it dirty cups, glasses, a bottle of whisky, a telephone. Letters,
documents, newspapers and children's toys on the floor.
CLIFTON has switched the light on. He's in a dressing gown. He
goes and answers the door. The baby's crying fades. Outside the
door is CROSBY, muffled against the cold.*

CROSBY. Hallo.

CLIFTON (*surprised*). Hallo.

CROSBY. I wondered if I could have a word.

CLIFTON. It's rather late.

CROSBY. It's rather urgent.

Slight pause.

CLIFTON. Do come in.

CLIFTON admits CROSBY, closes the door.

CROSBY. I'm sorry about the time.

CLIFTON. Well, we were up anyway. The baby.

Pause.

Drink? I'm afraid I've only got scotch.

CROSBY. Lovely.

CLIFTON. Lovely. (*He pours whiskies, gives one to CROSBY.
Pause.*) What a nasty day it's been.

CROSBY. I'm sorry. It's a social situation on which Emily Poste
is sadly mute. The proper etiquette on taking cocktails with
one's class enemy at one in the morning.

CLIFTON (*smiles, sits*). What do you want?

CROSBY. I want to collaborate.

Enter SANDY, wearing a nightie.

SANDY. Hallo —

CROSBY. Hallo.

CLIFTON. Ruth OK?

SANDY. Fine. She was hungry. Look, if it's not impolitic to ask —

CLIFTON (*stands*). I'm sorry. Peter Crosby, Tory candidate. My wife.

SANDY. I do have a name, Bob. And being your wife isn't the sum total of my existence.

CLIFTON. I'm sorry. Sandy. Who works for the Thawston Community Project and is, in her spare time, my wife.

SANDY (*sits*). Thank you. Hallo.

CROSBY. I'm pleased to meet you.

Pause. SANDY waves at CROSBY, to sit. He sits. Pause.

SANDY. Well, what a privilege. To be the witness to a cross-bench hobnob. What I think is known, in parliamentary parlance, as the 'usual channels'. Right?

CROSBY (*smiles*). That's right.

CLIFTON (*sits*). OK, then. What d'you want?

CROSBY. Yuh.

Slight pause.

You know they're coming out, tomorrow, the Asians at Barons?

CLIFTON. Yup. I do.

CROSBY. And that the whites'll try and break the picket?

CLIFTON. Yup again.

Pause.

CROSBY. Look, Bob. I'll be quite open. As you know, both parties, have traditionally attempted, well, to keep race out of politics. Put up a kind of — common front against the sort of demagogy that Nation Forward's using over Barons. Now, I just felt, it might be, both our interests, to declare this strike, well, out of bounds politically. . . For just the last three days. To — try and, salvage . . . Well. You know.

Slight pause.

That's all.

CLIFTON. You want it out of bounds.

CROSBY. That's right.

CLIFTON. Mm.

CROSBY. Well?

CLIFTON. Well, the common front. On race. Your deal, in '62. Then ours, a higher bid, the Kenyan Asians Bill, restricting entry purely on the grounds of colour. So, not to be outdone, the stakes go higher, back to you in '71, Keep Race out of Politics, Keep Blacks out of Britain.

CROSBY. Well, yes, but —

CLIFTON. But some people who won't play that poker game — who stick their necks out. I like to think I'm one of them. In fact, had quite a postbag on the subject. (*He picks up a pile of letters, waves them.*) Not just from the public, either. Party workers, saying they won't canvass. So, when you talk about mutual benefits, I would but mention that I've already made my stand. Selling out now won't help me one iota. You, on the other hand —

CROSBY. Well, I'm sorry, I'd hoped you'd take a more moderate . . .

CLIFTON. Oh, for —

CROSBY (*stands*). All right.

Slight pause.

You heard about Nation Forward's meeting? What they said?

CLIFTON. I heard.

CROSBY. And what they did? To hecklers?

CLIFTON. Yuh, that too.

Pause.

CROSBY. Well, then. Goodnight.

CLIFTON. I'll see you Thursday.

CROSBY. Yes. (*He puts down his empty glass.*) Thanks for the scotch.

CLIFTON. Don't mention it.

Exit CROSBY.

SANDY. Poor little man.

CLIFTON. Why?

SANDY. Charity. He's going to lose his uncle's seat.

CLIFTON (*stands*). I wouldn't bet on it. At the moment, it's a race to see which of us loses most to Nation Forward.

Pause.

SANDY. But of course you're right.

CLIFTON. Sometimes I wonder.

SANDY. Like when?

CLIFTON (*pouring another drink*). Like when I'm on the doorstep, confronting the massed Alf Garnetts of the West Midlands. (*Accent.*) Oh, ar, Mr Clifton, we're with you on import controls, gotta be right, but it's the darkies, i'n'it? I mean to say, we know they live twenty to a room and breed like flies and don't use toilet tissue —

SANDY. Shut up, Bob.

CLIFTON. Why?

SANDY. Cos you're making me angry.

CLIFTON. Why?

SANDY. Because you've no right to patronise people you know nothing about.

Pause.

CLIFTON. Oh, come on, love, I've just had Peter Crosby —

SANDY. I just get a little fed up with your assumptions about people you meet for two minutes on a doorstep once in a blue moon. Because, unlike you, I actually work in the field, and I meet ordinary people all the time.

CLIFTON. Well, bully for you.

SANDY. Working-class people.

CLIFTON. Even bullier.

SANDY. And if you don't think there are real problems in integrating large numbers of people from a totally different cultural background then you need your head examining.

Slight pause.

CLIFTON. Oh, sure, dead right. And so . . . This week control, next week call a halt, week after send 'em back —

SANDY. You do annoy me sometimes, Bob —

CLIFTON. Love, we're both tired —

SANDY. I'm not tired.

Pause.

CLIFTON. Um, to what do I owe . .

SANDY (*angry now*). Look, Bob. You make your great bloody statements about unrestricted immigration and institutional racism. Well, you can afford to.

CLIFTON. I can't, that's exactly —

SANDY. You can afford to. But you just take a walk, leave the car for once, take a walk round West Thawston. You might even stop occasionally and actually listen to what people are saying. You know, listen? Then you might find out.

CLIFTON. I know —

SANDY. You don't know, so I'll tell you. Widow I visit. Only white face in the street. No English shops any more. Can't buy an English newspaper. The butcher's gone. The kids smash up her windows. Yes, of course, you'll say, all kids do that, but when the street was white it didn't happen, Bob. So I call her a 'racist'?

CLIFTON. No —

SANDY. Old man. 'Bout 60. A T&G shop steward who refused to take a cut in bonus rates. What happened? Got the push, his job went to a Pakistani. He's a fascist?

CLIFTON. You know the answer. They're blaming the wrong people.

SANDY. Who should they blame? Themselves?

CLIFTON (*as much for his own benefit as hers*). You know perfectly well. That there was bad housing long before they came. That the worst housing in Britain's in Glasgow, with hardly any blacks. That the years of highest immigration were the years of fullest employment. That the people who are responsible for unemployment and bad housing are bosses and property sharks and very few of them are black. You know that. So why —

SANDY. Oh, great. Pavlov reaction. It's the system. So what do I do? Lead them to the bloody barricades?

SANDY. Well —

Crash, offstage.

SANDY. What's that?

The phone rings.

CLIFTON. You answer it.

CLIFTON goes. SANDY *picks up the phone.*

SANDY. Hallo? Paul. What? No, he's . . . All right. I'll tell him.

She puts down the phone, goes to exit, meets CLIFTON who enters holding a piece of paper. He stops her going through.

CLIFTON. I've checked. Ruth's all right. It's a brick through the window. And stuff, through — on the carpet.

SANDY. Stuff?

CLIFTON. Excrement. Human, shit.

SANDY. Oh Christ.

CLIFTON (*gives her the note*). And this.

SANDY (*reads*). Take care of your snivelling little whore-spawned bastard Clifton the dark nights are coming.

CLIFTON. 'Whore' as in 'H.O.A.R'.

SANDY. But not a bad stab at 'snivelling'.

CLIFTON. Who was that on the phone?

SANDY. Paul. He's heard Nation Forward are going to be at Barons, first thing. Breaking the picket.

Pause.

CLIFTON. Now that is all we need. (*He sits.*) Another uncompromising stance? And hallo Peter Crosby, Honourable Member.

SANDY (*kneels beside CLIFTON, takes his hand. Very gently*). Bob. Once — you may remember, you said, about the Party. Why you're in it.

CLIFTON. Mm?

SANDY. You said, despite — oh, all the right wingers, all the selling out, you said at least, at least there was a chance of changing things. Of, really, changing things. You could have joined some, tiny, fringe, some two-horsed revolution, kept your ideas pure, you said, but at the price of never being any real use to anyone. You wished to be of use, you said, with all the compromise, retreat, the scorn that that implies.

CLIFTON *looks at* SANDY.

And that struck me as being rather brave.

CLIFTON *smiles at* SANDY.

Let's go to bed.

Slight pause.

CLIFTON. OK.

CLIFTON *stands and goes.* SANDY *moves to go, turns, looks round the room. She switches out the light.*

Scene Two

Dim lights. Outside the Foundry. Near the gates, KHERA, PATEL, PAUL, *perhaps other* PICKETS. *Placards:* DO NOT CROSS PICKET LINE, OUR FIGHT IS YOUR FIGHT, DON'T SCAB. *A few moments, then:*

KHERA (*out front*). Seven a.m. A winter's morning, picket line. For most of us, the first. And some surprise, we're doing it at all.

Enter PLATT *and a Police* INSPECTOR, *with possibly, other* POLICE *on one side of the stage.* KHERA *looks at them.*

But here we are.

He joins the other PICKETS.

PATEL (*to* PAUL). Police, with Platt.

PAUL. You bet.

PATEL *goes over to* KHERA, *talks to him.*

PLATT. They'll be here soon.

INSPECTOR. They will.

PLATT. Your tactics?

INSPECTOR. Keep well out. Long as they keep to peaceful giving or obtaining information, peaceful persuasion to work or not.

PLATT. Is that the law?

INSPECTOR. That is the law. I know their rights.

KHERA (*to* PAUL). What are they saying?

PAUL. I can't hear.

PLATT (*pointing at* PATEL). You see that one? The young one? He's the lad I mentioned.

INSPECTOR. Yes?

PLATT. With the interesting past.

Enter CLEAVER *and* LIZ, *the other side of the stage.*

KHERA. Nation Forward?

PATEL. Think it is.

PATEL has a word with PAUL, *who nods.*

INSPECTOR. And who are they?

PLATT. Dunno. Perhaps they're passers-by.

INSPECTOR. At seven in the morning? Passers-by?

PLATT. It's possible.

Enter TURNER *and* TONY, *with union jacks.*

INSPECTOR. With union jacks?

PLATT. I'm wrong. That's Turner. Nation Forward.

INSPECTOR. So it is.

PAUL (*to* PATEL). That's Turner.

PATEL. Yes.

KHERA. What now?

PATEL. Just wait.

Enter ATTWOOD *to centre stage.*

OK.

The PICKET *forms.*

PLATT. You're doing nothing?

INSPECTOR. As I said. We wait for an offence.

Pause. Then ATTWOOD *looks at his watch.*

ATTWOOD. Well. Half-past seven. Time for work. (*He walks to the* PICKETS.) Oh now look at this. (NATION FORWARD *move closer to* PICKETS.)

An unofficial picket-line.

The PICKETS *move closer together.*

Barring my path to work.

Pause.

Please let me pass. (*Suddenly, pulling at* KHERA.) Come on, Harry Krishna. Clear my road.

Freeze action.

KHERA. And I nearly did. When he said move, I nearly did, as reflex action, move to let him through. But then —

PATEL (*to* ATTWOOD). You scab.

KHERA. And then again —

PATEL (*pushing* ATTWOOD). You bastard scab.

KHERA. And then again.

PATEL (*pushing* ATTWOOD). You bastard blackleg scab.

ATTWOOD. Get your filthy hands off me, you dirty nig black scum.

PATEL (*takes* ATTWOOD *by the throat*). The name. The name's Prakash Patel. And, brother, we are staying in your road.

Freeze breaks.

PLATT (*quickly, marching over to the* PICKETS). Now, come on, lads, why not just let him through —

PATEL (*to* ATTWOOD, *referring to* PLATT). Now look, you, look. Look at his smiling face —

A whistle blows. NATION FORWARD *rush the* PICKETS *and blackout. At once, as pot hits* KERSHAW, *side of stage.*

KERSHAW. Unpleasant. But we got ten in. Unthinkable, to use these people, but. Impossible, not to. All other options closed. Unease, but then necessity. Better embrace the butcher, soil the bed, than perish with clean hands.

Blackout.

Scene Three

A police station. Most of the stage area is a corridor, lit. PAUL, *reading a crumpled newspaper, sits on a bench. To one side, an area representing an interview room. A* SUSPECT *sits at a table in this area, facing upstage. The* INSPECTOR *enters with* TONY.

INSPECTOR. There.

TONY *shrugs, sits on the bench. Exit* INSPECTOR. PAUL *puts down his paper, recognises* TONY.

PAUL. Tony.

TONY (*turns, recognises* PAUL). Paul.

Pause. It sinks in. They both laugh.

BOTH. Well, don't you meet —

TONY. People in the strangest places.

Pause. They laugh again.

PAUL. Well. How are you?

TONY. I'm fine. And you?

PAUL. Just, great, as well.

TONY. That's good.

PAUL. Apart, that is, from being stuck in here.

TONY. Ar. Right.

Pause.

PAUL (*mock confidential*). Um, look, bab, don't want to pry
   or anything, but, uh . . . what you doing here then?

TONY. Got arrested.

PAUL. Snap.

TONY. I'm waiting, to be charged.

PAUL. Well, snap again.

Slight pause.

Um — ?

TONY. Bit of aggro, up at Baron Castings.

Slight pause.

PAUL. Yuh?

TONY. You know, there's this dispute —

PAUL. Yes, sure, so . . . You were on picket line?

TONY. Of course I wasn't on the bloody picket line.

Slight pause.

Were there to break the bloody picket, weren't we?

PAUL. We?

TONY. Yuh, we. Nation Forward.

Pause.

PAUL. I was on the picket-line.

Pause. TONY laughs.

TONY. Oh, blimey —

PAUL. So what's funny?

TONY. Blimey. Paul McShane. Great fighter for the working-class. Siding with a gang of nigs to undercut the wages of his brother —

PAUL. Tony, that's a load —

TONY (*angry*). Why don't people ever realise? We didn't ask for it.

PAUL. For what?

TONY. Have Pakkies take our jobs and houses. Turning England's green and pleasant land into an Asian slum. We didn't —

PAUL. Green and pleasant? Yuh. Just like round here. With all them lovely trees and verdant foliage. You know, they had a poster in the war: This Is Your England, Fight For It. A picture of a village green. Thatched cottages. How many English soldiers died had ever seen a country cottage? Thatched or otherwise?

TONY. They did it, if you want to know, Paul, cos some people bat for their own side.

PAUL *laughs*.

PAUL. For Christ's sake, Tony, who have you been talking to?

TONY. No need to talk. I know it. Any white man knows it. In the blood.

PAUL. The blood?

TONY. The spirit of the Race.

Pause.

PAUL. Oh God. (*He stands and shouts off.*) Hey, Sergeant! Did you know, you got the bleeding Master Race in here? You can't do him for causing an affray . . .

Pause. PAUL *turns back to* TONY, *for his reaction.*

TONY (*quiet, calm*). You really don't know, do you?

PAUL. What?

TONY. Your real enemy.

PAUL. Well, actually, I do take the old-fashioned view, that for the working-class the enemy's —

TONY. Oh, ar. The bosses. Which?

PAUL. Well? Answer?

TONY. Have a sniff, Paul. Got a nose. Can smell the alien stink. Or can't you?

PAUL. Oh, sure, yuh, can do. Smell the foul stench of all those black speculators. Those Pakky stockbrokers. Jamaican Managing Directors.

TONY. Not them, Paul.

PAUL. No, not them. The Ruling Class.

TONY. No, Paul. The Ruling Race.

Pause.

PAUL. All history's the struggle of the classes.

TONY. No. All history's the struggle of the races.

Pause.

PAUL. The workers of all races must unite.

TONY. The workers of all classes must unite.

Pause.

PAUL. Come down to it, the choice is socialism or barbarity.

TONY. Come down to it, it's Zionism, One-World Tyranny, or us.

Slight pause. TONY *stands.*

And when we win, get rid of them, there'll be no need for conflict. Class war. Strikes, and all. Then capital and labour work together, in the interests of the nation. Putting Britain first. The nation, over all.

Pause.

'Course, you can sneer. At race and blood. But everything you got, Paul, comes from that. Everything healthy, worthy, everything with any meaning, value, s'from the blood. Cos seed don't die, what we are doesn't die. Passed on. From generations, passed on, from the legions of the dead to legions of the living, legions of the future.

PAUL. Tony, last time they said that, it ended up with putting people into −

TONY (*simply*). No, no, Paul. It never happened. Auschwitz, n'all. Just factories. The holocaust, just photos forged. Invented by the Jews.

PAUL looks at TONY. TONY *still.*

PAUL. You Nazi.

TONY. Yuh. That's right.

Suddenly, PAUL *out front.*

PAUL. And, you know, it was like looking in a mirror, looking at him, me old mate, Tony. All correct, the same, identical. Just one thing wrong. Left's right. Class — race. As different as can be. The opposite. The bleeding wrong way round . . .

Lights cross-cut to INSPECTOR *and* SUSPECT. *We now see the* SUSPECT *is* PATEL. INSPECTOR *holding an Indian passport.*

INSPECTOR. Right, Mr Patel. Let's go through it just once more. You claim you entered when?

Blackout.

Scene Four

Lights on a Pakistani restaurant. A couple of tables. CLIFTON *and* SANDY *are sitting eating.* PAUL *and* KHERA *have just come in, are standing.*

PAUL. They've arrested Prakash Patel.

CLIFTON. What?

PAUL. And they're reckoning to do me for assault.

Slight pause.

CLIFTON. Sit down.

PAUL *and* KHERA *sit.*

PAUL. Now look, Bob, if you rang the dailies, now, you could get a statement in tomorrow morning, demanding his release —

CLIFTON. Patel's being done for assault?

PAUL (*impatient*). No, he's —

CLIFTON. Thought you said —

KHERA. Illegal immigrant. Under the '71 Immigration Act. Easier than jailing strikers. Just fly them back to India.

SANDY. But there's an amnesty.

KHERA. It doesn't cover. He's an overstayer, came in as a student, just didn't go back.

CLIFTON. Poor sod.

PAUL. So you see, Bob, it'd be great, day before polling —

CLIFTON. Where is he?

PAUL. At the copshop.

CLIFTON. And they found out —

PAUL. Platt. It has to be. The bastard knew, and shopped him.

CLIFTON (*non-commital*). Yuh.

Slight pause.

PAUL. Well?

CLIFTON (*businesslike*). Right. Now, he's an overstayer, yuh?

PAUL. Well, so they say.

CLIFTON. But he is?

PAUL. Well, I suppose so.

CLIFTON. So, in fact, he's breaking the law.

Pause.

PAUL. Well, yuh —

CLIFTON. Now that does make it rather difficult.

PAUL. Why?

SANDY. Because, if he's breaking the law, Bob obviously can't demand his release.

PAUL. Why not?

SANDY. Obviously.

Pause.

PAUL (*to* CLIFTON). But it's just what you been saying all along. Oppose the Immigration Act.

SANDY. That's not what you're asking him to do.

PAUL. Yes, it is. Here's a case, a guy —

SANDY. Bob's asking for the law to be changed, not broken.

Pause.

PAUL (*to* CLIFTON). Well, say something.

CLIFTON. What do you want me to say.

PAUL. Well, actually, that your good lady is talking through the back of her neck.

Pause.

CLIFTON. She isn't.

PAUL. Oh, I see.

CLIFTON. No you don't. So I'll explain.

PAUL. I'm all ears.

Slight pause. Strain in CLIFTON's *voice.*

CLIFTON. Now. I'm standing for election as a legislator, right? That is the job-description. And I'm doing that, can only do that, if I believe that laws should be made, OK? And that it's possible to change society by making them.

PAUL. But —

CLIFTON. So how, if that has any meaning, can I say that once they're made we shouldn't keep them?

PAUL. Well, what 'bout me? Assault, on Fascists.

SANDY. Paul, the law can't not protect a guy just cos you happen to regard him as a Fascist.

Pause.

CLIFTON. It's just a matter, simple, of the rule of law.

SANDY. You've got to see the problem, Paul.

PAUL. I can. I'm talking to it. It's sitting there, stuffing its face with chicken byriani.

Pause.

CLIFTON. The law's a car, Paul. Goes whichever way you steer it.

PAUL. So why, whoever's driving, does it always go one way?

Pause.

KHERA. There is a story, 'bout the rule of law. In Amritsar. 1919. A Brigadier-General, Dyer, ordered his troops to fire on a crowd of unarmed Indian demonstrators. Nearly 400 killed. Facts took some time to come out. Then, of course, Dyer was investigated. Strict legality. Censured. Asked to resign.

SANDY (*quietly*). 1919.

KHERA. That massacre. Defence of British rule in India.

SANDY (*quietly*). Which ended thirty years ago.

KHERA. Oh, yes, of course. I'm sorry.

Slight pause. As he speaks, softly, KHERA *looks at no-one, perhaps just playing with the ashtray on the table.*

I come from Jullundur, the Punjab. Sikh upbringing. Train the children to be quiet, subservient, respectful. So, to England, land of tolerance and decency, and found it hard to understand. But last year, I went home, on holiday, to India. Saw, with new eyes, just what the English did. And then I understood. There is more British capital in India, today, than 30 years ago.

It runs quite deep. Even the poor, white British, think that they, not just their masters, born to rule. And us, the blacks, the Irish, all of us — a lesser breed, without the Rule of Law.

But that's your problem.

He stands. To SANDY.

You'll forgive me. I'm on picket duty, seven in the morning. (*He goes.*)

Long pause.

PAUL. Well, that's put you —

CLIFTON. Did you see Crosby, in the Evening Post? Feared some of his remarks might have been misinterpreted. Wanted to make it clear, completely opposed to any further coloured immigration. Already signs of, social strain.

PAUL. Well, by tomorrow, there'll be one less, won't there?

Slight pause.

Ar, I saw it.

CLIFTON (*hands* PAUL *a note*). You won't have seen this. Came through the window last night. Accompanied by a brick and a neat little pile of excreta.

PAUL *reads the note.*

PAUL. So you retreat? Because of this? You see what these bastards can do, and you retreat?

SANDY. Ruth's eight months old, Paul.

PAUL. Oh, ar. And doubtless the law will give her every protection.

CLIFTON (*loses his temper*). You know, sometimes, Paul, your self-righteousness reaches a pitch of messianic fervour that I find quite terrifying.

PAUL. Oh, ar?

CLIFTON. Ar. And that's surprising. Because what you're doing isn't very difficult. It's rather easy, comfortable, your anger, rather cosy, in its steel-eyed way. Because you think in absolutes, in dogmas, you needn't face the real fights, the real, mucky struggles, you keep clean. And if your — sterile constructs ever touch the real world and its diseases, they're cocooned in rubber, scrubbed a thousand times, to keep them pure.

Pause.

PAUL (*quietly, gently, a genuine need to explain*). You know, there's a funny moment, comes to you, you see your real friends. Came to me, a meeting of the Barons strikers. Oh, yuh, sure, all clenched fists and synthetic Maoist fervour.

Just, amid all that, some people learning. Talking, for the first time, 'bout just how to do it, working out, quite slowly, tortuously, quite frustrating, you know, for us old pros, to sit there and listen to it all.

But it is listening to people grow. Learning that it's possible for them to make their future. Bit like the morning. Sun comes up, so slow, can't see it's changing. But it's growing lighter. Think of that.

Their fault. No turning back. The need, to be our own. To change, the real world.

He stands.

Tara.

Exit PAUL.

SANDY. Well done.

CLIFTON. Hm. In two days' time we'll know. What profits it a man to lose his party's soul.

SANDY. You haven't.

CLIFTON. Well, I didn't have much choice.

SANDY. You did.

CLIFTON. Well, still.

Slight pause.

I better win.

Blackout.

Scene Five

In the darkness, we hear the voice of the MAYORESS of Taddley, through a mike.

MAYORESS'S VOICE. I, the undersigned, being the Returning Officer for the Parliamentary Constituency of Taddley, hereby give notice that the total number of votes cast for each candidate was as follows:

Lights. The Election Result. Standing from left to right: CLEAVER, TONY, TURNER, PLATT, EMMA, CROSBY, MAYORESS, WILCOX, CLIFTON, SANDY, PAUL and KHERA. The first three and last two slightly apart. EMMA is CROSBY's wife, WILCOX is a Liberal. As the MAYORESS announces the result, PLATT and SANDY note the figures down. A VOICE identifies the candidates.

MAYORESS. Clifton, Robert John —

VOICE. Labour.

MAYORESS. Ten thousand and ninety-six.

A splatter of applause. CLIFTON looks worried, the TORIES pleased.

Crosby, Peter Sanderson —

VOICE. Conservative.

MAYORESS. Eleven thousand —

Big applause. CROSBY can't believe it. EMMA kisses him. CLIFTON shakes his hand. MAYORESS attempts.

Eleven thousand, eight hundred and thirty-two; Turner, Dennis . . . Turner, Dennis . . .

Applause dies.

Turner, Dennis Stephen —

VOICE. Nation Forward.

Sudden burst of chanting: 'Nation Forward, Nazi Party'. Dies.

MAYORESS. Six thousand nine hundred and ninety-three.

Applause. Booing. NATION FORWARD *look delighted.*

Wilcox, Diana —

VOICE. Liberal.

MAYORESS. One thousand and fifty-two.

A little applause. SANDY *gives* CLIFTON *the note and kisses him.* CROSBY, PLATT *and* EMMA *confer. As:*

And that the undermentioned person has been duly elected to serve as member for the said constituency: Peter Sanderson Crosby.

She turns to CROSBY, *shakes his hand.* CROSBY *taking over the mike, as* CLIFTON *speaks to* PLATT.

CLIFTON. Well done, Jim. Think we can conclude, they won you the election.

PLATT. Only if, took more from you than us, Bob. And who knows where the buggers come from.

CROSBY (*down the microphone*). Um —

Snap blackout. A very short time. Lights. The central section of people, and the microphone, have gone. Those left — TONY, CLEAVER *and* TURNER *on one side,* PAUL *and* KHERA *on the other, are left looking at the place where* CROSBY *stood. Then, as the lights fade down to dim, night lighting, the two groups become aware of each other. They look across the space. Edgy. Nervy. Then, on* PAUL *and* KHERA's *side, blocking their exit,* ATTWOOD *enters.* KHERA *and* PAUL *move towards centre. Pause. Then,* CLEAVER *taps* TURNER *on the shoulder, makes to go.* TURNER *not going.* CLEAVER *gestures him to follow.* TURNER *follows* CLEAVER *out.*

TONY. Well, here we are.

PAUL (*to* KHERA, *makes to go*). Come on.

TONY. Hi, Paul.

PAUL (*to* KHERA). Come on, mate.

TONY. And hallo, Paul's pet monkey.

Slight pause.

KHERA (*to* PAUL). No.

TONY. OK.

> TONY *goes for* KHERA, PAUL *to protect him*, ATTWOOD *for* PAUL. *Before he can get to* TONY, PAUL *aware of* ATTWOOD, *turns and knees him as* TONY *knocks* KHERA *down.* ATTWOOD *doubles up*, TONY *about to kick* KHERA *when he hears two clicks.* TONY *turns, thinking they come from behind him.*

TONY. Wha —

> *Quickly,* KHERA *slides one of the two flick-knives he holds across the floor to* PAUL. TONY *and* ATTWOOD *realise.* PAUL *picks up the knife, slashes at* ATTWOOD, *who manages to avoid the knife and runs out.* TONY *tries to stamp on* KHERA's *hand, misses.* KHERA *up, slashes at* TONY's *face,* TONY *turns to run, faces* PAUL. *He stops. Blood is beginning to run down his cheek.* TONY *is looking very, very scared.*

KHERA. Right. Now tell me. Who you think you're doing all this for.

> *Blackout.*

Scene Six

Lights on a hospitality room in a merchant bank in the City of London. Leather chairs. On the wall, a huge, dark painting of the putting down of the Indian Mutiny. CLEAVER *sits.* TURNER *stands, looking at the picture. A moment or two. Then* CLEAVER *looks at his watch.* TURNER *touches the picture, feeling its texture. Then he turns to* CLEAVER.

CLEAVER. He said they might be late. A meeting — implications of the Deutschmark doing something or other.

TURNER. Oh, ar?

CLEAVER. Yes.

> TURNER *back to the painting.* CLEAVER *stands, goes to* TURNER.

TURNER. I was there, you know.

CLEAVER (*smiling*). In 1857?

TURNER. No, from 1945. In Calcutta, bastards stoned us. Lot of lads, the troops, you know, refused to fire. They saw it as a kind of, justified revenge. (*He nods to the painting.*) You know, for that, and all.

CLEAVER. Guilt complex. Liberal masochism. What we've got to —

TURNER. Oh, sure. It makes you sick.

Slight pause.

D'you suppose they'll —

Enter KERSHAW, ROLFE *and* CAROL, ROLFE's *secretary.*

KERSHAW. Richard, I'm sorry.

CLEAVER. Doesn't matter.

KERSHAW. Richard, this is Lewis Rolfe.

ROLFE *and* CLEAVER *shake hands.*

CLEAVER.) How d'you do.
ROLFE.   ) Hallo.

KERSHAW. And Dennis Turner, Lewis, who I think you've met.

ROLFE (*to* TURNER, *shaes his hand*). Indeed. Long time ago. Congratulations, Dennis.

TURNER. Thank you, sir.

ROLFE (*smiles*). No need for that.

KERSHAW. Well. 23 per cent. You'll be delighted.

TURNER. Well, low poll. But it's a start.

CLEAVER. A deposit saved is a deposit earned.

All smile.

ROLFE. Carol, any chance of sherry??

CAROL. Yes, of course. (*She goes.*)

ROLFE. Do, please sit.

All sit, except ROLFE.

KERSHAW (*to* TURNER). I imagine Richard's filled you in?

TURNER. He has.

Slight pause.

KERSHAW. Well, then.

CLEAVER. We need to know your reasons.

KERSHAW. Yes, of course.

Enter CAROL *with a tray of sherry which she passes round. Then she goes out.*

ROLFE. Right, gentlemen. In answer to your question.

Slight pause.

We are under threat. The British Nation, and its enterprise. The two are indivisible. A blow at one's a blow against the other. We face a common threat, we face a common enemy. We have a common need.

A glue. To stick the nation to itself. And, yes, to make its enterprise secure. Unite the Durham miner with the Surrey stockbroker. The East End navvy with the Scottish laird. An ideology.

We know what we've been offered. Liberalism. From whatever source. A community of tolerance, compassion, moderation. Tolerance of crime, permissiveness. Compassion for the multi-coloured misfits of the world. And moderation, military reserve, low profile, in the face of insurrection. To a point when gangrene's gone so deep that — we must think about extremes.

You offer an extreme. An old idea. Not merely nation. Race. Roots deeply twined into the universal gut. To bind the barrel fast with hoops of steel.

Not pale. Not weak. Not atrophied. Red, white and blue — in tooth and claw. (*Half-smiling.*) Mm?

CLEAVER. There's more to it than that, of course.

KERSHAW. Fighting the Reds, wherever they appear. The schools, the factories.

CLEAVER. Why not the police?

KERSHAW. The police don't know. They're isolated. You — the Reds are on your streets. You know.

CLEAVER. The army?

ROLFE. Can contain, perhaps. They can't destroy.

CLEAVER. We also combat international capital.

KERSHAW. We also need protection.

CLEAVER. If it means control?

ROLFE. You scratch us, we'll scratch you.

CLEAVER. You'd sacrifice the 'free' of enterprise?

KERSHAW. Yes, to preserve the privacy of property.

> *Pause.*

> One doesn't, like, the dentist.

> *Slight pause.*

> But to save the tooth

ROLFE. Physicians. Army, police. Just tranquilize, to numb the pain. You — surgeons. Use the passions. And rechannel the hot blood, and send it gushing down another artery.

> *Pause.*

CLEAVER. Conditions.

KERSHAW (*sharply*). There's no question of conditions. There's no question of a deal.

> *Slight pause.*

> But if you ask . . .

> *Slight pause.*

> A tendency, among your people, shall we say, a little too far to port?

CLEAVER. Oh, yes. Our little group of Racial Trotskyites. Well, Maxwell and his Bolshie band aren't with us any more.

KERSHAW. I see.

CLEAVER. It is our view that the working class need not be wooed by slogans drawn from Marxism. Indeed, it is our view they *can't* be wooed by any such approach.

ROLFE. Indeed.

CLEAVER. So. Money?

KERSHAW. No, not yet. Not yet at all.

> *Pause.*

CLEAVER. Is this — approach, just you?

KERSHAW. Oh, yes. Just us. Hardly United Vehicles. Not now.

ROLFE. Hardly the Metropolitan Investment Trust. Not now. Not yet.

TURNER *suddenly looks up.*

CLEAVER. I see. Of course —

TURNER. What did you say?

ROLFE. I'm sorry?

TURNER. What did you say, your firm —

ROLFE. The Metropolitan Investment Trust.

KERSHAW. Shall we continue over lunch?

CLEAVER (*stands*). Why not.

ROLFE. Let's go.

> *He gestures the* COMPANY *out.* CLEAVER, KERSHAW *and* ROLFE *exit, leaving* TURNER, *who is forgotten in the general exodus. As they go,* ROLFE *to* CLEAVER, *conversationally.*

ROLFE. I thought we'd try a new place on Cornhill. That's if you don't mind Italian . . .

> *They're gone.* TURNER *goes and looks at the painting. Enter* CAROL, *with a tray, to collect the sherry glasses.*

CAROL. Oh, I'm sorry. I thought you'd all —

TURNER. They have.

CAROL. Are you not lunching?

TURNER. No.

> *Slight pause.*

CAROL. Fine.

> TURNER *is still looking at the painting.* CAROL *collects the sherry glasses. When she's finished, to* TURNER, *conversationally, about the painting.*

CAROL. Ghastly, isn't it?

TURNER. It's him.

CAROL. I'm sorry?

TURNER. Didn't realise. Your boss.

CAROL. My boss?

TURNER. That he's the Metropolitan Investment Trust.

CAROL. I don't quite see —

TURNER. The people took my livelihood away.

Slight pause.

You may not notice it. I'm suffering a gross deficiency of greed.

Slight pause.

You're right.

CAROL: What's right?

TURNER. It's ghastly.

Enter CLEAVER.

CLEAVER. Dennis? What's the matter? Aren't you coming?

TURNER. No.

CAROL. He said — we took his —

CLEAVER stops her with a gesture. She shrugs and goes. CLEAVER to TURNER:

CLEAVER. Dennis. I understand. I know exactly how I feel. I feel that way as well.

TURNER looks at him.

Of course it's disappointing. Pinned our hopes. The crock of gold.

TURNER understands CLEAVER.

But, Dennis. In the long term. When their precious law and order falls apart, the cities burn, the centre cannot hold . . . When it's the ultra-left or us . . .

Slight pause.

'Whatever barriers we may encounter . . . However long the journey, hard the road . . .' What on earth can stop us now?

A long pause. Then TURNER, to CLEAVER.

TURNER. So tell me. Tell me. *Tell me.*

Suddenly, lights change. CLEAVER and TURNER lit from behind in silhouette. A VOICE is heard; gentle, quiet, insistent. It is the voice of ADOLF HITLER.

ADOLF HITLER. Only one thing could have stopped our

Movement: if our adversaries had understood its principle, and had smashed, with the utmost brutality, the nucleus of our new Movement.

Slight pause.

Hitler. Nuremburg. Third of September, 1933.

Blackout.

Printed in the United States
47532LVS00001B/26

9 780413 152206